Poverty and Economic Justice

Poverty and Economic Justice

A *Philosophical Approach*

edited by
Robert H. Hartman

Paulist Press New York/Ramsey

Library of Congress
Catalog Card Number: 83-82020

ISBN: 0-8091-2597-8

Published by Paulist Press
545 Island Road, Ramsey, N.J. 07446

Printed and bound in the
United States of America

Contents

Acknowledgements

The Publisher gratefully acknowledges the use of the following materials:
"*Why We Need Socialism in America*" *by Michael Harrington from* Dissent *(May/ June 1970);* "*Alternative Conceptions of Poverty and Their Implications for Income Maintenance*" *by Seymour Spilerman and David Elesh from* Social Problems *(Winter, 1971);* Norman E. Bowie and Robert L. Simon, The Individual and Political Philosophy: An Introduction to Social and Political Philosophy, © 1977, pp. 190-212, *reprinted by permission of Prentice-Hall, Inc., Englewood Cliffs, N.J.; excerpts from* Religion and Economic Responsibility *by Walter G. Muelder (New York: Charles Scribner's Sons, 1953), reprinted with the permission of Charles Scribner's Sons;* "*The Christian Faith and the Economic Life in Liberal Society*" *by Reinhold Niebuhr from* Faith and Politics, *R.H. Stone, editor, reprinted by permission of George Braziller, Inc.; permission to reprint* "*Of Population*" *by William Goodwin and excerpts from* Ethics and the Theology of Liberation *(Enrique Dussel) was granted by Orbis Books; excerpts from* A Theory of Justice *by John Rawls, Cambridge Mass.: The Belknap Press of Harvard University Press, copyright © 1971 by the President and Fellows of Harvard College were reprinted by permission of the publishers;* "*Neutralizing the Disinherited: Some Psychological Aspects of Understanding the Poor*" *by Lee Rainwater from* Psychological Factors in Poverty *edited by Vernon L. Allen (Chicago: Markham Publishing Company, 1970) is reprinted by permission of Lee Rainwater;* "*Looking at Poverty from Radical, Conservative and Liberal Perspectives*" *by Howard M. Wachtel from* Review of Radical Political Economics *(Vol. 3, No. 3, pp. 1-19);* "*Approaches to the Reduction of Poverty*" *by Robert J. Lampman from* American Economic Review *(May, 1965, Vol. 55, No. 2, pp. 521-529); excerpts from* "*Economic Philosophy and Distribution of Income*" *by Mary Fish and Vergil Williams from* The Midwest Quarterly; "*The Alleviation of Poverty*" *by Milton Friedman from* Capitalism and Freedom *is reprinted by permission of The University of Chicago Press, copyright © 1962;* "*The Positive Functions of Poverty*" *by Herbert Gans from* American Journal of Sociology, *copyright © 1972 by Herbert Gans. Reprinted from* More Equality *by Herbert Gans, by permission of Pantheon Books, a Division of Random House, Inc.;* "*Blaming the Victim*" *by William Ryan from chapter one of* Blaming the Victim *by William Ryan, copyright © 1971 by William Ryan, reprinted by permission of Pantheon Books, a Division of Random House, Inc.;* "*The Salvation of Superpersonal Forces*" *from* A Theology for the Social Gospel *by Walter Rauschenbusch, copyright 1917 by Macmillan Publishing Co., Inc., renewed 1945 by Pauline E. Rauschenbusch, is reprinted by permission of Macmillan;* "*A Strategy to End Poverty*" *by Richard A. Cloward and Frances Fox Piven from* Nation, *copyright © 1966 by Nation magazine, The Nation Associates, Inc.; selections from* Anarchy, State and Utopia *by Robert Nozick, copyright © 1974 by Basic Books, Inc., New York, are reprinted by permission of the publisher.*

vii

Introduction

A. Why Study Poverty?

Poverty is a continuing embarrassment to America. That the richest nation on earth should contain a fairly large number of poor within its population seems to contradict the very creed of opportunity and egalitarianism upon which it was founded. Michael Harrington has aptly termed the poor "the other America" because it is the America we usually do not see and perhaps do not want to see. One of the ways in which human beings attempt to handle unpleasant problems and facts is to deny that they are real problems and facts in the first place. Thus there are those who see poverty as a pseudo-concept, the invention of social scientists and humanitarian liberals. Or they see it as a purely relative term—the poor in relation to the dominant and affluent middle class, but not poor in comparison with the starving masses in Africa or the peasants in Latin America. At least the poor in America have television!

Granted the relativity of poverty there still remain some serious conditions and misshapened lives that cannot be so easily dismissed. There are families and individuals lacking in the basic things that make for a minimally viable existence: nutrition, shelter, clothing, education, health care, and productive work. For some these deficiencies are only temporary and experienced in part; recent studies have shown that a significant proportion of those receiving some kind of assistance one year are off the dole the next, and that they move back and forth across the poverty line as economic conditions fluctuate. Others, however, remain poor year in and year out. Unemployed and unemployable, lacking in basic skills, burdened with families they cannot adequately care for, struggling with ill health and the surrounding conditions that cause it, these are the poor whose plight has improved by little in response to the efforts of our society. And year after year they have been studied, put on charts and graphs, made the subject of lectures, articles and books, defended and chastised by the social workers and economists. Most recently they have become, along with all who receive public assistance, the topic of great debate in the offices of government as the budgets are prepared for coming fiscal years.

All of the political rhetoric of the latter and "fact-finding" of the former, however, may distract us from addressing the subject of poverty in its deeper dimensions. For the study of poverty entails underlying attitudes, premises and beliefs relating to some larger issues. The need, therefore, is

3

to take a fresh look at poverty not as an isolated phenomenon but as one that occurs within the broader framework of economic justice with its questions of rights, production and distribution, freedom and responsibility, and the good of society as a whole.

B. Why Philosophy and Poverty?

The inquiry into poverty's existence and origins is usually considered to be the province of the social sciences. Through empirical investigation not only are we able to determine the various components of what it means to be poor—the social, behavioral, cultural and economic factors—but we can also study the operational systems that tend to produce poverty. The philosopher cannot neglect this kind of research and its findings, but wants to go a step further. He or she wants to make us aware of how our very perception of the social realities is a structured awareness. Controlling the eyes that see are theories and beliefs which involve some important philosophical assumptions. Together these form a set of lenses through which we perceive and experience the things we do.

Gunnar Myrdal, among others, has long maintained that even within the social sciences are valuations, and that we should stop treating these disciplines as though they occupy a position of disinterested neutrality. In fact many if not most of the controversies about poverty stem from differences in the value assumptions and goals that in turn derive from philosophies about man and society. Their very implications have direct bearing upon, and often control, the answers given to such basic questions as to whether poverty is inevitable, whether it is desirable, what causes it, what obligations it entails, whether we can put an end to it and whether we should even try to, and what kinds of economic and social systems are to be preferred over others.

The dimensions of our perception have been insightfully explored by Norwood Russell Hanson in his study of the conceptual foundations of the natural sciences, *Patterns of Discovery*. Hanson begins by asking whether two observers, in this case the astronomers Johann Kepler and Tycho Brahe, see the same sun at dawn rising in the east, Kepler being a Copernican with the view that the sun is fixed and the earth revolving around it, and Tycho a Ptolemaic believing the opposite. Hanson answers: No, they do not see the same sun. For seeing is an experience and not merely a picture on the retina. We see as persons, not as eyes. And we "see-as," recognize this configuration *as* something which we name and understand according to the context of our theory, and are prepared to "see-as" by virtue of our previous experience.

What we bring to the event of seeing is therefore as important as the data at hand, if not more so. For not only is our seeing perspectival in its very essence, but it is also "theory-laden." The astronomers cannot help but see the sun *as* a certain kind of phenomenon and *that* it is in certain relationships to other bodies in the universe according to their particular theoretical outlooks. The sun takes on different meanings for Kepler and Brahe. These meanings are not added on after the experience of observation takes place but just *are* the very meaning of that experience. Without the structural components of observation one could not speak of "the sun" at all, let alone of "the sun rising in the east."

Let us make up our own example to fit the subject matter at hand. Two persons, A and B, go to Appalachia and observe the poor living there. A looks at their life and condition and sees them *as* social misfits, indolent, lacking in initiative and other personal characteristics that make for success. A sees the poor as deficient in their own makeup, and the absence of inner qualities accounts for the poor's condition. B, on the other hand, sees the poor in different dimensions. They are the unfortunate victims of a society that creates the conditions fostering poverty. In this view the causal agents are not inside the skins of the poor themselves but in the prevailing forces that create unemployment, poor educational opportunities, lack of available jobs, and in the leviathan presence of a coal industry that has been allowed to dominate the lives and destiny of the people in that region.

The difference between A and B cannot be settled by looking at the "facts," for each is already viewing the facts in a certain way. Both might even be social workers who have gone into the area to study the people and recommend the kind of assistance that should or should not be given. Both may be compassionate, sensitive individuals. But the difference between them is critical because it leads to different courses of action. Which perspective is the more valid is a matter of conceptual debate involving beliefs, value systems, and theory analysis.

A philosophical approach wants to look at the implicit components of our seeing so that what is implicit is brought to the light of consciousness and can be examined. It wants to do this for at least three reasons. First, just as Socrates said that the unexamined life is not worth living, so unexamined beliefs are not worth holding. Only as we become aware of their presence and influence and then subject them to open analysis can we hold them with good reason. Second is the advantage of gaining for our consideration some alternative views so that we may compare our own beliefs with others and benefit from that comparison. Whether we end up with the same beliefs, a new set, or a combination of old and new, we have at least weighted the relative merits and demerits of contrasting perspectives. Finally, any such inquiry should lead to the making of intelligent choices rather than ones founded upon unquestioned assumptions and prejudices. The choice of beliefs is critical since they form the conceptual framework within which we define and interpret poverty and determine the appropriate action to be taken.

The selections that follow have been chosen because they offer a wide variety of perspectives on economic justice and poverty. In Section II the stage is set for contemporary debate by the historical writers represented who lay out for us the fundamental issues. Economics as a study in itself emerges from the age of Adam Smith and becomes a subject of serious and sometimes heated debate during the eighteenth and nineteenth centuries. As you read through these essays you sense that one concern comes more and more to occupy the center of the stage: that of the distribution of wealth among all members of society. Note also how certain philosophical assumptions underlie what is being said: beliefs about natural law, the character of history, the motivations of men and women. These in turn lead to certain conclusions about what can and what cannot be changed in the economic arrangements. Section III deals with religious approaches which at the same time involve a great deal of philosophical thinking. They have as their key concern the relationship between the individual and the society and world in which he or she lives and the responsibilities each bears toward the other. The writings reflect different social and political backgrounds of which the reader needs to be aware. Section IV begins with two general theories of justice that deal in broadest terms with the conflicting rights of individuals and of individuals with the society in which they live, and concludes with an essay on economic justice in particular. The selections are somewhat longer than those of the other sections because they aim at presenting their philosophical concepts clearly and accurately and at drawing out some of their implications. Section V gets more specific in its dealing with perceptions of the poor in our own society. The first and second essays expose some of the preconceptions that get built into the way in which we see the poor, while the third examines some of the roles that the poor play in our society. The fourth article of the section is an introduction to theory-making about the poor. It begins with an overview of attitudes and definitions, moves on to three perspectives that are common today—the conservative, liberal and radical—and concludes with a study of the practical implications for formulating strategies that different theories have. Section VI presents some of the solutions to poverty and economic injustice that have been proposed in recent years. Although they are all arguments for certain measures to be taken and appeal to our sense of practicality, they are based upon theory and ideology. Note that some of them aim at the reduction or alleviation of poverty while others would end poverty altogether. Which is truly possible leads us back to the central theme of this study, namely, that poverty and the approaches we take toward it involve a philosophical examination of our beliefs and concepts and cannot be considered matters of empirical data alone.

II. Historical Perspectives: Selections from Past Thinkers

People began to think seriously about economics about the time of Adam Smith because the ownership and control of wealth was changing hands. A new middle class that profited from trade, commerce and industry was replacing that of the landed aristocracy who for centuries had controlled the treasuries of nations because of their vast estates and positions of authority over lesser lords and servants. In some countries, like England, the royal lands were made public domain and available to enterprising citizens. Inheritance became less a title to wealth as the manufacture and exchange of goods, based on an ethic of work, investment and saving, took its place. Adam Smith provided a rationale for the emerging prosperous class. The market for obtaining wealth he saw as an open one in which potentially everyone could participate simply by pursuit of self-interest. Seeing no absolute or final conflict between the interests of the self and those of others, Smith believed that the interplay of the two would strike a balance within both the individual and the society at large. His theory, however, applied especially to the person who owned and operated his or her own business and was self-employed. What about the laborers without capital who depended upon employment by others and who worked to create capital for someone else? Smith treated them on the same level as the entrepreneur, but his successors saw that their efforts did not produce the natural harmony in which the interests and needs of all were met that was supposed to result. The laboring class tended to remain poor, and Malthus introduced another natural law to account for this fact, the law of population by which the poor paid dearly because of their lack of sexual restraint. As they increased the population the food supply diminished, producing misery and starvation. Because such was the law of God, however, it was not mankind's place to interfere. In answer to this dark doctrine William Godwin invoked another law, that of compassion and responsibility. To exculpate the owners and employers was to make a mockery of the very religion Malthus appealed to. David Ricardo reformulated Malthus' thesis by taking it out of the religious context and putting it into a secular one. He, too, saw the poor as too irrational to exercise self-control, but their penalty is the result of the ''iron law of wages,'' purely a matter of economics.

The appeal to ''nature'' in all of the above and its corresponding abhorrence at the thought of any interference with the economic machinery was seriously questioned by Thomas Paine. Capitalism as he saw it dealt with the question of wealth's distribution only from the standpoint of the capitalist and not from that of all members of society. Are there not human rights that transcend economy and that pertain to humans as humans? Should not society see to it that these rights are protected? Paine takes us back to the fundamental question of how the inequalities of wealth within a society are to be dealt with and offers a different solution entirely. John Stuart Mill, a genius at making logical distinctions, attempted to reconcile the claims of capitalist theory with those of Paine. While the production of wealth may be based on what nature provides and ordains, the distribution of it is a social matter and calls for human responsibility. The duty of government to deal with inequities is reaffirmed, and the economic system is to be judged by its observable consequences. Robert Owen, however, presents a model by which the capitalist *qua* capitalist can deal with the inequalities and social ills of the industrial age by taking positive measures of reform. In so doing he adds cooperation to competition as a basic motivation, expanding self-interest considerably to embrace the well-being of others.

Owen was to remain the exception among capitalists rather than the rule as Karl Marx readily saw. In Marx the competitive drive in capitalism becomes uncontrollable and ends in self-destruction. No economy is possible, he thinks, so long as we divide up interests into the atomic units of individuals, for the vast inequalities that are engendered will not be tolerated by history. The future belongs to those who have suffered the most. They, the proletariat or oppressed working class, are alone capable of true cooperation and universal interests which are the hallmarks of true justice. For Marx no amount of modification can save capitalism; its total demise is the precondition of the new age of communism which he equates with the ideal ''harmony''—the very concept Adam Smith had used to describe the new age of capitalism!

A. Adam Smith

The name Adam Smith is synonymous with classical laissez-faire economics. A clergyman and scholar, Smith was professor of moral philosophy at Glasgow College in his native Scotland. His views were very much influenced by the age of the Enlightenment, which took a rosy view of man and his world. Economic justice was the natural harmony that would result from the fulfillment of two conditions: (1) that supply and demand on the open market be left to find their natural equilibrium, and (2) that each individual act simply from his or her own self-interest. The laws of economy were seen as an extension of the divine moral law which would regulate and adjust the competing interests among all classes of society, so that even the poorest would have incentive to work and earn the highest wage obtainable. And the higher the wages the more industrious the worker, and the more the general population would prosper.

Yet Smith perceived that the sources of wealth and poverty alike were not due to nature alone but were social in character as well. Providing education for the children of the common folk was a novel idea for that time, but it offered a welcome alternative to the fatalism of those who saw in poverty only the law of God at work. Nevertheless questions remain. To leave the open market up to providence and the harmony of interests to natural forces is an act of faith in itself. Might not the structure and purpose of a particular society play a role in the outcome? Moreover, a glance at the capitalist nations of the world, including our own, reveals that there is and has been persistent poverty. Looking back to the turn of the century when competition was virtually unbridled, we find that as the wealth of the few increased the plight of the many worsened and produced some of the most sordid conditions imaginable.

Smith's theory, therefore, leads us to ask some fundamental questions. It bids us to ponder afresh all the factors that help to determine the outcome of capitalism. In particular it calls for a look at the modifications that have been made in capitalist countries to the original doctrine and that have mitigated the harshness of unequal distributions.

The Wealth of Nations

The real recompence of labour, the real quantity of the necessaries and conveniences of life which it can produce to the labourer, has, during the course of the present century, increased perhaps in a still greater proportion than its money price. Not only grain has become somewhat cheaper, but many other things, from which the industrious poor derive an agreeable and wholesome variety of food, have become a great deal cheaper.

The great improvements in the coarser manufactures of both linen and woollen cloth furnish the labourers with cheaper and better cloathing; and those in the manufactures of the coarser metals, with cheaper and better instruments of trade, as well as with many agreeable and convenient pieces of household furniture.

Is this improvement in the circumstances of the lower ranks of the people to be regarded as an advantage or as an inconveniency to the society? The answer seems at first sight abundantly plain. Servants, labourers and workmen of different kinds, make up the far greater part of every great political society. But what improves the circumstances of the greater part can never be regarded as an inconveniency to the whole. No society can surely be flourishing and happy, of which the far greater part of the members are poor and miserable. It is but equity, besides, that they who feed, cloath and lodge the whole body of the people, should have such a share of the produce of their own labour as to be themselves tolerably well fed, cloathed and lodged.

Poverty, though it no doubt discourages, does not always prevent marriage. It seems even to be favourable to generation. A half-starved Highland woman frequently bears more than twenty children, while a pampered fine lady is often incapable of bearing any, and is generally exhausted by two or three. Barrenness, so frequent among women of fashion, is very rare among those of inferior station. Luxury in the fair sex, while it inflames perhaps the passion for enjoyment, seems always to weaken, and frequently to destroy altogether the powers of generation.

But poverty, though it does not prevent the generation, is extremely unfavourable to the rearing of children. The tender plant is produced, but in so cold a soil, and so severe a climate, soon withers and dies. It is not uncommon, I have been frequently told, in the Highlands of Scotland for a mother who has borne twenty children not to have two alive. Several officers of great experience have assured me, that so far from recruiting their regiment, they have never been able to supply it with drums and fifes from all the soldiers' children that were born in it. A greater number of fine children, however, is seldom seen any where than about a barrack of soldiers. Very few of them, it seems, arrive at the age of thirteen or fourteen. In some places one half the children born die before they are four years of age; in many places before they are seven; and in almost all places before they are nine or ten. This great mortality, however, will every where be found chiefly among the children of the common people, who cannot afford to tend them with the same care as those of better station. Though their marriages are generally more fruitful than those of people of fashion, a smaller proportion of their children arrive at maturity. In foundling hospitals, and among the children brought up by parish charities, the mortality is still greater than among those of the common people.

Every species of animals naturally multiplies in proportion to the means of their subsistence, and no species can ever multiply beyond it. But in civilized society it is only among the inferior ranks of people that the scantiness of subsistence can set limits to the further multiplication of the human species; and it can do so in no other way than by destroying a great part of the children which their fruitful marriages produce.

The liberal reward of labour, by enabling them to provide better for their children, and consequently to bring up a greater number, naturally tends to widen and extend those limits. It deserves to be remarked too, that it necessarily does this as nearly as possible in the proportion which the demand for labour requires. If this demand is continually increasing, the reward of labour must necessarily encourage in such a manner the marriage and multiplication of labourers, as may enable them to supply that continually increasing demand by a continually increasing population. If the reward should at any time be less than what was requisite for this purpose, the deficiency of hands would soon raise it; and if it should at any time be more, their excessive multiplication would soon lower it to this necessary rate. The market would be so much under-stocked with labour in the one case, and so much over-stocked in the other, as would soon force back its price to that proper rate which the circumstances of the society required. It is in this manner that the demand for men, like that for any other commodity, necessarily regulates the production of men; quickens it when it goes on too slowly, and stops it when it advances too fast. It is this demand which regulates and determines the state of propagation in all the different countries of the world, in North America, in Europe, and in China; which renders it rapidly progressive in the first, slow and gradual in the second, and altogether stationary in the last. . . .

The liberal reward of labour, therefore, as it is the effect of increasing wealth, so it is the cause of increasing population. To complain of it, is to lament over the necessary effect and cause of the greatest public prosperity.

It deserves to be remarked, perhaps, that it is in the progressive state, while the society is advancing to the further acquisition, rather than when it has acquired its full complement of riches, that the condition of the labouring poor, of the great body of the people, seems to be the happiest and the most comfortable. It is hard in the stationary, and miserable in the declining state. The progressive state is in reality the cheerful and the hearty state to all the different orders of the society. The stationary is dull; the declining melancholy.

The liberal reward of labour, as it encourages the propagation, so it increases the industry of the common people. The wages of labour are the encouragement of industry, which, like every other human quality, improves in proportion to the encouragement it receives. A plentiful subsistence increases the bodily strength of the labourer, and the comfortable hope of bettering his condition, and of ending his days perhaps in ease and plenty, animates him to exert that strength to the utmost. Where wages are high, accordingly, we shall always find the workmen more active, diligent, and expeditious than where they are low. . . .

The difference of natural talents in different men is, in reality, much less than we are aware of; and the very different genius which appears to distinguish men of different professions, when grown up to maturity, is not upon many occasions so much the cause, as the effect of the divisions of labour. The difference between the most dissimilar characters, between a philosopher and a common street porter, for example, seems to arise not so much from nature, as from habit, custom, and education. When they came into the world, and for the first six or eight years of their existence, they were, perhaps, very much alike, and neither their parents nor playfellows could perceive any remarkable difference. About that age, or soon after, they come to be employed in very different occupations. The difference of talents comes then to be taken notice of, and widens by degrees, till at last the vanity of the philosopher is willing to acknowledge scarce any resemblance. But without the disposition to truck, barter, and exchange, every man must have procured to himself every necessary and conveniency of life which he wanted. All must have had the same duties to perform, and the same work to do, and there could have been no such difference of employment as could alone give occasion to any great difference of talents. . . .

The education of the common people requires, perhaps in a civilized and commercial society, the attention of the public more than that of people of some rank and fortune. People of some rank and fortune are generally eighteen or nineteen years of age before they enter upon that particular business, profession, or trade, by which they propose to distinguish themselves in the world. They have before that full time to acquire, or at least to fit themselves for afterwards acquiring, every accomplishment which can recommend them to the public esteem, or render them worthy of it. Their parents or guardians are generally sufficiently anxious that they should be so accomplished, and are, in most cases, willing enough to lay out the expence which is necessary for that purpose. If they are not always properly educated, it is seldom from the want of expence laid out upon their education; but from the improper application of that expence. It is seldom from the want of masters; but from the negligence and incapacity of the masters who are to be had, and from the difficulty, or rather from the impossibility which there is, in the present state of things, of finding any better. The employments too in which people of some rank or fortune spend the greater part of their lives, are not, like those of the common people, simple and uniform. They are almost all of them extremely complicated, and such as exercise the head more than the hands. The understandings of those who are engaged in such employments can seldom grow torpid for want of exercise. The employments of people of some rank and fortune, besides, are seldom such as harass them from morning to night. They generally have a good deal of leisure, during which they may perfect themselves in every branch either of useful or ornamental knowledge of which they may have laid the foundation, or for which they may have acquired some taste in the earlier part of life.

It is otherwise with the common people. They have little time to spare for education. Their parents can scarce afford to maintain them even in infancy. As soon as they are able to work, they must apply to some trade by which they can earn their subsistence. That trade too is generally so simple and uniform as to give little exercise to the understanding; while, at the same time, their labour is both so constant and so severe, that it leaves them little leisure and less inclination to apply to, or even to think of any thing else.

But though the common people cannot, in any civilized society, be so well instructed as people of some rank and fortune, the most essential parts of education, however, to read, write, and account, can be acquired at so early a period of life, that the greater part even of those who are to be bred to the lowest occupations, have time to acquire them before they can be employed in those occupations. For a very small expence the public can facilitate, can encourage, and can even impose upon almost the whole body of the people, the necessity of acquiring those most essential parts of education.

The public can facilitate this acquisition by establishing in every parish or district a little school, where children may be taught for a reward so moderate, that even a common labourer may afford it; the master being partly, but not wholly paid by the public; because, if he was wholly, or even principally paid by it, he would soon learn to neglect his business.

The Wealth of Nations, New York: Random House (Modern Library edition), 1937, pp. 78–81, 15–16, 736–737.

B. Thomas Robert Malthus

If ever there was a gloomy prophet to appear on the economic scene it was Thomas Malthus. Extending Adam Smith's natural law to fit the strategies of the Industrial Revolution,· Malthus concluded that the ill fate of the laboring class was due to the inexorable law of population growth. The more the masses reproduce, which is their irresistible tendency, the more they increase disproportionately in relation to the food supply. Human moral restraint is called for, but the ignorant and slothful folk of the factories are scarcely capable of it, short of letting nature take its course to famine, disease, unemployment and unrest. There is an Augustinian element here: sexuality becomes a curse for most members of the human race since they do not check their passions. The sin of Adam now takes on a new social dimension and provides a fresh rationale for the suffering caused by the machine age.

Malthus (1766–1834), a clergyman and professor of history and political economy, provided the operators and owners of industry in England with a moral justification for the slums and human wreckage their economic practices produced. He wrote in the wake of the French Revolution which he feared might put ideas into the heads of the lower classes on his side of the English Channel. Since poverty was a discipline for wantonness, to relieve the poor of their plight or to raise their wages would only aid and abet their indulgence and bring more mouths to feed into their grim world. The Poor Law of 1834 echoed such sentiments. No relief was to be granted except to those in workhouses. There the husbands and wives were segregated, and the conditions, vividly described by the novelist Charles Dickens, were the worst of the period.

Thus the new class of wealth created by Adam Smith's laissez-faire doctrine could pursue its gain with abandon. No need to worry about subhuman wages and conditions—they were the law of God at work!

An Essay on the Principle of Population

I think I may fairly make two postulata.

First, That food is necessary to the existence of man.

Secondly, That the passion between the sexes is necessary and will remain nearly in its present state.

These two laws, ever since we have had any knowledge of mankind, appear to have been fixed laws of our nature, and, as we have not hitherto seen any alteration in them, we have no right to conclude that they will ever cease to be what they now are, without an immediate act of power in that Being who first arranged the system of the universe, and for the advantage of his creatures, still executes, according to fixed laws, all its various operations.

I do not know that any writer has supposed that on this earth man will ultimately be able to live without food. But Mr. Godwin has conjectured that the passion between the sexes may in time be extinguished. As, however, he calls this part of his work a deviation into the land of conjecture, I will not dwell longer upon it at present than to say that the best arguments for the perfectibility of man are drawn from a contemplation of the great progress that he has already made from the savage state and the difficulty of saying where he is to stop. But towards the extinction of the passion between the sexes, no progress whatsoever has hitherto been made. It appears to exist in as much force at present as it did two thousand or four thousand years ago. There are individual exceptions now as there always have been. But, as these exceptions do not appear to increase in number, it would surely be a very unphilosophical mode of arguing, to infer merely from the existence of an exception, that the exception would, in time, become the rule, and the rule the exception.

Assuming then, my postulata as granted, I say that the power of population is indefinitely greater than the power in the earth to produce subsistence for man.

Population, when unchecked, increases in a geometrical ratio. Subsistence increases only in an arithmetical ratio. A slight acquaintance with numbers will show the immensity of the first power in comparison of the second.

By that law of our nature which makes food necessary to the life of man, the effects of these two unequal powers must be kept equal.

· This implies a strong and constantly operating check on population from the difficulty of subsistence. This difficulty must fall some where and must necessarily be severely felt by a large portion of mankind.

Through the animal and vegetable kingdoms, nature has scattered the seeds of life abroad with the most profuse and liberal hand. She has been comparatively sparing in the room and the nourishment necessary to rear them. The germs of existence contained in this spot of earth, with ample food and ample room to expand in, would fill millions of worlds in the course of a few thousand years. Necessity, that imperious all pervading law of nature, restrains them within the prescribed bounds. The race of plants and the race of animals shrink under this great restrictive law. And the race of man cannot, by any efforts of reason, escape from it. Among plants and animals its effects are waste of seed, sickness, and premature death. Among mankind, misery and vice. The former, misery, is an absolutely necessary consequence of it. Vice is a highly probable consequence, and we therefore see it abundantly prevail, but it ought not, perhaps, to be called an absolutely necessary consequence. The ordeal of virtue is to resist all temptation to evil.

This natural inequality of the two powers of population and of production in the earth and that great law of our nature which must constantly keep their effects equal form the great difficulty that to me appears insurmountable in the way to the perfectibility of society. All other arguments are of slight and subordinate consideration in comparison of this. I see no way by which man can escape from the weight of this law which pervades all animated nature. No fancied equality, no agrarian regulations in their utmost extent, could remove the pressure of it even for a single century. And it appears, therefore, to be decisive against the possible existence of a society, all the members of which should live in ease, happiness, and comparative leisure, and feel no anxiety about providing the means of subsistence for themselves and families.

Consequently, if the premises are just, the argument is conclusive against the perfectibility of the mass of mankind.

I have thus sketched the general outline of the argument, but I will examine it more particularly, and I think it will be found that experience, the time source and foundation of all knowledge, invariably confirms its truth.

I said that population, when unchecked, increased in a geometrical ratio, and subsistence for man in an arithmetical ratio.

Let us examine whether this position be just.

I think it will be allowed that no state has hitherto existed (at least that we have any account of) where the manners were so pure and simple, and the means of subsistence so abundant, that no check whatever has existed to early marriages, among the lower classes, from a fear of not providing well for their families, or among the higher classes, from a fear of lowering their condition in life. Consequently in no state that we have yet known has the power of population been left to exert itself with perfect freedom.

Whether the law of marriage be instituted or not, the dictate of nature and virtue seems to be an early attachment to one woman. Supposing a liberty of changing in the case of an unfortunate choice, this liberty would not affect population till it arose to a height greatly vicious; and we are now supposing the existence of a society where vice is scarcely known.

In a state therefore of great equality and virtue, where pure and simple manners prevailed, and where the means of subsistence were so abundant that no part of the society could have any fears about providing amply for a family, the power of population being left to exert itself unchecked, the increase of the human species would evidently be much greater than any increase that has been hitherto known.

In the United States of America, where the means of subsistence have been more ample, the manners of the people more pure, and consequently the checks to early marriages fewer than in any of the modern states of Europe, the population has been found to double itself in twenty-five years.

This ratio of increase, though short of the utmost power of population, yet as the result of actual experience, we will take as our rule, and say, that population, when unchecked, goes on doubling itself every twenty-five years or increases in a geometrical ratio. . . .

Taking the population of the world at any number, a thousand millions, for instance, the human species would increase in the ratio of——1, 2, 4, 8, 16, 32, 64, 128, 256, 512, &c. and subsistence as——1, 2, 3, 4, 5, 6, 7, 8, 9, 10, &c. In two centuries and a quarter, the population would be to the means of subsistence as 512 to 10, in three centuries as 4096 to 13, and in two thousand years the difference would be almost incalculable, though the produce in that time would have increased to an immense extent.

No limits whatever are placed to the productions of the earth; they may increase for ever and be greater than any assignable quantity; yet still the power of population being a power of a superior order, the increase of the human species can only be kept commensurate to the increase of the means of subsistence by the constant operation of the strong law of necessity acting as a check upon the greater power.

The effects of this check remain now to be considered.

Among plants and animals the view of the subject is simple. They are all impelled by a powerful instinct to the increase of their species, and this instinct is interrupted by no reasoning or doubts about providing for their offspring. Wherever therefore there is liberty, the power of increase is exerted, and the super-abundant effects are repressed afterwards by want of room and nourishment, which is common to animals and plants, and among animals, by becoming the prey of others.

The effects of this check on man are more complicated. Impelled to the increase of his species by an equally powerful instinct, reason interrupts his career and asks him whether he may not bring beings into the world, for whom he cannot provide the means of subsistence. In a state of equality, this would be the simple question. In the present state of society, other considerations occur. Will he not lower his rank in life? Will he not subject himself to greater difficulties than he at present feels? Will he not be obliged to labour harder? and if he has a large family, will his utmost exertions enable him to support them? May he not see his offspring in rags and misery, and clamouring for bread that he cannot give them? And may he not be reduced to the grating necessity for forfeiting his independence and of being obliged to the sparing hand of charity for support?

These considerations are calculated to prevent, and certainly do prevent, a very great number in all civilized nations from pursuing the dictate of nature in an early attachment to one woman. And this restraint almost necessarily, though not absolutely so, produces vice. Yet in all societies, even those that are most vicious, the tendency to a virtuous attachment is so strong that there is a constant effort towards an increase of population. This constant effort as constantly tends to subject the lower classes of the society to distress and to prevent any great permanent amelioration of their condition.

The way in which these effects are produced seems to be this.

We will suppose the means of subsistence in any country just equal to the easy support of its inhabitants. The constant effort towards population, which is found to act even in the most vicious societies, increases the number of people before the means of subsistence are increased. The food therefore which before supported seven millions must now be divided among seven millions and a half or eight millions. The poor consequently must live much worse, and many of them be reduced to severe distress. The number of labourers also being above the proportion of the work in the market, the price of labour must tend toward a decrease, while the price of provisions would at the same time tend to rise. The labourer therefore must work harder to earn the same as he did before. During this season of distress, the discouragements to marriage and the difficulty of rearing a family are so great that population is at a stand. In the mean time the cheapness of labour, the plenty of labourers, and the necessity of an increased industry amongst them, encourage cultivators to employ more labour upon their land, to turn up fresh soil, and to manure and improve more completely what is already in tillage, till ultimately the means of subsistence become in the same proportion to the population as at the period from which we set out. The situation of the labourer being then again tolerably comfortable, the restraints to population are in some degree loosened, and the same retrograde and progressive movements with respect to happiness are repeated.

This sort of oscillation will not be remarked by superficial observers, and it may be difficult even for the most penetrating mind to calculate its periods. Yet that in all old states some such vibration does exist, though from various transverse causes, in a much less marked, and in a much more irregular manner than I have described it, no reflecting man who considers the subject deeply can well doubt. . . .

The next inquiry would be in what way we ought practically to proceed. The first grand obstacle which presents itself in this country is the system of the poor-laws, which has been justly stated to be an evil in comparison of which the national debt, with all its magnitude of terror, is of little moment. The rapidity with which the poor's rates have increased of late years presents us indeed with the prospect of such an extraordinary proportion of paupers in the society as would seem to be incredible in a nation flourishing in arts, agriculture, and commerce, and with a government which has generally been allowed to be the best that has hitherto stood the test of experience.

I have reflected much on the subject of the poor-laws, and hope therefore that I shall be excused in venturing to suggest a mode of their gradual abolition to which I confess that at present I can see no material objection. Of this indeed I feel nearly convinced that, should we ever become so fully sensible of the widespreading tyranny, dependence, indolence, and unhappiness which they create as seriously to make an effort to abolish them, we shall be compelled by a sense of justice to adopt the principle, if not the plan, which I shall mention. It seems impossible to get rid of so extensive a system of support, consistently with humanity, without applying ourselves directly to its vital principle, and endeavouring to counteract that deeply-seated cause which occasions the rapid growth of all such establishments and invariably renders them inadequate to their object.

As a previous step even to any considerable alteration in the present system, which would contract or stop the increase of the relief to be given, it appears to me that we are bound in justice and honour formally to disclaim the *right* of the poor to support.

To this end, I should propose a regulation to be made, declaring that no child born from any marriage, taking place after the expiration of a year from the date of the law, and no illegitimate child born two years from the same date, should ever be entitled to parish assistance. And to give a more general knowledge of this law, and to enforce it more strongly on the minds of the lower classes of people, the clergyman of each parish should, after the publication of banns, read a short address stating the strong obligation on every man to support his own children; the impropriety, and even immorality, of marrying without a prospect of being able to do this; the evils which had resulted to the poor themselves from the attempt which had been made to assist by public institutions in a duty which ought to be exclusively appropriated to parents; and the absolute necessity which had at length appeared of abandoning all such institutions, on account of their producing effects totally opposite to those which were intended.

This would operate as a fair, distinct, and precise notice, which no man could well mistake; and, without pressing hard on any particular individuals, would at once throw off the rising generation from that miserable and helpless dependence upon the government and the rich, the moral as well as physical consequences of which are almost incalculable.

After the public notice which I have proposed had been given, and the system of poor-laws had ceased with regard to the rising generation, if any man chose to marry, without a prospect of being able to support a family, he should have the most perfect liberty so to do. Though to marry, in this case, is, in my opinion, clearly an immoral act, yet it is not one which society can justly take upon itself to prevent or punish; because the punishment provided for it by the laws of nature falls directly and most severely upon the individual who commits the act, and through him, only more remotely and feebly, on the society. When nature will govern and punish for us, it is a very miserable ambition to wish to snatch the rod from her hand and draw upon ourselves the odium of executioner. To the punishment therefore of nature he should be left, the punishment of want. He has erred in the face of a most clear and precise warning, and can have no just reason to complain of any person but himself when he feels the consequences of his error. All parish assistance should be denied him; and he should be left to the uncertain support of private charity. He should be taught to know that the laws of nature, which are the laws of God, had doomed him and his family to suffer for disobeying their repeated admonitions; that he had no claim of *right* on society for the smallest portion of food, beyond that which his labour would fairly purchase; and that if he and his family were saved from feeling the natural consequences of his imprudence he would owe it to the pity of some kind benefactor, to whom, therefore, he ought to be bound by the strongest ties of gratitude.

If this system were pursued, we need be under no apprehensions that the number of persons in extreme want would be beyond the power and the will of the benevolent to supply. The sphere for the exercise of private charity would, probably, not be greater than it is at present; and the principal difficulty would be to restrain the hand of benevolence from assisting those in distress in so indiscriminate a manner as to encourage indolence and want of foresight in others.

With regard to illegitimate children, after the proper notice had been given, they should not be allowed to have any claim to parish assistance, but be left entirely to the support of private charity. If the parents desert their child, they ought to be made answerable for the crime. The infant is, comparatively speaking, of little value to the society, as others will immediately supply its place.

An Essay on the Principle of Population, edited by Philip Appleman. New York: W.W. Norton, 1976, pp. 19–21, 23–25, 134–136.

C. William Godwin

The Essay on Population *of Malthus was written in reply to the ideas of William Godwin (1756–1836), an English political thinker. At one time Godwin, too, was a cleric, although he later turned toward the idea of the Enlightenment and professed the faith of reason, equality, and human perfectibility. A different view of human nature emerges from his rebuttal to Malthus, one that regards man as the molder of his destiny and capable of learning from experience. No one, he thought, is so devoid of rationality as to persist in a course of action that brings about his or her own ruin. Thus even among the humblest folk the natural drives will be put under the reins of discretion and prudence, preventing the logarithmic population explosion that Malthus so gloomily forecast.*

The Malthuisian treatment of the poor also came under Godwin's attack. "Mr. Malthus's is not the religion of the Bible," he declared. "On the contrary it is in diametrical opposition to it." For Christianity cannot allow for placing absolute rights in the hands of owners, giving them total license when it comes to dealing with other human beings. Such is to ignore the recurring theme of compassion that runs through the biblical teaching as well as the theme of stewardship over possessions.

Godwin appeals to another kind of natural law, that which formed the foundation of the philosophical movement of the Enlightenment. The natural light of reason burns in every soul, no matter how dimly, and it provides a ground for hope. The more men learn from it the more perfect and harmonious their societies will become. Both reason and religion, therefore, offer a basis for restraint, stemming the tides of greed and poverty.

Of Population

There was an old maxim, the repetition of which has been attended with some compunction in the minds of the tender-hearted and humane.

"He that will not work, neither shall he eat."

But Mr. Malthus's proscription is of a very different sort, and includes, 1. man in his infancy and childhood, whose little hands are yet incapable of the labour that should procure him the necessaries of life: 2. the aged, whom length of years, and the hardships they have endured, have finally rendered as feeble as helpless infancy: 3. the sick, the cripple, the maimed, and those who labour under one or other of those diseases, which make the most fearful part of the picture of human life: 4. those who, being both able and willing to work, are yet, by the ill constitution of the society

25

of which they are members, or by some of those revolutions to which perhaps all societies are liable, unable to procure employment. These are the persons, whom "in justice and honour" we are bound to inform, that they have no claim of right to the assistance of their prosperous neighbours.

There is no need of informing them, that they have no right, founded in political law, to assistance, except in those countries, and to that extent, where and to which a provision is made for that purpose, as by the poor-laws of England.

But Mr. Malthus's appeal is to a very different jurisdiction. He denies that they have any right in morality to the assistance of their neighbours.

There are two heads and springs of moral duty, as far as this country of England is concerned; the first of which is to be found in the records of the Christian religion, and the other in the instructions we derive from the light of nature. I should not think myself justifiable on the present occasion in over-looking the first.

The lessons of Christianity on this subject are plain and incontrovertible. We are there taught to "love our neighbours as ourselves," and to "do unto others as we would they should do unto us." When an ingenuous young man came to Jesus Christ, desirous to be instructed in his duties, he was referred to the commandment, and, having answered, "All these have I kept from my youth up; what lack I yet?" Christ bade him, "Go, sell all that he had, and give to the poor:" upon which "the young man went away sorrowful; for he had great possessions."

There is a kind of Oriental boldness in this, at least considered as a general exposition of the moral law: for it would be reasonable to answer, If it is my duty to render the greatest benefit to my fellow-creatures, and if my mind is well prepared to discharge this duty, it will probably be better done, by my devoting my income to this purpose, than by at once divesting myself of the principal.

But nothing can be more clear than the general tenour of revelation in this question. By it we are instructed that we are stewards, not proprietors, of the good things of this life, we are forbidden to pamper our appetites or our vanity, we are commanded to be fellow-workers with and impartial ministers of the bountiful principle of nature, and we are told that, when we have done all, we have done nothing of which we have any right to boast.

Such are the dictates of the Christian revelation in this particular: and in all this there is nothing new, nothing that the light of nature did not as clearly and imperiously prescribe, to every one who was willing conscientiously to enquire into the law of morality. . . .

To the rich also he [Malthus] has read an important lesson. A great portion of this class of society are sufficiently indisposed to acts of charity, and eminently prone to the indulgence of their appetites and their vanity.

But hitherto they had secretly reproached themselves with this, as an offence against God and man. Mr. Malthus has been the first man to perform the grateful task of reconciling their conduct and their consciences, and to shew them that, when they thought they were allowing themselves in vice, they were in reality conferring a most eminent and praiseworthy benefit upon the community. . . .

His plan is that of a law, "declaring, that no child born from any marriage, taking place after the expiration of a year from the date of the law, and no illegitimate child born two years from the same date, shall ever be entitled to parish assistance." "This," he says, "would amount to a fair, distinct and precise notice, which no man could well mistake." "No individual would be either deceived or injured and consequently no person could have a just right to complain."

For my own part, I profess myself at a loss to conceive of what earth the man was made, by whom this sentence was penned.

In the question of a child to be born into the world, and of the fortune that shall attend it, there are two parties concerned, the child and its parents. I own I was ignorant enough to imagine that the child was the most deeply concerned of the two.

Tristram Shandy has trifled in a very whimsical way with the idea of a scheme for baptising children before they are born. Mr. Malthus is the first man that has proposed the proclaiming children, and putting them out of the protection of the law, before they are born, for the purpose of preventing them from complaining afterwards. What has his "fair, distinct and precise notice" to do with them?. . .

Here then is a child that perishes with want perhaps as soon as he is born. Or he may drag on the load of existence for a varied length of way, from one to fourscore years. However long he may exist, he shall bear about him for ever the miseries, which arise from his being half-famished in the first stage of existence. And Mr. Malthus comes and tells him he "has no right to complain," for a "fair, distinct and precise notice" was given two years before he was born.

If Mr. Malthus and his disciples were to tell him, that general considerations of human weal, and the "principle of population" required that he should be thus deserted, that would be somewhat different. But to say, that a "fair, distinct and precise notice" was given two years before he was born, and "*therefore* no person has a just right to complain," what a mockery is it! . . .

But let us follow a little more closely Mr. Malthus's scheme for the gradual abolition of the poor-laws.

"To give a more general knowledge of this law, and to inforce it more strongly on the minds of the lower classes of people, I should propose that the clergyman of each parish should, after the publication of the bans of marriage, read a short address, stating the strong obligation on every man to support his own children; the impropriety, and even immorality, of marrying without a prospect of being able to do this; the evils which had resulted to the poor themselves, from the attempt which had been made to assist by public institutions in a duty which ought to be exclusively appropriated to parents; and the absolute necessity which had at length appeared of abandoning all such institutions, on account of their producing effects totally opposite to those which had been intended.

"This would operate as a fair, distinct and precise notice, which no man could well mistake."

It must be admitted that this is a strong measure. It strips human life of all those pleasing hues, and all that fascinating appearance, which, if not genuine, has at least served to reconcile thousands to their fate. Marriage is the grand holiday of our human nature, and, if the rest of the path-way of life is too often involved in horrors or in shades, this is the white spot, the little gleam of pure sunshine, which compensates for a thousand other hardships and calamities. It is indeed a bitter homily to the poor man, that Mr. Malthus proposes. However fair may be his hopes, no one who lives by the sweat of his brow, can be sure that he shall always be able, without assistance, to support a family. . . .

Never certainly was there so comfortable a preacher as Mr. Malthus. No wonder that his book is always to be found in the country-seats of the court of aldermen, and in the palaces of the great. Very appropriately has a retreat been provided for him by the commercial sovereigns of the regions of the East. What a revolution does his theory produce in the interior sentiments of the human breast! There were vices on the earth before Malthus. Men abounding in the good things of this world, indulged themselves unsparingly in all those caprices, which they well knew the mass of their species condemned, and which they more than suspected were worthy of condemnation. But they had a monitor, not only on their shelves, but in their bosoms, which said: "Rejoice, O thou rich man, in thy wealth; and let thy heart cheer thee in the multitude of thy possessions; walk thou in the ways of thy heart, and in the sight of thy eyes: but know, that for all these things God will bring thee into judgment."

Mr. Malthus has reversed all this. He has undertaken to shew, that while they thought they were giving way to their vices, and were drawing down the "curses, not loud, but deep," of the bystanders, they were in reality public benefactors, and that the more they wasted, the more they saved. He has encouraged them to persist in their generous plan of conduct, undismayed by the lamentable misconstructions of their starving fellow-creatures. Nature (not Mr. Malthus's Nature) had planted within us a secret monitor, which, when we wandered from the path of decency and duty, admonished us with a soft and gentle, but articulate voice, and bade us recollect ourselves. But Mr. Malthus stimulates us to drive away this better genius. He reconciles us to the worst and most prodigal appetites of our sensual faculty, and bids us call them by the names of patriotism and philanthropy. It is sufficiently remarkable that, when he enumerates the eleven ways in which vice and misery act to keep down the excess of population, he does not betray his cause, or put the extravagance of the rich and great into his catalogue. It is true, for this it seems is not vice.

Of Population: An Enquiry Concerning the Power of Increase in Numbers of Mankind, Being an Answer to Mr. Malthus's Essay on That Subject. London, 1820.

D. David Ricardo

It was David Ricardo (1772–1823) who put capitalism in the classical form that has come down to us. Having immersed himself in Adam Smith's thought, he set out to revise and improve upon the master's magnum opus, The Wealth of Nations. But Ricardo takes a different approach. Whereas Smith's writing is scholarly, wide-ranged, and given to the whole realm of social and moral ideas, Ricardo comes to the subject of economics from the world of business. His treatment is more techni-cal, setting out to solve problems of limited scope, and following a deductive method which gives his work the tone of a scientific treatise. For fifty years he dom-inated the school of classical economics in Britain. His attractiveness was due in part to the rigor of his method since it offered explanatory laws that covered a wide range of economic phenomena, and in part to his normative principles that happily coincided with the moral code and self-interest of the industrialists and middle class as a whole.

Ricardo pressed the ramifications of Malthus' theory of population into more specific economic principles. His formulation of the "iron law of wages" was to have a lasting impact, not only upon the laissez-faire capitalists, but also upon Karl Marx, the latter adapting it into a doctrine that preached the necessary breakdown of capitalism. Wages, said Ricardo, always tend toward the level of subsistence, providing barely enough for the working family to eat on. Any increase in wages will produce a corresponding rise in the birth rate. But this in turn swells the avail-able working force beyond demand, thus producing a wage downturn. Thus nature itself insists on equilibrium, for as the wages of the worker decrease, so does the birth rate. Then the death rate rises through starvation and disease.

Like Malthus, Ricardo had little faith in the working poor exercising self-re-straint. The thin ray of hope that they would learn the lesson and have fewer chil-dren was overshadowed by the evidence of their past behavior.

Political Economy

On Wages

Labour, like all other things which are purchased and sold, and which may be increased or diminished in quantity, has its natural and its market price. The natural price of labour is that price which is necessary to enable the labourers, one with another, to subsist and to perpetuate their race, without either increase or diminution.

The power of the labourer to support himself, and the family which may be necessary to keep up the number of labourers, does not depend on the quantity of money which he may receive for wages, but on the quantity of food, necessaries, and conveniences become essential to him from habit which that money will purchase. The natural price of labour, therefore, depends on the price of the food, necessaries, and conveniences required for the support of the labourer and his family. With a rise in the price of food and necessaries, the natural price of labour will rise; with the fall in their price, the natural price of labour will fall.

With the progress of society the natural price of labour has always a tendency to rise, because one of the principal commodities by which its natural price is regulated has a tendency to become dearer from the greater difficulty of producing it. As, however, the improvements in agriculture, the discovery of new markets, whence provisions may be imported, may for a time counteract the tendency to a rise in the price of necessaries, and may even occasion their natural price to fall, so will the same causes produce the correspondent effects on the natural price of labour.

The natural price of all commodities, excepting raw produce and labour, has a tendency to fall in the progress of wealth and population; for though, on one hand, they are enhanced in real value, from the rise in the natural price of the raw material of which they are made, this is more than counterbalanced by the improvements in machinery, by the better division and distribution of labour, and by the increasing skill, both in science and art, of the producers.

The market price of labour is the price which is really paid for it, from the natural operation of the proportion of the supply to the demand; labour is dear when it is scarce and cheap when it is plentiful. However much the market price of labour may deviate from its natural price, it has, like commodities, a tendency to conform to it.

It is when the market price of labour exceeds its natural price that the condition of the labourer is flourishing and happy, that he has it in his power to command a greater proportion of the necessaries and enjoyments of life, and therefore to rear a healthy and numerous family. When, however, by the encouragement which high wages give to the increase of population, the number of labourers is increased, wages again fall to their natural price, and indeed from a reaction sometimes fall below it.

When the market price of labour is below its natural price, the condition of the labourers is most wretched: then poverty deprives them of those comforts which custom renders absolute necessaries. It is only after their privations have reduced their number, or the demand for labour has increased, that the market price of labour will rise to its natural price, and that the labourer will have the moderate comforts which the natural rate of wages will afford. . . .

It is not to be understood that the natural price of labour, estimated even in food and necessaries, is absolutely fixed and constant. It varies at different times in the same country, and very materially differs in different countries. It essentially depends on the habits and customs of the people. An English labourer would consider his wages under their natural rate, and too scanty to support a family, if they enabled him to purchase no other food than potatoes, and to live in no better habitation than a mud cabin; yet these moderate demands of nature are often deemed sufficient in countries where "man's life is cheap" and his wants easily satisfied. Many of the conveniences now enjoyed in an English cottage would have been thought luxuries at an earlier period of our history. . . .

The friends of humanity cannot but wish that in all countries the labouring classes should have a taste for comforts and enjoyments, and that they should be stimulated by all legal means in their exertions to procure them. There cannot be a better security against a superabundant population. In those countries where the labouring classes have the fewest wants, and are contented with the cheapest food, the people are exposed to the greatest vicissitudes and miseries. They have no place of refuge from calamity; they cannot seek safety in a lower station; they are already so low that they can fall no lower. On any deficiency of the chief article of their subsistence there are few substitutes of which they can avail themselves and dearth to them is attended with almost all the evils of famine. . . .

These, then, are the laws by which wages are regulated, and by which the happiness of far the greatest part of every community is governed. Like all other contracts, wages should be left to the fair and free competition of the market, and should never be controlled by the interference of the legislature.

The clear and direct tendency of the poor laws is in direct opposition to these obvious principles: it is not, as the legislature benevolently intended, to amend the condition of the poor, but to deteriorate the condition of both poor and rich; instead of making the poor rich, they are calculated to make the rich poor; and whilst the present laws are in force, it is quite in the natural order of things that the fund for the maintenance of the poor should progressively increase till it has absorbed all the net revenue of the country, or at least so much of it as the state shall leave to us, after satisfying its own never-failing demands for the public expenditure.

This pernicious tendency of these laws is no longer a mystery, since it has been fully developed by the able hand of Mr. Malthus; and every friend to the poor must ardently wish for their abolition. Unfortunately, however, they have been so long established, and the habits of the poor have been so formed upon their operation, that to eradicate them with safety from our political system requires the most cautious and skilful management. It is agreed by all who are most friendly to a repeal of these laws that, if it be desirable to prevent the most overwhelming distress to those for whose benefit they were erroneously enacted, their abolition should be effected by the most gradual steps.

It is a truth which admits not a doubt that the comforts and well-being of the poor cannot be permanently secured without some regard on their part, or some effort on the part of the legislature, to regulate the increase of their numbers, and to render less frequent among them early and improvident marriages. The operation of the system of poor laws has been directly contrary to this. They have rendered restraint superfluous, and have invited imprudence, by offering it a portion of the wages of prudence and industry.

The nature of the evil points out the remedy. By gradually contracting the sphere of the poor laws; by impressing on the poor the value of independence, by teaching them that they must look not to systematic or casual charity, but to their own exertions for support, that prudence and forethought are neither unnecessary nor unprofitable virtues, we shall by degrees approach a sounder and more healthful state.

No scheme for the amendment of the poor laws merits the least attention which has not their abolition for its ultimate object; and he is the best friend of the poor, and to the cause of humanity, who can point out how this end can be attained with the most security, and at the same time with the least violence. . . .

On Machinery

Ever since I first turned my attention to questions of political economy, I have been of opinion that such an application of machinery to any branch of production as should have the effect of saving labour was a general good, accompanied only with that portion of inconvenience which in most cases attends the removal of capital and labour from one employment to another. It appeared to me that, provided the landlords had the same money rents, they would be benefited by the reduction in the prices of some of the commodities on which those rents were expended, and which reduction of price could not fail to be the consequence of the employment of machinery. The capitalist, I thought, was eventually benefited precisely in the same manner. He, indeed, who made the discovery of the machine, or who first usefully applied it, would enjoy an additional advantage by making great profits for a time; but, in proportion as the machine came into general use, the price of the commodity produced would, from the effects of competition, sink to its cost of production, when the capitalist would get the same money profits as before, and he would only participate in the general advantage as a consumer, by being enabled, with the same money revenue, to command an additional quantity of comforts and enjoyments. The class of labourers also, I thought, was equally benefited by the use of machinery, as they would have the means of buying more commodities with the same money wages, and I thought that no reduction of wages would take place because the capitalist would have the power of demanding and employing the same quantity of labour as before, although he might be under the necessity of employing it in the production of a new or, at any rate, of a different commodity. If, by improved machinery, with the employment of the same quantity of labour, the quantity of stockings could be quadrupled, and the demand for stockings were only doubled, some labourers would necessarily be discharged from the stocking trade; but as the capital which employed them was still in being, and as it was the interest of those who had it to employ it productively, it appeared to me that it would be employed on the production of some other commodity useful to the society, for which there could not fail to be a demand; for I was, and am, deeply impressed with the truth of the observation of Adam Smith, that "the desire for food is limited in every man by the narrow capacity of the human stomach, but the desire of the conveniences and ornaments of building, dress, equipage, and household furniture, seems to have no limit or certain boundary." As, then, it appeared to me that there would be the same demand for labour as before, and that wages would be no lower, I thought that the labouring class would, equally with the other classes, participate in the advantage, from the general cheapness of commodities arising from the use of machinery.

These were my opinions, and they continue unaltered, as far as regards the landlord and the capitalist; but I am convinced that the substitution of machinery for human labour is often very injurious to the interests of the class of labourers.

My mistake arose from the supposition that whenever the net income of a society increased, its gross income would also increase; I now, however, see reason to be satisfied that the one fund, from which landlords and capitalists derive their revenue, may increase, while the other, that upon which the labouring class mainly depend, may diminish, and therefore it follows, if I am right, that the same cause which may increase the net revenue of the country may at the same time render the population redundant, and deteriorate the condition of the labourer. . . .

All I wish to prove is that the discovery and use of machinery may be attended with a diminution of gross produce; and whenever that is the case, it will be injurious to the labouring class, as some of their number will be thrown out of employment, and population will become redundant compared with the funds which are to employ it.

The Principles of Political Economy and Taxation, London: J.M. Dent and Sons, Ltd., 1973, pp. 52–63, 263–271.

E. Thomas Paine

Here is another voice from the age of the Enlightenment, but sounding a different note altogether from that of Adam Smith. Paine (1737–1809) was sympathetic to the French Revolution and published the Rights of Man *as a defense and extension of it. Among those rights were economic ones, since in his eyes a man's political rights are well-nigh meaningless to an empty stomach. When his work first appeared in England, it met with strong approval, especially among those who championed the cause of the lower classes, and it sold close to 200,000 copies its first year. But the government authorities detected an odor of sedition in it and ordered the work banned, seeking the author's arrest and imprisonment. Paine fled to France, then to America, where he met with a more favorable reception among political leaders. His work, however, survived even in England and became the backbone of the British labor movement.*

Note the change in perspective: where Smith saw both poverty and wealth in society as the result of natural forces (in particular, the economic laws of freedom and competition creating a natural harmony), Paine saw them as the consequences of social and political policies. He questioned the divine right of capitalism and especially the inequities it created. The selections included here foreshadow the modern welfare system with its comprehensive program for all ages. Paine cannot be called a socialist, however; in fact he does not deal with the question of the ownership of productive forces but only with the distribution of wealth. He attempts to show that the tax system, if not the creator of poverty, is at least its perpetuator, and that its overhaul could go a long way toward eliminating poverty altogether. Many of his suggestions find their echo in the social legislation of the twentieth century in this country.

Paine helps to sharpen the dilemma of modern-day considerations in economic justice with its conflict of values. On the one hand are the advantages of individual freedom and the rights of each member of society to pursue his or her own interest and gain in a free competitive market; on the other are the social values of providing general sustenance, employment, and security to all members of the society. How much of one shall we sacrifice for the sake of the other? What kind of balance should be struck between them? These are questions that relate not only to what Smith and Paine have to say but to most of the others that follow. They are continuing concerns of economic justice.

Rights of Man

When, in countries that are called civilized, we see age going to the work-house, and youth to the gallows, something must be wrong in the system of government. It would seem, by the exterior appearance of such countries, that all was happiness; but there lies hidden from the eye of common observation, a mass of wretchedness that has scarcely any other chance than to expire in poverty or infamy. Its entrance into life is marked with the presage of its fate; and until this is remedied, it is in vain to punish.

Civil government does not consist in executions; but in making that provision for the instruction of youth, and the support of age, as to exclude, as much as possible, profligacy from the one, and despair from the other. Instead of this, the resources of a country are lavished upon kings, upon courts, upon hirelings, imposters, and prostitutes; and even the poor themselves, with all their wants upon them, are compelled to support the fraud that oppresses them.

Why is it that scarcely any are executed but the poor? The fact is a proof, among other things, of a wretchedness in their condition. Bred up without morals, and cast upon the world without a prospect, they are the exposed sacrifice of vice and legal barbarity. The millions that are superfluously wasted upon governments are more than sufficient to reform those evils, and to benefit the condition of every man in the nation, not included within the purlieus of a court. This I hope to make appear in the progress of this work.

It is the nature of compassion to associate with misfortune. In taking up this subject, I seek no recompense—I fear no consequences. Fortified with that proud integrity that disdains to triumph or to yield, I will advocate the Rights of Man. . . .

Before the coming of the Hanoverians, the taxes were divided in nearly equal proportions between the land and articles of consumption, the land bearing rather the largest share; but since that era, nearly thirteen millions annually of new taxes have been thrown upon consumption. The consequence of which has been a constant increase in the number and wretchedness of the poor, and in the amount of the poor-rates.

Yet here again the burden does not fall in equal proportions on the aristocracy with the rest of the community. Their residences, whether in town or country, are not mixed with the habitations of the poor. They live apart from distress, and the expense of relieving it. It is in the manufacturing towns and laboring villages that those burdens press the heaviest; in many of which it is one class of poor supporting another.

Several of the most heavy and productive taxes are so contrived as to give an exemption to this pillar, thus standing in its own defense. The tax upon beer brewed for sale does not affect the aristocracy, who brew their own beer free of this duty. It falls only on those who have not conveniency or ability to brew, and who must purchase it in small quantities.

But what will mankind think of the justice of taxation, when they know, that this tax alone, from which the aristocracy are from circumstances exempt, is nearly equal to the whole of the land-tax, being in the year 1788, (and it is not less now), £1,666,152, and with its proportion of the taxes on malt and hops, it exceeds it. That a single article thus partially consumed, and that chiefly by the working part, should be subject to a tax equal to that on the whole rental of a nation, is, perhaps, a fact not to be paralleled in the history of revenues. . . .

Were an estimation to be made of the charge of the aristocracy to a nation, it will be found nearly equal to that of supporting the poor. The Duke of Richmond alone (and there are cases similar to his) takes away as much for himself as would maintain two thousand poor and aged persons. Is it, then, any wonder that under such a system of government, taxes and rates have multiplied to their present extent?

In stating these matters, I speak an open and disinterested language, dictated by no passion but that of humanity. To me, who have not only refused offers, because I thought them improper, but have declined rewards I might with reputation have accepted, it is no wonder that meanness and imposition appear disgusting. Independence is my happiness, and I view things as they are, without regard to place or person; my country is the world, and my religion is to do good. . . .

At the time when the taxes were very low, the poor were able to maintain themselves; and there were no poor-rates. In the present state of things, a laboring man, with a wife and two or three children, does not pay less than between seven and eight pounds a year in taxes. He is not sensible of this, because it is disguised to him in the articles which he buys, and he thinks only of their dearness; but as the taxes take from him, at least, a fourth part of his yearly earnings, he is consequently disabled from providing for a family, especially if himself, or any of them, are afflicted with sickness.

The first step, therefore, of practical relief, would be to abolish the poor-rates entirely, and, in lieu thereof, to make a remission of taxes to the poor to double the amount of the present poor-rates, *viz.*, four millions annually out of the surplus taxes. By this measure, the poor would be benefited two millions, and the housekeepers two millions. This alone would be equal to a reduction of one hundred and twenty millions of the national debt, and consequently equal to the whole expense of the American War.

It will then remain to be considered, which is the most effectual mode of distributing the remission of four millions.

It is easily seen, that the poor are generally composed of large families of children, and old people unable to labor. If these two classes are provided for, the remedy will so far reach to the full extent of the case, that what remains will be incidental, and, in a great measure, fall within the compass of benefit clubs, which, though of humble invention, merit to be ranked among the best of modern institutions.

Admitting England to contain seven millions of souls; if one-fifth thereof are of that class of poor which need support, the number will be one million four hundred thousand. Of this number, one hundred and forty thousand will be aged poor, as will be hereafter shown, and for which a distinct provision will be proposed.

There will then remain one million two hundred and sixty thousand, which, at five souls to each family, amount to two hundred and fifty-two thousand families, rendered poor from the expense of children and the weight of taxes. . . .

To provide for . . . persons, who at one time or other of their lives, after fifty years of age, may feel it necessary or comfortable to be better supported, than they can support themselves, and that not as a matter of grace and favor, but of right. . . .

This support, as already remarked, is not of the nature of charity, but of a right. Every person in England, male or female, pays on an average of taxes, two pounds eight shillings and sixpence per annum from the day of his (or her) birth; and if the expense of collection be added, he pays two pounds, eleven shillings and sixpence; consequently, at the end of fifty years, he has paid one hundred and twenty-eight pounds fifteen shillings; and at sixty, one hundred and fifty-four pounds ten shillings.

Converting, therefore, his (or her) individual tax into a tontine, the money he shall receive after fifty years, is but little more than the legal interest of the net money he has paid. . . .

After all the above cases are provided for, there will still be a number of families who, though not properly of the class of poor, yet find it difficult to give education to their children, and such children, under such a case, would be in a worse condition than if their parents were actually poor. A nation under a well regulated government should permit none to remain uninstructed. It is monarchial and aristocratical governments, only, that require ignorance for their support.

Suppose then four hundred thousand children to be in this condition, which is a greater number than ought to be supposed, after the provisions already made, the method will be:

To allow for each of those children ten shillings a year for the expense of schooling, for six years each, which will give them six months schooling each year, and half a crown a year for paper and spelling books. . . .

Cases are continually occurring in a metropolis different from those which occur in the country, and for which a different, or rather an additional mode of relief is necessary. In the country, even in large towns, people have a knowledge of each other and distress never rises to that extreme height it sometimes does in a metropolis. There is no such thing in the country as persons, in the literal sense of the word, starved to death, or dying with cold from the want of a lodging. Yet such cases, and others equally as miserable, happen in London.

Many a youth comes up to London full of expectations, and little or no money, and unless he gets employment he is already half undone; and boys bred up in London without any means of a livelihood, and, as it often happens, of dissolute parents, are in a still worse condition, and servants long out of place are not much better off. In short, a world of little cases is continually arising, which busy or affluent life knows not of, to open the first door to distress. Hunger is not among the postponable wants, and a day, even a few hours, in such a condition, is often the crisis of a life of ruin.

These circumstances, which are the general cause of the little thefts and pilferings that lead to greater, may be prevented. . . . The plan then will be:

First, To erect two or more buildings, or take some already erected, capable of containing at least six thousand persons, and to have in each of these places as many kinds of employment as can be contrived, so that every person who shall come, may find something which he or she can do.

Secondly, To receive all who shall come, without inquiring who or what they are. The only condition to be, that for so much or so many hours work, each person shall receive so many meals of wholesome food, and a warm lodging, at least as good as a barrack. That a certain portion of what each person's work shall be worth shall be reserved, and given to him, or her, on their going away; and that each person shall stay as long, or as short time, or come as often as he chooses, on these conditions. . . .

Notwithstanding the great modes of relief which the best instituted and best principled government may devise, there will still be a number of smaller cases, which it is good policy as well as beneficence in a nation to consider.

Were twenty shillings to be given to every woman immediately on the birth of a child, who should make the demand, and none will make it whose circumstances do not require it, it might relieve a great deal of instant distress. . . .

And twenty shillings to every new married couple who should claim in like manner. . . .

Also [money] to be appropriated to defray the funeral expenses of persons, who, traveling for work, may die at a distance from their friends. By relieving parishes from this charge, the sick stranger will be better treated.

I shall finish this part of my subject with a plan adapted to the particular condition of a metropolis, such as London. . . .

By the operation of this plan, the poor laws, those instruments of civil

torture, will be superseded, and the wasteful expense of litigation prevented. The hearts of the humane will not be shocked by ragged and hungry
children, and persons of seventy and eighty years of age begging for bread.
The dying poor will not be dragged from place to place to breathe their last,
as a reprisal of parish upon parish.

Widows will have maintenance for their children, and will not be
carted away, on the death of their husbands, like culprits and criminals; and
children will no longer be considered as increasing the distress of their parents. The haunts of the wretched will be known, because it will be to their
advantage; and the number of petty crimes, the offspring of distress and
poverty, will be lessened. The poor, as well as the rich, will then be interested in the support of government, and the cause and apprehension of riots
and tumults will cease.

Ye who sit in ease, and solace yourselves in plenty, and such there are
in Turkey and Russia, as well as in England, and who say to yourselves,
"Are we not well off," have ye thought of these things? When ye do, ye
will cease to speak and feel for yourselves alone.

Rights of Man—Part Second, in William M. Van der Weyde, ed., *The Life and*
Works of Thomas Paine. **New Rochelle, N.Y.: Thomas Paine National Historical Asso-**
ciation, 1926, Volume VII, pp. 15–16, 26–28, 32, 51–66.

F. John Stuart Mill

Although Mill (1806–1873) was an advocate of the classical theory of economics in his early years, he abhorred its dismal implications for the common man. He recognized, however, that the theory's fundamental premises had to be revised if it was to lead to better consequences. Mill was primarily a philosopher and moralist. He sought to infuse Utilitarianism with a humanitarian spirit and served as an active member of Parliament where he championed the working class and helped to enact important social legislation in its behalf. Recognizing that true liberty and happiness were not purely private matters, he championed public education for all, universal suffrage, women's rights, restrictions on the working hours for children, the creation of labor unions, and the imposition of an inheritance tax on the rich as measures to mitigate the inequalities of wealth.

The selections below contain two important points. The first is that the forces that control production of wealth are not the same as those that govern its distribution. Wealth is created by laws that are very much like physical laws. Nature directly affects the process, first by the character of material things, and second by the physical and mental properties of the producers themselves. Thus the laws that govern production seem fairly strict and unalterable. In contrast, the underlying factors that govern the distribution of wealth are social and historical, and therefore a matter of human contrivance and custom. The distinction was a crucial one for Mill. It meant that poverty within a capitalist society was not the result of forces working outside man's control; rather it was the product of the way that society chose to allocate its wealth and property.

Perhaps the persons who made up that society were not consciously aware of that choice, or even of the fact that a choice was being made. Its lack of visibility was due to that fact that it is embodied in the laws, the institutions and habits, and the prevailing codes and ideologies that form the mentality of that society.

The other selection contains Mill's discussion of communism which he judges, in comparison with capitalism, according to utilitarian norms. Which system produces the greatest benefits, not only in terms of material well-being, but also in terms of personal freedom? Which would provide security but without sacrificing a wide degree of diversity among men? Mill insists that the only true comparison is between the principles of the two systems, not their practices which fall short of these principles. The ultimate test is whether the proposals of communism are preferable to a more humane form of capitalism in which the consequences set forth in the doctrines of Malthus and Ricardo are avoided.

In answering this question note how Mill revises the notion of economy itself. No longer is it a self-sufficient, all-embracing system whose ends we are bound to serve whether we wish to or not, and whose laws remain wholly outside the province of human control. Economy, including capitalistic forms of it, is to be servant rather than master. Its practices are to be submitted to critical judgment in terms of the total ends of society and of its individual members. Such an instrumental view meant the abandonment of a wholly laissez-faire approach and recognized that laws and government belong to a higher level of responsibility for men's ills and fortunes. As we read Mill, we are bound to ask whether he went far enough—whether the forces that produce wealth may not also be a matter of human contrivance along with those of distribution. If so, then the laws of economy would seem to be even more contingent than he thought.

Political Economy

The principles which have been set forth in the first part of this Treatise, are, in certain respects, strongly distinguished from those, on the consideration of which we are now about to enter. The laws and conditions of the production of wealth, partake of the character of physical truths. There is nothing optional, or arbitrary in them. Whatever mankind produce, must be produced in the modes, and under the conditions, imposed by the constitution of external things, and by the inherent properties of their own bodily and mental structure. Whether they like it or not, their productions will be limited by the amount of their previous accumulation, and, that being given, it will be proportional to their energy, their skill, the perfection of their machinery, and their judicious use of the advantages of combined labor. Whether they like it or not, a double quantity of labor will not raise, on the same land, a double quantity of food, unless some improvement takes place in the processes of cultivation. Whether they like it or not, the unproductive expenditure of individuals will *pro tanto* tend to impoverish the community, and only their productive expenditure will enrich it. The opinions, or the wishes, which may exist on these different matters, do not control the things themselves. We cannot, indeed, foresee to what extent the modes of production may be altered, or the productiveness of labor increased, by future extensions of our knowledge of the laws of nature, suggesting new processes of industry of which we have at present no conception. But howsoever we may succeed in making for ourselves more space within the limits set by the constitution of things, we know that there must be limits. We cannot alter the ultimate properties either of matter or mind, but can only employ those properties more or less successfully, to bring about the events in which we are interested.

It is not so with the Distribution of Wealth. That is a matter of human institution solely. The things once there, mankind, individually or collectively, can do with them as they like. They can place them at the disposal of whomsoever they please, and on whatever terms. Further, in the social state, in every state except total solitude, any disposal whatever of them can only take place by the consent of society, or rather of those who dispose of its active force. Even what a person has produced by his individual toil, unaided by anyone, he cannot keep, unless by the permission of society. Not only can society take it from him, but individuals could and would take it from him, if society only remained passive; if it did not either interfere *en masse,* or employ and pay people for the purpose of preventing him from being disturbed in the possession. The distribution of wealth, therefore, depends on the laws and customs of society. The rules by which it is determined, are what the opinions and feelings of the ruling portion of the community make them, and are very different in different ages and countries; and might be still more different, if mankind so chose. . . .

Whatever may be the merits or defects of these various schemes, they cannot be truly said to be impracticable. No reasonable person can doubt that a village community, composed of a few thousand inhabitants cultivating in joint ownership the same extent of land which at present feeds that number of people, and producing by combined labor and the most improved processes the manufactured articles which they required, could raise an amount of productions sufficient to maintain them in comfort; and would find the means of obtaining, and if need be, exacting, the quantity of labor necessary for this purpose, from every member of the association who was capable of work.

The objection ordinarily made to a system of community of property and equal distribution of the produce, that each person would be incessantly occupied in evading his fair share of the work, points, undoubtedly, to a real difficulty. But those who urge this objection, forget to how great an extent the same difficulty exists under the system on which nine-tenths of the business of society is now conducted. The objection supposes, that honest and efficient labor is only to be had from those who are themselves individually to reap the benefit of their own exertions. But how small a part of all the labor performed in England, from the lowest paid to the highest, is done by persons working for their own benefit. From the Irish reaper or hodman to the chief justice or the minister of state, nearly all the work of society is remunerated by day wages or fixed salaries. A factory operative has less personal interest in his work than a member of a Communist association, since he is not, like him, working for a partnership of which he is himself a member. . . . Even the laborer who loses his employment by idleness or negligence, has nothing worse to suffer, in the most unfavorable case, than the discipline of a workhouse, and if the desire to avoid this be a sufficient motive in the one system, it would be sufficient in the other. I am not undervaluing the strength of the incitement given to labor when the whole or a large share of the benefit of extra exertion belongs to the laborer. But under the present system of industry this incitement, in the great majority of cases, does not exist. If Communistic labor might be less vigorous than that of a peasant proprietor, or a workman laboring on his own account, it would probably be more energetic than that of a laborer for hire, who has no personal interest in the matter at all. The neglect by the uneducated classes of laborers for hire, of the duties which they engage to perform, is in the present state of society most flagrant. Now it is an admitted condition of the Communist scheme that all shall be educated: and this being supposed, the duties of the members of the association would doubtless be as diligently performed as those of the generality of salaried officers in the middle or higher classes; who are not supposed to be necessarily unfaithful to their trust, because so long as they are not dismissed, their pay is the same in however lax a manner their duty is fulfilled. Undoubtedly, as a general rule, remuneration by fixed salaries does not in any class of functionaries produce the maximum of zeal: and this is as much as can be reasonably alleged against Communistic labor.

That even this inferiority would necessarily exist, is by no means so certain as is assumed by those who are little used to carry their minds beyond the state of things with which they are familiar. Mankind are capable of a far greater amount of public spirit than the present age is accustomed to suppose possible. History bears witness to the success with which large bodies of human beings may be trained to feel the public interest their own. And no soil could be more favorable to the growth of such a feeling, than a Communist association, since all the ambition, and the bodily and mental activity, which are now exerted in the pursuit of separate and self-regarding interests, would require another sphere of employment, and would naturally find it in the pursuit of the general benefit of the community. The same cause, so often assigned in explanation of the devotion of the Catholic priest or monk to the interest of his order—that he has no interest apart from it—would, under Communism, attach the citizen to the community. And independently of the public motive, every member of the association would be amenable to the most universal, and one of the strongest of personal motives, that of public opinion. The force of this motive in deterring from any act or omission positively reproved by the community, no one is likely to deny; but the power also of emulation, in exciting to the most strenuous exertions for the sake of the approbation and admiration of others, is borne witness to by experience in every situation in which human beings publicly compete with one another, even if it be in things frivolous, or from which the public derive no benefit. A contest, who can do most for the common good, is not the kind of competition which Socialists repudiate. To what extent, therefore, the energy of labor would be diminished by Communism, or whether in the long run it would be diminished at all, must be considered for the present an undecided question.

Another of the objections to Communism is similar to that, so often urged against poor-laws: that if every member of the community were assured of subsistence for himself and any number of children, on the sole condition of willingness to work, prudential restraint on the multiplication of mankind would be at an end, and population would start forward at a rate which would reduce the community through successive stages of increasing discomfort to actual starvation. There would certainly be much ground for this apprehension if Communism provided no motives to restraint, equivalent to those which it would take away. But Communism is precisely the state of things in which opinion might be expected to declare itself with great intensity against this kind of selfish intemperance. Any augmentation of numbers which diminished the comfort or increased the toil of the mass, would then cause (which now it does not) immediate and unmistakable inconvenience to every individual in the association; inconvenience which could not then be imputed to the avarice of employers, or the unjust privileges of the rich. In such altered circumstances opinion could not fail to reprobate, and if reprobation did not suffice, to repress by penalties of some description, this or any other culpable self-indulgence at the expense of the community. The Communistic scheme, instead of being peculiarly open to the objection drawn from danger of over-population, has the recommendation of tending in an especial degree to the prevention of that evil.

A more real difficulty is that of fairly apportioning the labor of the community among its members. There are many kinds of work, and by what standard are they to be measured one against another? Who is to judge how much cotton spinning, or distributing goods from the stores, or bricklaying, or chimney sweeping, is equivalent to so much ploughing? The difficulty of making the adjustment between different qualities of labor is so strongly felt by Communist writers, that they have usually thought it necessary to provide that all should work by turns at every description of useful labor: an arrangement which by putting an end to the division of employments, would sacrifice so much of the advantage of co-operative production as greatly to diminish the productiveness of labor. Besides, even in the same kind of work, nominal equality of labor would be so great a real inequality, that the feeling of justice would revolt against its being enforced. All persons are not equally fit for all labor; and the same quantity of labor is an unequal burden on the weak and the strong, the hardy and the delicate, the quick and the slow, the dull and the intelligent.

But these difficulties, though real, are not necessarily insuperable. The apportionment of work to the strength and capacities of individuals, the mitigation of a general rule to provide for cases in which it would operate harshly, are not problems to which human intelligence, guided by a sense of justice, would be inadequate. And the worst and most unjust arrangement which could be made of these points, under a system aiming at equality, would be so far short of the inequality and injustice with which labor (not to speak of remuneration) is now apportioned, as to be scarcely worth counting in the comparison. We must remember too that Communism, as a system of society, exists only in idea; that its difficulties, at present, are much better understood than its resources; and that the intellect of mankind is only beginning to contrive the means of organizing it in detail, so as to overcome the one and derive the greatest advantage from the other.

If, therefore, the choice were to be made between Communism with all its chances, and the present state of society with all its sufferings and injustices; if the institution of private property necessarily carried with it as a consequence, that the produce of labor should be apportioned as we now see it, almost in an inverse ratio to the labor—the largest portions to those who have never worked at all, the next largest to those whose work is almost nominal, and so in a descending scale, the remuneration dwindling as the work grows harder and more disagreeable, until the most fatiguing and exhausting bodily labor cannot count with certainty on being able to earn even the necessaries of life; if this, or Communism, were the alternative, all the difficulties, great or small, of Communism would be but as dust in the balance. But to make the comparison applicable, we must compare Communism at its best, with the *régime* of individual property, not as it is, but as it might be made. The principle of private property has never yet had a fair trial in any country; and less so, perhaps, in this country than in some others. The social arrangements of modern Europe commenced from a distribution of property which was the result, not of just partition, or acquisition by industry, but of conquest and violence: and notwithstanding what industry has been doing for many centuries to modify the work force, the system still retains many and large traces of its origin. The laws of property have never yet conformed to the principles on which the justification of private property rests. They have made property of things which never ought to be property, and absolute property where only a qualified property ought to exist. They have not held the balance fairly between human beings, but have heaped impediments upon some, to give advantage to others; they have purposely fostered inequalities, and prevented all from starting fair in the race. That all should indeed start on perfectly equal terms, is inconsistent with any law of private property: but if as much pains as has been taken to aggravate the inequality of chances arising from the natural working of the principle, had been taken to temper that inequality by every means not subversive of the principle itself; if the tendency of legislation had been to favor the diffusion, instead of the concentration of wealth—to encourage the subdivision of the large masses, instead of striving to keep them together; the principle of individual property would have been found to have no necessary connection with the physical and social evils which almost all Socialist writers assume to be inseparable from it.

Private property, in every defence made of it, is supposed to mean, the guarantee to individuals, of the fruits of their own labor and abstinence. The guarantee to them of the fruits of the labor and abstinence of others, transmitted to them without any merit or exertion of their own, is not of the essence of the institution, but a mere incidental consequence, which when it reaches a certain height, does not promote, but conflicts with the ends which render private property legitimate. To judge of the final destination of the institution of property, we must suppose everything rectified, which causes the institution to work in a manner opposed to that equitable principle, of proportion between remuneration and exertion, on which in every vindication of it that will bear the light, it is assumed to be grounded. We must also suppose two conditions realized, without which neither Communism nor any other laws or institutions could make the condition of the mass of mankind other than degraded and miserable. One of these conditions is, universal education; the other, a due limitation of the numbers of the community. With these, there could be no poverty even under the present social institutions: and these being supposed, the question of Socialism is not, as generally stated by Socialists, a question of flying to the sole refuge against the evils which now bear down humanity; but a mere question of comparative advantages, which futurity must determine. We are too ignorant either of what individual agency in its best form, or Socialism in its best form, can accomplish, to be qualified to decide which of the two will be the ultimate form of human society.

If a conjecture may be hazarded, the decision will probably depend mainly on one consideration, viz., which of the two systems is consistent with the greatest amount of human liberty and spontaneity. After the means of subsistence are assured, the next in strength of the personal wants of human beings is liberty; and (unlike the physical wants, which as civilization advances become more moderate and more amenable to control) it increases instead of diminishing in intensity, as the intelligence and the moral faculties are more developed. The perfection both of social arrangements and of practical morality would be, to secure to all persons complete independence and freedom of action, subject to no restriction but that of not doing injury to others: and the education which taught or the social institutions which required them to exchange the control of their own actions for any amount of comfort or affluence, or to renounce liberty for the sake of equality, would deprive them of one of the most elevated characteristics of human nature. It remains to be discovered how far the preservation of this characteristic would be found compatible with the communistic organization of society. No doubt, this, like all the other objections to the Socialist schemes, is vastly exaggerated. The members of the association need not be required to live together more than they do now, nor need they be controlled in the disposal of their individual share of the produce, and of the probably large amount of leisure which, if they limited their production to things really worth producing, they would possess. Individuals need not be chained to an occupation, or to a particular locality. The restraints of Communism would be freedom in comparison with the present condition of the majority of the human race. The generality of laborers in this and most other countries, have as little choice of occupation or freedom of locomotion, are practically as dependent on fixed rules and on the will of others, as they could be on any system short of actual slavery; to say nothing of the entire domestic subjection of one-half the species, to which it is the signal honor of Owenism and most other forms of Socialism that they assign equal rights, in all respects, with those of the hitherto dominant sex. But it is not by comparison with the present bad state of society that the claims of Communism can be estimated; nor is it sufficient that it should promise greater personal and mental freedom than is now enjoyed by those who have not enough of either to deserve the name. The question is whether there would be any asylum left for individuality of character; whether public opinion would not be a tyrannical yoke; whether the absolute dependence of each on all, and surveillance of each by all, would not grind all down into a tame uniformity of thoughts, feelings, and actions. This is already one of the glaring evils of the existing state of society, notwithstanding a much greater diversity of education and pursuits and a much less absolute dependence of the individual on the mass, than would exist in the Communistic *régime*. No society in which eccentricity is a matter of reproach, can be in a wholesome state. It is yet to be ascertained whether the Communistic scheme would be consistent with that multiform development of human nature, those manifold unlikenesses, that diversity of tastes and talents, and variety of intellectual points of view, which not only form a great part of the interest of human life, but by bringing intellects into a stimulating collision, and by presenting to each innumerable notions that he would not have conceived of himself, are the mainspring of mental and moral progression.

Political Economy, Volume I. Revised Edition. New York: The Colonial Press, 1899, pp. 196–197, 200–208.

G. Robert Owen

Robert Owen (1771–1858) was an unusual combination of capitalist and social reformer. Self-made and self-educated, he owned one of the largest cotton mills in Scotland at New Lanark by the time he was twenty-nine. There he sought to prove that the laissez-faire system could be benevolent as well as profitable by making New Lanark a model community for the mill workers. New and better houses were built, streets were paved, fuel was made available at low cost, free medical care was provided, and all forms of punishment within the factory were abolished. The first preschool nursery in Britain was established, as well as free schools for children five to ten years old. The workday shrank from seventeen to ten hours, and children were not allowed to work in the factories until the age of ten—instead of seven.

Owen's experimental community was a clear success, but it was not copied by other industrialists. Nor was his plan for cooperative villages adopted by Parliament, part of which is presented here. Clearly he was ahead of his time in his dream of replacing competition with cooperatives organized by workers and consumers. New Harmony, Indiana was his attempt to implement his ideas on this side of the Altantic, a utopian community that met with much less success than New Lanark.

At the foundation of Owen's secular communitarianism was his persistent belief that poverty and degradation were the consequences of social environment and not of natural conditions. Change the environment—provide decent homes, education, health care, and a sense of participation in the community and production of wealth—and the motivation and character of the individual will change also. Thus he raises a major philosophical challenge to the likes of Malthus and Ricardo who see the worker's conditions as the natural results of capitalism—i.e., part of the unchangeable order of things. Owen in essence is saying that capitalism can be held responsible for the conditions it creates, and these conditions can be changed. But he is also interjecting a new element within the idea of capitalism itself. It is that competition can be supplemented with cooperative endeavors and these, while not destroying the profit-making motive, can channel and mitigate its effects to the benefit of those who historically have stood to suffer the most from its excesses.

Report to the House of Commons

My Lords and Gentlemen, having been requested by you to draw up a detailed Report of a Plan for the general Relief of the Manufacturing and Labouring Poor, I have the honour to submit the following.

In order to do justice to this interesting subject, it is necessary to trace the operation of those leading causes, to which the distress now existing to an unprecedented extent in this country, and in other countries in no very slight degree, is to be ascribed: the evil will be found to flow from a state of things to which the progress of society has given birth;—a development of this will therefore suggest the means of counteracting it.

The immediate cause of the present distress is the depreciation of human labour. This has been occasioned by the general introduction of mechanism into the manufactures of Europe and America; but principally into those of Britain, where the change was greatly accelerated by the inventions of Arkwright and Watt. . . .

I proceed, therefore, with the subject, and shall endeavour to show in what manner advantageous employment can be found for all the poor and working classes, under an arrangement which will permit mechanical improvements to be carried to any extent.

Under the existing laws, the unemployed working classes are maintained by, and consume part of the property and produce of, the wealthy and industrious, while their powers of body and mind remain unproductive. They frequently acquire the bad habits which ignorance and idleness never fail to produce; they amalgamate with the regular poor, and become a nuisance to society. . . .

. . . Any plan for the amelioration of the poor should combine means to prevent their children from acquiring bad habits, and to give them good ones—to provide useful training and instruction for them—to provide proper labour for the adults—to direct their labour and expenditure, so as to produce the greatest benefit to themselves and to society; and to place them under such circumstances as shall remove them from unnecessary temptations, and closely unite their interest and duty.

These advantages cannot be given either to individuals, or families, separately, or to large congregated numbers.

They can be effectually introduced into practice only under arrangements that would unite in one establishment a population of from 500 to 1500 persons, averaging about 1000. . . .

It is evident, that while the poor are suffered to remain under the circumstances in which they have hitherto existed, they, and their children with very few exceptions, will continue unaltered to succeeding generations.

In order to effect any radically beneficial change in their character, they must be removed from the influence of such circumstances, and placed under those which, being congenial to the natural constitution of man, and the well-being of society, cannot fail to produce that amelioration in their condition, which all classes have so great an interest in promoting.

Such circumstances, after incessant application to the subject, I have endeavoured to combine in the arrangement of the establishment represented in the drawings, so far as the present state of society will permit. These I will now attempt to explain more particularly.

Each lodging-room is to accommodate a man, his wife, and two children under three years of age; and to be such as will permit them to have much more comfort than the dwellings of the poor usually afford. It is intended that the children above three years of age should attend the school, eat in the mess-room, and sleep in the dormitories, the parents being of course permitted to see and converse with them at meals, and all other proper times. That before they leave school they shall be well instructed in all necessary and useful knowledge; that every possible means should be adopted to prevent the acquirement of bad habits, from their parents or otherwise; that no pains should be spared to impress upon them such habits and dispositions as may be most conducive to their happiness through life, as well as render them useful and valuable members of the community to which they belong.

It is proposed that the women should be employed, in the first place, in the care of their infants, and in keeping their dwellings in the best order. 2dly, In cultivating the gardens to raise vegetables for the supply of the public kitchen. 3dly, In attending to such of the branches of the various manufactures as women can well undertake; but not to be employed more than four or five hours in the day. 4thly, In making up clothing for the inmates of the establishment. 5thly, In attending occasionally, and in rotation, in the public kitchen, mess-rooms, and dormitories; and when properly instructed, in superintending some parts of the education of the children in the schools.

It is proposed that the elder children should be trained to assist in gardening and manufacturing for a portion of the day, according to their strength; and that the men should be employed, all of them, in agriculture, and also in manufactures or some other occupation for the benefit of the establishment.

The ignorance of the poor, their ill training, and want of a rational education, make it necessary that those of the present generation should be actively and regularly occupied through the day in some essentially useful work; yet in such a manner as that their employment should be healthy and productive. The plan which has been described will most amply admit of this. . . .

It is impossible to find language sufficiently strong to express the inconsistency, as well as the injustice, of our present proceedings towards the poor and working classes. They are left in gross ignorance. They are permitted to be trained up in habits of vice, and in the commission of crimes;

and, as if purposely to keep them in ignorance and vice, and goad them on to commit criminal acts, they are perpetually surrounded with temptations which cannot fail to produce all those effects.

The system, or rather want of system, which exists with regard to the management of the poor has been emphatically condemned by a long and painful experience.

The immense sums annually raised for their relief are lavished in utter disregard of every principle of public justice or economy. They offer greater reward for idleness and vice than for industry and virtue; and thus directly operate to increase the degradation and misery of the classes whom they are designed to serve. No sum, however enormous, administered after this manner, could be productive of any other result: rather will pauperism and wretchedness increase along with the increase of an expenditure thus applied.

The poor and unemployed working classes however cannot, must not, be abandoned to their fate, lest the consequences entail misfortune on us all. Instead of being left as they now are, to the dominion of ignorance, and to the influence of circumstances which are fatal to their industry and morals—a situation in which it is easy to perceive the inefficacy, or rather the injuriousness, of granting them a provision in a mere pecuniary shape— they should, on the contrary, be afforded the means of procuring a certain and comfortable subsistence by their labour, under a system which will not only direct that labour and its earnings to the best advantage, but, at the same time, place them under circumstances the most favourable to the growth of morals and of happiness. In short, instead of allowing their habits to proceed under the worst influence possible, or rather as it were to be left to chance, thus producing unintentionally crimes that render necessary the severities of our penal code,—let a system for the prevention of pauperism and of crimes be adopted, and the operation of our penal code will soon be restricted to very narrow limits.

The outlines of such a plan, it is presumed, have been, however imperfectly, suggested and sketched in this Report.

It may be hoped that the Government of this country is now sufficiently alive to the necessity of abandoning the principle on which all our legislative measures on this subject have hitherto proceeded; for no thing short of this can place the empire in permanent safety. Until the preventive principle shall become the basis of legislative proceedings, it will be vain to look for any measures beyond partial temporary expedients, which will leave society unimproved, or involve it in a much worse state. . . .

A summary of the advantages to be derived from the execution of such a plan may be presented under the following heads:

1. Expensive as such a system for the unemployed poor may appear to a superficial observer, it will be found on mature investigation by those who understand all the consequences of such a combination, to be by far the most economical that has yet been devised.

2. Many of the unemployed poor are now in a state of gross ignorance, and have been trained in bad habits,—evils which, under the present system, are likely to continue for endless generations. The arrangements proposed offer the most certain means, in a manner gratifying to all the parties interested, and to every liberal mind, of overcoming both their ignorance and their bad habits in one generation.

3. The greatest evils in society arise from mankind being trained in principles of disunion. The proposed measures offer to unite men in the pursuit of common objects for their mutual benefit, by presenting an easy practicable plan for gradually withdrawing the causes of difference among individuals, and of making their interest and duty very generally the same.

4. This system will also afford the most simple and effectual means of giving the best habits and sentiments to all the children of the unemployed poor, accordingly as society shall be able to determine what habits and sentiments, or what character, ought to be given to them.

5. It will likewise offer the most powerful means of improving the habits and general conduct of the present unemployed adult poor, who have been grossly neglected by society from their infancy.

6. Owing to the peculiar arrangement of the plan, it will give to the poor, in return for their labour, more valuable, substantial, and permanent comfort than they have ever yet been able to obtain.

7. In one generation it will supersede the necessity for poor rates, or any pecuniary gifts of charity, by preventing any one from being poor, or subject to such unnecessary degradation.

8. It will offer the means of gradually increasing the population of such unpopulous districts of Europe and America as may be deemed necessary;—of enabling a much greater population to subsist in comfort on a given spot, if requisite, than existed before;—in short, of increasing the strength and political power of the country in which it shall be adopted, more than tenfold.

9. It is so easy, that it may be put into practice with less ability and exertion than are necessary to establish a new manufacture in a new situation. Many individuals of ordinary talents have formed establishments which possess combinations much more complex. In fact, there would not be any thing required which is not daily performed in common society, and which, under the proposed arrangement, might not be much more easily accomplished.

10. It will effectually relieve the manufacturing and labouring poor from their present deep distress, without violently or prematurely interfering with the existing institutions of society.

11. It will permit mechanical inventions and improvements to be carried to any extent; for by the proposed arrangement every improvement in mechanism would be rendered subservient to, and in aid of, human labour.

12. and lastly. Every part of society would be essentially benefited by this change in the condition of the poor. Some plan founded on such principles as have been developed herein, appears absolutely necessary to secure the well-being of society; as well as to prevent the afflicting spectacle of thousands pining in want, and amidst a superabundance of means to well-train, educate, employ, and support in comfort, a population of at least four times the present numbers.

Report to the Committee of the Association for the Relief of the Manufacturing and Laboring Poor, Laid Before the Committee of the House of Commons on the Poor Laws. London 1817.

H. Karl Marx

Although the name of Karl Marx (1818–1883) is anathema to most Americans, it belongs to a figure who launched one of the most searching attacks on the theory and practice of capitalism. Marx concluded that injustice and poverty are no mere accidental by-products of the system; they are essential elements within it. The capitalist venture is founded on false premises from the beginning.

Marx sees all past history as a repetition of the master-slave relation, all, that is, except for a very early period which practiced primitive communism. This epoch, which he calls the Asiatic, saw the communal ownership of land, combined labor forces, and no private property. As soon as private property was introduced there arose a division between rich and poor, accompanied by a demand for available labor to serve the propertied masters. At first the laborers were secured by conquest in war and enslavement of the captives. But moving into the classical era of Greece and Rome, there arose complex institutions of government and law which kept the masses of domestic citizens in a state of bondage. The feudal and bourgeois periods that followed and bring us up to the time of Marx perpetuated vast inequalities among the classes and merely changed the institutions of oppression.

The real target of Marx's attack, however, was the system he observed at work in his own time—modern capitalism. Private property, the accumulation of wealth through profits by the few elite who owned industry, the paying of wages for labor—these practices constituted the real roadblock to any improvement in the worker's plight. Moreover, they were sowing the seeds of their own destruction. For capitalism operates according to laws as rigorous as those of a machine and grinds out inevitable effects. Wealth puts the entire locus of economic power at the disposal of the owners. Their power is absolute. The laboring class is reduced to a new kind of serfdom which in most respects, Marx thinks, is worse than the old form of it. Both the employed and unemployed are victimized, first because the supply of labor exceeds the demand and creates a large body of unemployed, and second because scarcity of jobs produces the lowest possible wage since labor is abundantly available to the industrialists. The laboring class is kept at a subsistence level, and the law of increased disproportion takes over: the wealthier and more powerful the owners become, the poorer and weaker labor becomes. Conditions thus ripen for revolution.

Marx never conceived of the possibility of poverty in the communist society once it was established. All able-bodied persons would be employed. Only the last vestiges of bourgeois mentality would produce sloth and idleness, for the change in ownership of the productive processes would release the ''natural'' impulses of the proletariat to work and to cooperate. Thus the problems of the poor would be solved axiomatically once the new order was established.

Capital

The labouring population therefore produces, along with the accumulation of capital produced by it, the means by which itself is made relatively
superfluous, is turned into a relative surplus population; and it does this to
an always increasing extent. This is a law of population peculiar to the capitalist mode of production; and in fact every special historic mode of production has its own special laws of population, historically valid within its
limits alone. An abstract law of population exists for plants and animals
only, and only in so far as man has not interfered with them.

But if a surplus labouring population is a necessary product of accumulation or of the development of wealth on a capitalist basis, this surplus
population becomes, conversely, the lever of capitalistic accumulation,
nay, a condition of existence of the capitalist mode of production. It forms
a disposable industrial reserve army, that belongs to capital quite as absolutely as if the latter had bred it at its own cost. Independently of the limits
of the actual increase of population, it creates, for the changing needs of the
self-expansion of capital, a mass of human material always ready for exploitation. With accumulation, and the development of the productiveness
of labour that accompanies it, the power of sudden expansion of capital
grows also; it grows, not merely because the elasticity of the capital already
functioning increases, not merely because the absolute wealth of society
expands, of which capital only forms an elastic part, not merely because
credit, under every special stimulus, at once places an unusual part of this
wealth at the disposal of production in the form of additional capital; it
grows, also, because the technical conditions of the process of production
themselves—machinery, means of transport, &c.—now admit of the rap-
idest transformations of masses of surplus product into additional means of
production. The mass of social wealth, overflowing with the advance of accumulation, and transformable into additional capital, thrusts itself frantically into old branches of production, whose market suddenly expands, or
into newly formed branches, such as railways, &c., the need for which
grows out of the development of the old ones. In all such cases, there must
be the possibility of throwing great masses of men suddenly on the decisive
points without injury of the scale of production in other spheres. Over-population supplies these masses. The course characteristic of modern industry, viz., a decennial cycle (interrupted by smaller oscillations), of periods
of average activity, production at high pressure, crisis and stagnation, depends on the constant formation, the greater or less absorption, and the re-
formation of the industrial reserve army of surplus population. In their turn,
the varying phases of the industrial cycle recruit the surplus population, and

become one of the most energetic agents of its reproduction. This peculiar course of modern industry, which occurs in no earlier period of human history, was also impossible in the childhood of capitalist production. The composition of capital changed but very slowly. With its accumulation, therefore, there kept pace, on the whole, a corresponding growth in the demand for labour. Slow as was the advance of accumulation compared with that of more modern times, it found a check in the natural limits of the exploitable labouring population, limits which could only be got rid of by forcible means to be mentioned later. The expansion by fits and starts of the scale of production is the preliminary to its equally sudden contraction; the latter again evokes the former, but the former is impossible without disposable human material, without an increase in the number of labourers independently of the absolute growth of the population. This increase is effected by the simple process that constantly "sets free" a part of the labourers; by methods which lessen the number of labourers employed in proportion to the increased production. The whole form of the movement of modern industry depends, therefore, upon the constant transformation of a part of the labouring population into unemployed or half-employed hands. . . .

The industrial reserve army, during the periods of stagnation and average prosperity, weighs down the active labour-army; during the periods of over-production and paroxysm, it holds its pretensions in check. Relative surplus-population is therefore the pivot upon which the law of demand and supply of labour works. It confines the field of action of this law within the limits absolutely convenient to the activity of exploitation and to the domination of capital. . . .

The relative surplus population exists in every possible form. Every labourer belongs to it during the time when he is only partially employed or wholly unemployed. Not taking into account the great periodically recurring forms that the changing phases of the industrial cycle impress on it, now an acute form during the crisis, then again a chronic form during dull times—it has always three forms, the floating, the latent, the stagnant.

In the centres of modern industry—factories, manufacturers, ironworks, mines, &c.—the labourers are sometimes repelled, sometimes attracted again in greater masses, the number of those employed increasing on the whole, although in a constantly decreasing proportion to the scale of production. Here the surplus population exists in the floating form.

In the automatic factories, as in all the great workshops, where machinery enters as a factor, or where only the modern divisions of labour is carried out, large numbers of boys are employed up to the age of maturity. When this term is once reached, only a very small number continue to find employment in the same branches of industry, whilst the majority are regularly discharged. This majority forms an element of the floating surplus-population, growing with the extension of those branches of industry. Part of them emigrates, following in fact capital that has emigrated. One consequence is that the female population grows more rapidly than the male, *teste* England. That the natural increase of the number of labourers does not satisfy the requirements of the accumulation of capital, and yet all the time is in excess of them, is a contradiction inherent to the movement of capital itself. It wants larger numbers of youthful labourers, a smaller number of adults. The contradiction is not more glaring than that other one that there is a complaint of the want of hands, while at the same time many thousands are out of work, because the division of labour chains them to a particular branch of industry.

The consumption of labour-power by capital is, besides, so rapid that the labourer, half-way through his life, has already more or less completely lived himself out. He falls into the ranks of the supernumeraries, or is thrust down from a higher to a lower step in the scale. It is precisely among the work-people of modern industry that we meet with the shortest duration of life. Dr. Lee, Medical Officer of Health for Manchester, stated "that the average age at death of the Manchester . . . upper middle class was 38 years, while the average age at death of the labouring class was 17; while at Liverpool those figures were represented as 35 against 15. It thus appeared that the well-to-do classes had a lease of life which was more than double the value of that which fell to the lot of the less favoured citizens." In order to conform to these circumstances, the absolute increase of this section of the proletariat must take place under conditions that shall swell their numbers, although the individual elements are used up rapidly. Hence, rapid renewal of the generations of labourers (this law does not hold for the other classes of the population). This social need is met by early marriages, a necessary consequence of the conditions in which the labourers of modern industry live, and by the premium that the exploitation of children sets on their production.

As soon as capitalist production takes possession of agriculture, and in proportion to the extent to which it does so, the demand for an agricultural labouring population falls absolutely, while the accumulation of the capital employed in agriculture advances, without this repulsion being, as in non-agricultural industries, compensated by a greater attraction. Part of the agricultural population is therefore constantly on the point of passing over into an urban or manufacturing proletariat, and on the look-out for circumstances favourable to this transformation. (Manufacture is used here in the sense of all non-agricultural industries). This source of relative surplus-population is thus constantly flowing. But the constant flow towards the towns presupposes, in the country itself, a constant latent surplus-population, the extent of which becomes evident only when its channels of outlet open to exceptional width. The agricultural labourer is therefore reduced to the minimum of wages, and always stands with one foot already in the swamp of pauperism.

The third category of the relative surplus-population, the stagnant, forms a part of the active labour army, but with extremely irregular employment. Hence it furnishes to capital an inexhaustible reservoir of disposable labour-power. Its conditions of life sink below the average normal level of the working class; this makes it at once the broad basis of special branches of capitalist exploitation. It is characterized by maximum of working time, and minimum of wages. We have learnt to know its chief form under the rubric of "domestic industry." It recruits itself constantly from the supernumerary forces of modern industry and agriculture, and specially from those decaying branches of industry where handicraft is yielding to manufacture, manufacture to machinery. Its extent grows, as with the extent and energy of accumulation, the creation of a surplus population advances. But it forms at the same time a self-reproducing and self-perpetuating element of the working class, taking a proportionally greater part in the general increase of that class than the other elements. In fact, not only the number of births and deaths, but the absolute size of the families stands in inverse proportion to the height of wages, therefore to the amount of means of subsistence of which the different categories of labourers dispose. This law of capitalistic society would sound absurd to savages, or even civilized colonists. It calls to mind the boundless reproduction of animals individually weak and constantly hunted down.

The lowest sediment of the relative surplus-population finally dwells in the sphere of pauperism. Exclusive of vagabonds, criminals, prostitutes, in a word, the "dangerous" classes, this layer of society consists of three categories. First, those able to work. One need only glance superficially at the statistics of English pauperism to find that the quantity of paupers increases with every crisis, and diminishes with every revival of trade. Second, orphans and pauper children. These are candidates for the industrial reserve-army, and are, in times of great prosperity, as 1860, *e.g.*, speedily and in large numbers enrolled in the active army of labourers. Third, the demoralized and ragged, and those unable to work, chiefly people who succumb to their incapacity for adaptation, due to the division of labour; people who have passed the normal age of the labourer; the victims of industry, whose number increases with the increase of dangerous machinery, of mines, chemical works, &c., the mutilated, the sickly, the widows, &c. Pauperism is the hospital of the active labour-army and the dead weight of the industrial reserve-army. Its production is included in that of the relative surplus-population, its necessity in theirs; along with the surplus-population, pauperism forms a condition of capitalist production, and of the capitalist development of wealth. It enters into the *faux frais* of capitalist production; but capital knows how to throw these, for the most part, from its own shoulders on to those of the working-class and the lower middle class.

The greater the social wealth, the functioning capital, the extent and energy of its growth, and, therefore, also the absolute mass of the proletariat and the productiveness of its labour, the greater is the industrial reserve-army. The same causes which develop the expansive power of capital, develops also the labour-power at its disposal. The relative mass of the industrial reserve-army increases therefore with the potential energy of wealth. But the greater this reserve-army in proportion to the active labour-army, the greater is the mass of a consolidated surplus-population, whose misery is in inverse ratio to its torment of labour. The more extensive, finally, the lazurus-layers of the working-class, and the industrial reserve-army, the greater is official pauperism. *This is the absolute general law of capitalist accumulation.* Like all other laws it is modified in its working by many circumstances, the analysis of which does not concern us here.

The folly is now patent of the economic wisdom that preaches to the labourers the accommodation of their number to the requirements of capital. The mechanism of capitalist production and accumulation constantly effects this adjustment. The first word of this adaptation is the creation of a relative surplus-population, or industrial reserve-army. Its last word is the misery of constantly extending strata of the active army of labour, and the dead weight of pauperism.

The law by which a constantly increasing quantity of means of production, thanks to the advance in the productiveness of social labour, may be set in movement by a progressively diminishing expenditure of human power, this law, in a capitalist society—where the labourer does not employ the means of production, but the means of production employ the labourer—undergoes a complete inversion and is expressed thus: the higher the productiveness of labour, the greater is the pressure of the labourers on the means of employment, the more precarious, therefore, becomes their condition of existence, viz., the sale of their own labour-power for the increasing of another's wealth, or for the self-expansion of capital. The fact that the means of production, and the productiveness of labour, increase more rapidly than the productive population, expresses itself, therefore, capitalistically in the inverse form that the labouring population always increases more rapidly than the conditions under which capital can employ this increase for its own self-expansion.

We saw [earlier], when analysing the production of relative surplus-value; within the capitalist system all methods for raising the social productiveness of labour are brought about at the cost of the individual labourer; all means for the development of production transform themselves into means of domination over, and exploitation of, the producers; they mutilate the labourer into a fragment of a man, degrade him to the level of an appendage of a machine, destroy every remnant of charm in his work and turn it into a hated toil; they estrange from him the intellectual potentialities of the labour-process in the same proportion as science is incorporated in it as an independant power; they distort the conditions under which he works, subject him during the labour-process to a despotism the more hateful for its meanness; they transform his life-time into working-time, and drag his wife and child beneath the wheels of the Juggernaut of capital. But all methods for the production of surplus value are at the same time methods of accumulation; and every extension of accumulation becomes again a means for the development of those methods. It follows therefore that in proportion as capital accumulates, the lot of the labourer, be his payment high or low, must grow worse. The law, finally, that always equilibrates the relative surplus-population, or industrial reserve army, to the extent and energy of accumulation, this law rivets the labourer to capital more firmly than the wedges of Vulcan did Prometheus to the rock. It establishes an accumulation of misery, corresponding with accumulation of capital. Accumulation of wealth at one pole is, therefore, at the same time accumulation of misery, agony of toil, slavery, ignorance, brutality, mental degradation, at the opposite pole, *i.e.*, on the side of the class that produces its own product in the form of capital.

Capital, **Karl Marx. New York: Random House, pp. 692–695, 701, 703–709.**

III. Religious Perspectives

Both Judaism and Christianity insist upon an obligation to the poor in their ethical teaching. Turning first to Jewish thought we find two themes running through the Hebraic scriptures. One is stewardship which defines the terms of the use of property and wealth. In the story of creation in Genesis where God gives man dominion over the earth, it is intended that the use of the earth will be one in which man remains responsible to God. Humans are not given an absolute right to the things they own and use, and their abuse brings about dire consequences. The covenant of God with man is a promise of freedom (including sovereignty) but within the moral context established within the covenant. Poor management constitutes a breach. Our current emphasis on ecology is a contemporary version of this theme. To abuse the environment is to bring havoc upon human existence and threaten the well-being of the entire race.

The other theme is that of active concern for the poor. More than once we find the injunction to "open wide your hand to your brother, to the needy and to the poor" (Dt 15:11). The laws of the Torah are specific in setting forth obligations of the field and vineyard owners to share the harvest with the poor. When reaping grain the owner is to leave a portion to be reaped by the poor. They shall also gather any stalks that fall from the hand of the reaper. After the gathering is completed a sheaf of grain is to be left behind for the poor. The same duties are incumbent upon the vineyard lords. The poor are to be allowed to gather any grapes dropped during the harvest and to pick any not joined together in clusters on the vine. The distinctive teaching of the Torah is that all such gifts are the property of the poor and as such cannot be withheld from them by the owner. Nor can the latter select the recipients since all the poor have the right to share them. Beyond these continual gifts the Torah obligates the owners of fields and vineyards to give a tithe or tenth of all their produce every third year. In biblical times the proportion of income going to the poor was considerable since agriculture was the principle livelihood.

The Jewish teaching does not consider these goods as "charity" in the modern sense of handouts that depend sheerly upon the good will of the giver. The Hebrew word for "charity" is Zedakkah, and its primary meaning is "justice," underscoring the fact that giving to the needy is a duty and not merely a matter of personal feeling or disposition. The donor is to look upon the recipient as having the same flesh—the same hungers, thirsts, and nakedness—as oneself. Anonymous gifts are the most suitable, for then the dignity of the poor is protected. Even the harvester in dropping grain for the poor is not to look back, and the true benefactor will remove all his workers from the field before sundown so that the poor have time to gather unobserved.

The original intent of the Jewish law was far from legalistic. It was to duplicate on the human level the likeness of God as manifest in the covenant: a God of love, mercy, and compassion. Duty was to spring from inner character and not from some external and alien force. The Hebrew prophets had much to say about those who fulfill the law externally only but lack the heart required of those who truly obey God out of love. Such hypocrisy does not go unnoticed! Love is of soul and body, thought and action.

When we come to the Christian idea of charity we find a continuation and fulfillment of the same ideas in the teaching and life of Jesus. Although love is conceived as transcending the prescribed duties of the law, it does not do away with responsibility. There are still obligations among persons, but these are translated into a joyous self-giving, one that does not measure out its acts or calculate its costs. Yet the danger that has plagued Christianity almost from the very beginning has been its tendency to sentimentalize love and render it ineffective against the ills and inequities that societies have incorporated within their structures. In emphasizing the transcendent quality of love over justice, the requirements of justice have often been pushed aside and forgotten.

At its best Christianity has held love and justice together in a lively tension, one in which each requires the other but at the same time resists being swallowed up by the other. Without justice love becomes merely a dispositional quality; without love justice becomes expediency or legalism or both. The unending task of Christians has been to relate these two principles to particular cases in such a way that the integrity of both has been preserved. Here, however, there is need for help and it has sometimes been lacking. What is required, as William Temple among others has pointed out, are "middle axioms," those subordinate rules that connect the ultimate principles such as loving one's neighbor as oneself to the immediate situation in which we are to act. Middle axioms would guide us in exercising good judgment and instruct us in the kind of consequences produced by our acts that are in keeping with the spirit and substance of the Christian faith.

The separation of love and justice, however, is a persistent pattern in our history and it has taken a number of forms. It has led to a divorce between private and public morality in which personal and social conduct are at variance with one another. And this in turn has produced a split between the sphere of ethics and that of economics, the fruits of which we have inherited. With the advent of Adam Smith's philosophy, it was thought that moral decisions within the economy not only were unnecessary but would disrupt the whole system. The Invisible Hand of the free market was regarded as a moral force itself, acting as a providential instrument of adjustment and embodying a wisdom higher than any collective sum of human wisdom. The only requirement made of the individual was that of pursuing self-interest, something he was hardly in need of being told to do. The fundamental laws of economics were thought to operate autonomously, like those of Newton's science which charted the universe as a divinely constructed machine complete and ultimately perfect in all of its workings.

Laissez-faire philosophy gained ascendency because of important historical changes. Foremost among them was the emergence and spectacular success of the middle class which broke away from a system of values based on land ownership and created a new kind of wealth in money and trade. Here, for the first time, the possibility of financial gain was open to a large proportion of the population. Capitalism offered a kind of economic democracy. Ordinary persons of unsuspected talents and energies were able to secure wealth; they needed no special title or recognition, no patronage on the part of those holding noble rank. Distribution of wealth depended upon effort and use of opportunity. Thus it seemed that so long as basic education was provided so that all members of society could become players in the market game, the outcome would be just, and anyone who remained poor would do so through self-inflicted sloth or indulgence.

Such, at least, became the laissez-faire creed even though its more thoughtful proponents never intended to rid economics of ethics altogether. But the separation of the two became more established as economics was conceived to be more and more a "science," a discipline of measured values that pushed normative questions outside its purview. Matters of production and distribution became the business of the specialist with his charts, graphs, and formulae. The moralist came to be regarded as an inept meddler whose attempts to bring economics under ethical control only tended to throw the system out of order.

There are recent signs, however, that moral considerations are gaining a new credence. Witness, for example, the increase in courses being offered on college and university campuses dealing with business ethics, consumer and environmental issues, and a minimum standard of living. Questions are being asked about government fiscal policy, especially the proposed and approved budget cuts in programs that benefit the lower-income segments of our society. There is growing concern also over the conditions in the third world, especially in Latin America, where a vast endless peasantry has been held down by a powerful and wealthy elite, and where the distribution of wealth has taken on dimensions of global impact.

In the selections below are voices that have reaffirmed the need for ethical considerations in economic affairs. They are at one in affirming that the handling of wealth is a concern of society at large and not merely of the specialist. Walter Rauschenbusch, high priest of the social gospel movement, lived and wrote in an America in which the vast inequalities of wealth reached their zenith. The pitiful wages paid by industry in the early years of the twentieth century kept a vast proportion of the population in penury. Rauschenbusch saw that the Christianity generally preached in the churches was not even addressing the economic conditions of the time. His emphasis upon the social teachings of the Gospel was an antidote to a religion that had been restricted to the private lives of individuals. Walter Muelder comes out of this same tradition. His theme of social responsibility puts a focus on the need for the corporate and collective forms of life to be held accountable for the establishment of justice. In *Pacem in Terris,* the encyclical from Pope John XXIII, we find one of the most eloquent statements in recent times of human rights. Here the idea of social responsibility takes on a global context. The selection from the Oxford Conference Report, although written earlier than John's encyclical, develops the concept of justice as it applies to the social and economic order within a Christian context and shows how, without justice, the ethic of love is out of touch with this order. Reinhold Niebuhr spent a lifetime dealing with these two norms, love and justice, showing how they are both necessary for the full Christian life and how they interrelate. The selection included here is one of the more concise statements he has written on that subject. Liberation theology comes out of the struggle of oppressed and underdeveloped peoples who have never known anything like a democratic process through which to voice their grievances. The demands for social justice become more strident in the writings of the theologians represented here, Enrique Dussel and Denis Goulet. The social gospel is carried to new lengths in which the Christian is called to identify himself, as did Jesus, with the forces of revolution against intransigent centers of political power. It is a doctrine that is likely to bring great personal cost and suffering. There is a decided shift throughout these sections toward an increasingly activist role in the historical process to bring about change.

A. Walter Rauschenbusch

Walter Rauschenbusch (1861–1918) was the foremost spokesman of the social gospel movement in its early years. Born in Rochester, New York, of a long line of German clergymen, he was reared in the Protestant pietistic tradition which stressed inward faith and outward acceptance of the social order. But his experience in New York City brought about a radical change. His first church where he was to serve for eleven years was located right next to Hell's Kitchen, a slum area that received wide notoriety because of its sordid conditions. Nothing could have rudely awakened him more from his pietistic slumbers. Subsequently he joined the causes of social reform and worked with the Christian Socialist movement, although he never became a member of the Socialist Party. His sympathies were for a fundamental change in the structure of American capitalism, and for a time Henry George was his mentor. As he reached the age of thirty-five he was called to a professorship at Rochester Theological Seminary where he launched a vigorous career in writing, lecturing and traveling to lend active support to various social causes.

Rauschenbusch saw the economic institutions of society as the most challenging to Christian ethics. They above others had remained unregenerate in their practices, especially in their treatment of the common man. Many of the personal and social sins such as alcohol and prostitution were related to a capitalism that drove working people to seek escape from the drudgery it produced. Were capitalist industries to be brought under "the law of Christ" instead of "the law of Mammon," Rauschenbusch believed, not only would the sins of the flesh begin to disappear but the causes for which the laboring class was striving would be achieved: decent wages, health and retirement benefits, fairer distribution of the wealth, and the like.

The social gospel movement was important in America because it was a vigorous attempt to recast the key ideas of the Christian faith into terms that came to grips with the urbanized institutional centers of power. Its new anthropology borrowed from the secular socialist thought that arose in the latter half of the nineteenth century: that the inner nature of man is highly affected and molded by the prevailing institutions of society, that even our moral and religious thinking is shaped by them, and that the Christian Gospel must address these and criticize them much as the Old Testament prophets assailed the policies and court structures of their rulers.

Rauschenbusch called for a conversion of the "superpersonal forces" in our society. Repentance, atonement and salvation applied to them as well as to individuals. By preaching sin, judgment and redemption—all familiar themes in the evangelical tradition of Protestantism—he hoped to see American capitalism usher in a new age of economic reform. He underestimated the resistance of such institutions to change, however, and overestimated their ability to act on something other than self-interest. Only after the Great Depression would it be seen—by Reinhold Niebuhr—that persuasion was not enough and that some form of coercion was needed to bring about social justice.

The Salvation of the Super-Personal Forces

In discussing the doctrine of sin we faced the fact that redemption will have to deal not only with the weakness of flesh and blood, but with the strength of principalities and powers. Beyond the feeble and short-lived individual towers the social group as a super-personal entity, dominating the individual, assimilating him to its moral standards, and enforcing them by the social sanctions of approval or disapproval.

When these super-personal forces are based on an evil principle, or directed toward an evil purpose, or corrupted by some controlling group interest which is hostile to the common good, they are sinners of sublimer mould, and they block the way of redemption. They are to us what demonic personalities were to earlier Christian minds. Men of religious vision have always seen social communities in that way. The prophets dealt with Israel and Judah, with Moab and Assyria, as with personalities having a continuous life and spirit and destiny. Jesus saw Jerusalem as a man might see a beloved woman who is driven by haughtiness and self-will into tragic ruin.

In our age these super-personal social forces present more difficult problems than ever before. The scope and diversity of combination is becoming constantly greater. The strategy of the Kingdom of God is short-sighted indeed if it does not devote thought to their salvation and conversion.

The salvation of the composite personalities, like that of individuals, consists in coming under the law of Christ. A few illustrations will explain how this applies.

Two principles are contending with each other for future control in the field of industrial and commercial organization, the capitalistic and the co-operative. The effectiveness of the capitalistic method in the production of wealth is not questioned; modern civilization is evidence of it. But we are also familiar with capitalistic methods in the production of human wreckage. Its one-sided control of economic power tempts to exploitation and oppression; it directs the productive process of society primarily toward the creation of private profit rather than the service of human needs; it demands autocratic management and strengthens the autocratic principle in all social affairs; it has impressed a materialistic spirit on our whole civilization.

On the other hand organizations formed on the co-operative principle are not primarily for profit but for the satisfaction of human wants, and the aim is to distribute ownership, control, and economic benefits to a large number of co-operators.

The difference between a capitalistic organization and a co–operative comes out clearly in the distribution of voting power. Capitalistic joint stock companies work on the plan of "one share, one vote." Therewith power is located in money. One crafty person who has a hundred shares can outvote ninety-nine righteous men who have a share apiece, and a small minority can outvote all the rest if it holds a majority of stock. Money is stronger than life, character, and personality.

Co-operatives work on the plan of "one man, one vote." A man who holds one share has as much voting power as a man with ten shares; his personality counts. If a man wants to lead and direct, he can not do it by money power; he must do it by character, sobriety, and good judgment. The small stockholders are not passive; they take part; they must be persuaded and taught. The superior ability of the capable can not outvote the rest, but has to train them. Consequently the co-operatives develop men and educate a community in helpful loyalty and comradeship. This is the advent of true democracy in economic life. Of course the co-operative principle is not a sovereign specific; the practical success of a given association depends on good judgment and the loyalty of its constituents. But the co-operatives, managed by plain men, often with little experience, have not only held their own in Europe against the picked survivors of the capitalistic competitive battle, but have forged steadily ahead into enormous financial totals, have survived and increased even during the war, and by their helpful moral influence have gone a long way to restore a country like Ireland which had long been drained and ruined by capitalism.

Here, I think, we have the difference between saved and unsaved organizations. The one class is under the law of Christ, the other under the law of mammon. The one is democratic and the other autocratic. Whenever capitalism has invaded a new country or industry, there has been a speeding up in labor and in the production of wealth, but always with a trail of human misery, discontent, bitterness, and demoralization. When co-operation has invaded a country there has been increased thrift, education, and neighborly feeling, and there has been no trail of concomitant evil and no cries of protest. The men in capitalistic business may be the best of men, far superior in ability to the average committee member of a co-operative, but the latter type of organization is the higher, and when co-operation has had as long a time to try out its methods as capitalism, the latter will rank with feudalism as an evil memory of mankind.

Super-personal forces are saved when they come under the law of Christ. A State which uses its terrible power of coercion to smite and crush offenders as a protection to the rest, is still under brutal law. A State which deals with those who have erred in the way of teaching, discipline, and restoration, has come under the law of Christ and is to that extent a saved community. "By their fruits ye shall know them." States are known by their courts and prisons and contract labor systems, or by their juvenile courts and parole systems. A change in penology may be an evidence of salvation.

A State which uses its superior power to overrun a weaker neighbor by force, or to wrest a valuable right of way from it by instigating a *coup d' état*, or uses intimidation to secure mining or railway concessions or to force a loan at usurious rates on a half-civilized State, is in mortal sin. A State which asks only for an open door and keeps its own door open in return, and which speaks as courteously to a backward State as to one with a big fleet, is to that extent a Christian community. . . .

The salvation of the super-personal beings is by coming under the law of Christ. The fundamental step of repentance and conversion for professions and organizations is to give up monopoly power and the incomes derived from legalized extortion, and to come under the law of service, content with a fair income for honest work. The corresponding step in the case of governments and political oligarchies, both in monarchies and in capitalistic semi-democracies, is to submit to real democracy. Therewith they step out of the Kingdom of Evil into the Kingdom of God.

"The Salvation of the Super-Personal Forces," from his *A Theology for the Social Gospel*. New York: Macmillan, 1922.

B. Walter Muelder

The idea of the "responsible society" is taken from the first assembly's report of the World Council of Churches (1948) which attempted to move beyond the conflict between capitalist and communist ideas. Muelder attempts to draw out the ethical applications of this idea and, in particular, to define the economic responsibilities it suggests. He resists divorcing economics from the cultural whole of which it is a part and affirms economic values as instrumental rather than ends in themselves. They are to serve the larger ends of human dignity. The brief excerpt from his work provides the succinct statement of one who has taken the social gospel seriously and translated it into a contemporary approach to the essential activities of a modern economy.

Walter Muelder, b. 1907, like Niebuhr and Rauschenbusch, was born of German immigrants and raised in the pietistic tradition. He served as dean of Boston University School of Theology and held a chair in Christian ethics there for two decades. He has been active in the ecumenical movement since its inception in 1948.

The Responsible Society

Economic philosophy and science are significant parts of man's quest to understand truth, the common good, and the means of achieving both. If economic thought and institutions attempt to be divorced from the larger meanings found in the integral functions of religion, they belie the interpenetration of value and fact which exists everywhere in nature and society. Expedient economics may shipwreck religious goals. Only where fact and value are united can intelligent decision be made. The purpose of economics is to help men make intelligent decisions regarding the means of community life. If men are scientific in their descriptions of fact and unscientific in their approach to values, they are very foolish. The fact that values are hard to handle scientifically does not alter the need for such work, but only challenges thought to create an adequate philosophy of value. Economics thus points beyond description to decision in the light of an adequate philosophy of world community. Economic philosophy has to do with the intelligent and coherent understanding of means and their relation to community goals.

God who has created all things and all men has made them to interpenetrate and to be interdependent. He has not distributed natural resources evenly over the world. He has made man-power itself as the greatest natural resource. Man is both economic power and the subject who controls economic power. The world of economic life is not primarily a world of things, but of people in relation to each other with respect to the things they need, i.e. need in relation to basic goals. From the outset, then, religion in relation to economic life deals with the interdependent life of mankind as it seeks to meet its needs confronting nature and value.

Our religious postulates stress, then, the sacredness of the person under God. They view man not as a bundle of interests and desires, primarily, but as a creature of needs, some of which can be met by economic acts, but most of which are non-economic. An economics of need focuses the power of a community differently from an economics of self-interest or of sensate desire. Central in the economic implications of ethical monotheism is the notion of the responsible community. Men are spiritually equal, they are created metaphysically free and morally to be free, and they are called to solve their problems and meet their needs in responsible community.

In the United States of America there has been growing tension between those who defend, with a kind of absolute loyalty, the so-called "free enterprise" system and those who hold to the extension of the so-called "welfare state." The virtue put forward prominently by the first group is freedom; that of the second is social justice. From the standpoint of Judaic and Christian theism both types of loyalty may, in fact, be idolatry. There is a tendency to worship at the shrine of the "free market" as there is also at the shrine of security "from the cradle to the grave." The principles of free-market enterprise are not ordinances of God as can be seen from the instability of an economy based solely on a free price system. Moreover, even under "free enterprise" many welfare services must be supplied by the community to its citizens through the good offices of government. On the other hand, welfare can also become an idol when it becomes a dogmatic rejection of the merits of market freedom or fails to face the problems of power and the bureaucratic state. Both groups tend to idolatry in the provincialism of their perspectives, by their lack of self-criticism, by their falling prey to specialized interest groups, by their unwillingness to seek both pluralistic good in the light of the overall economy and general welfare as reflected in all the real needs of the least members of the interdependent community.

The religious conception of an economically responsible society, as we shall develop it, is one in which men freely acknowledge responsibility to inclusive justice and public order; one in which economic goals are not divorced from the welfare of society they ought to serve; one in which political authority and economic power are responsible both to God and the people; one in which economic activities are understood as means to larger ends but in which the person can nevertheless actualize himself; one in which the people have freedom to control, to criticize and to reform their political and economic institutions; one in which power is widely distributed throughout the whole community and one in which justice and equality of opportunity are established for all. The religious conception is an integral conception in which the church is both a conserver, a critic and an inspirer of creative approaches to the meeting of human needs. It is a conception in which economic life finds its rightful place in a doctrine of redemption for men both in history and beyond.

"The Responsible Society," from his *Religion and Economic Responsibility*. New York: Scribner's, 1953.

C. Pope John XXIII

Although the papacy of John XXIII was brief (1959–1963), it had an enormous impact upon all of Christendom, both Catholic and Protestant. From John came two important encyclicals, Mater et Magistra (1961) and Pacem in Terris (1963), which breathed new life into the Church. They were augmented by the work of the Second Vatican Council (1962–1965) which John convened and infused with his own charismatic presence. Vatican II called for a democratizing of Church organization, addressed non-Catholics as "men of good will" and called non-Catholic Christians separated "brethren" rather than heretics. It opened up dialogue with persons of secular learning and called on Christians to learn from the world of science and technology. And in ethics it dwelt less on the ascetic virtues versus the non-ascetic life and more on private possession versus the sharing of goods among all mankind.

In the selection below from Pacem in Terris (Peace on Earth), Pope John offers one of the strongest affirmations in recent times of basic universal rights and their corresponding duties. We have included only those parts that pertain to economic justice. They do not pretend to solve the problems of distribution and poverty, but they set the framework of values and principles within which to work, and they provoke a number of questions for further discussion: What are the means necessary to ensure these rights? What changes in existing societies might be entailed? What are the true ends to be sought by economy and government? What is the proper relationship between private property and public responsibility? Finally, what does the encyclical suggest as to how our religious and ethical principles should apply to the decisions and functions of individuals within society?

Peace on Earth
(Pacem in Terris)

Order Between Men

Every man is a person with rights and duties

FIRST of all, it is necessary to speak of the order which should exist between men. Any human society, if it is to be well-ordered and productive, must lay down as a foundation this principle, namely, that every human being is a person, that is, his nature is endowed with intelligence and free-will. By virtue of this, he has rights and duties of his own, flowing directly and simultaneously from his very nature, which are therefore universal, inviolable and inalienable.

If we look upon the dignity of the human person in the light of divinely

revealed truth, we cannot help but esteem it far more highly; for men are re-
deemed by the blood of Jesus Christ, they are by grace the children and
friends of God and heirs of eternal glory.

Rights

The right of life and a worthy standard of living. Beginning our discussion of the rights of man, we see that every man has the right to life, to
bodily integrity, and to the means which are necessary and suitable for the
proper development of life; these are primarily food, clothing, shelter, rest,
medical care, and finally the necessary social services. Therefore a human
being also has the right to security in cases of sickness, inability to work,
widowhood, old age, unemployment, or in any other case in which he is deprived of the means of subsistence through no fault of his own.

Economic rights. Human beings have the natural right to free initiative
in the economic field, and the right to work.

Indissolubly linked with those rights is the right to working conditions
in which physical health is not endangered, morals are safeguarded, and
young people's normal development is not impaired. Women have the right
to working conditions in accordance with their requirements and their duties as wives and mothers.

From the dignity of the human person, there also arises the right to
carry on economic activities according to the degree of responsibility of
which one is capable. Furthermore—and this must be specially emphasized—there is the right to a working wage, determined according to cri-
terions of justice, and sufficient, therefore, in proportion to the available
resources, to give the worker and his family a standard of living in keeping
with the dignity of the human person. In this regard, Our Predecessor Pius
XII said: *"To the personal duty to work imposed by nature, there corresponds and follows the natural right of each individual to make of his work
the means to provide for his own life and the lives of his children; so profoundly is the empire of nature ordained for the preservation of man."* The
right to private property, even of productive goods, also derives from the
nature of man. This right, as We have elsewhere declared, *"is a suitable
means for safeguarding the dignity of the human person and for the exercise of responsibility in all fields; it strengthens and gives serenity to family
life, thereby increasing the peace and prosperity of the State."*

However, it is opportune to point out that there is a social duty essentially inherent in the right of private property.

Rights and duties necessarily linked in the one person. The natural
rights with which We have been dealing are, however, inseparably con-

nected, in the very person who is their subject, with just as many respective duties; and rights as well as duties find their source, their sustenance and their inviolability in the natural law which grants or enjoins them.

For example, the right of every man to life is correlative with the duty to preserve it; his right to a decent standard of living with the duty of living it becomingly; and his right to investigate the truth freely, with the duty of seeking it and of possessing it ever more completely and profoundly.

The proper balance between population, land and capital. As everybody knows, there are countries with an abundance of arable land and a scarcity of man-power, while in other countries there is no proportion between natural resources and the capital available. This demands that peoples should set up relationships of mutual collaboration, facilitating the circulation from one to the other of capital, goods, and man-power.

Here we deem it opportune to remark that, whenever possible, the work to be done should be taken to the workers, not vice versa.

In this way a possibility of a better future is offered to many persons without being forced to leave their own environment in order to seek residence elsewhere, which almost always entails the heart-ache of separation and difficult periods of adjustment and social integration.

D. The Oxford Conference

It was world events that brought the Christian churches together to launch the ecumenical movement rather than a religious impetus to discover a common faith. The Oxford Conference, representing the first formal attempt to move toward unity, met in response to the unsettling events of the 1930's. War clouds were already gathering on the horizon when it convened in 1937. The peace settlement after World War I had failed to produce a viable political order in Europe. Widespread depression and the inability of democratic leadership to deal with the pressing problems it produced led to a severe loss of confidence. Out of this vacuum emerged totalitarianism under the banners of nazism and fascism whose ideologies of nationalism and military power gave the people a new sense of cause but whose aggressive policies threatened the entire Western world. In addition, the Bolshevik revolution had been transformed into a permanent reign of terror. The Marxist criticisms of Christianity, democracy and capitalism were finding a sympathetic ear outside Russia and added to the social unrest in the West.

What was the proper response of Christians to these events and forces? A number of concerned leaders representing churches from several countries called a Conference on Church, Community and State at Oxford, England. Their task was to set forth some norms for dealing with the new goliaths at loose in the world. They were drawn together by the ethical issues and the need for a shared Christian basis in dealing with them. The conference formulated some principles which would bridge the gap between the general norm of love and the particular situation with all of its complexities. Rather than retreat into a shell of religious platitudes they called upon the churches to establish guidelines by which to judge the new ideologies and systems and to suggest ways for appropriate Christian action.

Note in the report a change in tone and emphasis. There is little of the optimism expressed by Rauschenbusch in his call for converting the super-personal forces and bringing to earth the Kingdom of God. There is heavier accent on human sin, collective greed and ambition, and the need for a humbler acknowledging that the power for change comes from God and not from man. The divine healing and forgiving grace are needed if we are to avoid falling into the same pitfalls as those we condemn. Especially striking is the relationship between love and justice enunciated here. In it one can detect the influence of Reinhold Niebuhr, one of the leaders of the conference.

The Oxford Conference Report

The relative and departmental standard for all the social arrangements and institutions, all the economic structures and political systems, by which the life of man is ordered is the principle of justice. Justice, as the ideal of a harmonious relation of life to life, obviously presupposes the sinful tendency of one life to take advantage of another. This sinful tendency it seeks to check by defining the rightful place and privilege which each life must have in the harmony of the whole and by assigning the duty of each to each. Justice does not demand that the self sacrifice itself completely for the neighbor's good, but seeks to define and to maintain the good which each member of the community may rightfully claim in the harmony of the whole.

The principle of justice has both a positive and a negative significance. Negatively, principles of justice restrain evil and the evildoer. They must therefore become embodied in systems of coercion which prevent men from doing what sinful ambition, pride, lust and greed might prompt them to do. This necessary coercion is itself a root of new evils, since its exercise involves power and power tempts the possessor to its unrighteous use. Furthermore, coercion may rouse resentment among those coerced even when its purpose is a necessary social end. The use of power and coercion cannot therefore be regarded by Christians as ultimately desirable. Criticism against its abuses must be constantly maintained. On the other hand, it cannot be assumed that the practice of Christian love will ever obviate the necessity for coercive political and economic arrangements.

The laws of justice are not purely negative. They are not merely "dikes against sin." The political and economic structure of society is also the mechanical skeleton which carries the organic element in society. Forms of production and methods of cooperation may serve the cause of human brotherhood by serving and extending the principle of love beyond the sphere of purely personal relations.

The commandment of love therefore always presents possibilities for individuals beyond the requirements of economic and social institutions. There is no legal, political or economic system so bad or so good as to absolve individuals from the responsibility to transcend its requirements by acts of Christian charity. Institutional requirements necessarily prescribe only the minimum. Even in the best possible social system they can only achieve general standards in which the selfishness of the human heart is taken for granted and presupposed. But the man who is in Christ knows a higher obligation which transcends the requirements of justice—the obligation of a love which is the fulfillment of the law.

The love which is the fulfillment of the law is, however, no substitute for law, for institutions or for systems. Individual acts of charity within a given system of government or economics may mitigate its injustices and increase its justice. But they do not absolve the Christian from seeking the best possible institutional arrangement and social structure for the ordering of human life. Undue emphasis upon the higher possibilities of love in personal relations, within the limits of a given system of justice or an established social structure, may tempt Christians to allow individual acts of charity to become a screen for injustice and a substitute for justice. Christianity becomes socially futile if it does not recognize that love must will justice and that the Christian is under an obligation to secure the best possible social and economic structure, in so far as such structure is determined by human decisions.

The relation of the commandment of love to the justice of political and economic systems is twofold. It is an ideal which reaches beyond any possible achievements in the field of political relations, but it is nevertheless also a standard by which various schemes of justice may be judged. In attempting to deal with political and economic problems, the Christian must therefore be specially on his guard against two errors.

The one is to regard the realities of social justice incorporated in given systems and orders as so inferior to the law of love that the latter cannot be a principle of discrimination among them but only a principle of indiscriminate judgment upon them all. This error makes Christianity futile as a guide in all those decisions which Christians, like other people, must constantly be making in the political and economic sphere. Practically, it gives the advantage to established systems as against the challenge of new social adventures and experiments; for it tempts Christians to make no decisions at all, and such efforts to reserve decision become in practice decisions in favor of the status quo.

The other error is to identify some particular social system with the will of God or to equate it with the kingdom of God. When conservatives insist on such an identification in favor of the status quo, they impart to it a dangerous religious sanction which must drive those who challenge it into a secular revolt against religion itself. If, on the other hand, this identification is made in the interests of a new social order, it will lead to the same complacency which the critic deprecates in the old social situation. Every tendency to identify the kingdom of God with a particular social structure or economic mechanism must result in moral confusion for those who maintain the system and in disillusionment for those who suffer from its limitations. The former will regard conformity with its standards as identical with the fulfillment of the law, thus falling into the sin of pharisaism. The latter will be tempted to a cynical disavowal of the religion because it falsely gives absolute worth to partial values and achievements. Both errors are essentially heretical from the point of view of Christian faith. The one denies the reality of the kingdom of God in history; the other equates the kingdom of God with the processes of history. In the one case, the ultimate and eternal destiny of human existence, which transcends history, is made to support an attitude of indifference toward historical social issues; in the other case, the eternal destiny of human existence is denied or obscured. The law of love which is the standard of the Christian life is properly to be regarded as being at the same time a present reality and an ultimate possibility. It is not only a criterion of judgment in all the fateful decisions which men must make in history, but also an indictment against all historical achievements.

As a criterion of judgment upon the relative merits of economic arrangements and social structures, the law of love gives positive guidance in terms of justice, even though it transcends the realities of all possible social structures. The obligation to love our neighbors as ourselves places clearly under condemnation all social and economic systems which give one man undue advantage over others. It must create an uneasy conscience (for example) in all Christians who are involved in a social system which denies children, of whatever race or class, the fullest opportunity to develop whatever gifts God has given them and makes their education depend upon the fortuitous circumstance of a father's possession or lack of means to provide the necessary funds. It must challenge any social system which provides social privileges without reference to the social functions performed by individuals, or which creates luxury and pride on the one hand and want and insecurity on the other. It makes the conscience of Christians particularly uneasy in regard to the deprivation of basic security for large masses of human beings.

Points at Which the Christian Understanding of Life Is Challenged

At the beginning of this part of the report attention should be called to the potentialities for good in the economic order. Situations vary in different parts of the world but in many countries it already seems possible, through the full utilization of the resources of the new technology and through the release of human productive power, to remove the kind of poverty which is crippling to human personality. There is a sense in which poverty is a relative matter and hence in any situation would be present in some form; but we are thinking of the poverty which would be regarded in any age as denying the physical necessities of life. The abolition of such poverty now seems to depend on the human organization of economic life, rather than on factors given in nature or on what might be called the inevitable constitution of every economic order. But the possibility of economic "plenty" has this moral importance, that to an increasing extent it makes the persistence of poverty a matter for which men are morally responsible. This possibility marks off our time from the period of the New Testament and from other periods in which Christian thinking about economic life has been formulated. In the light of it the direction of Christian effort in relation to the economic order should henceforth be turned from charitable paternalism to the realization of more equal justice in the distribution of wealth. Moreover, Christians who live in the more privileged geographical areas must recognize that the securing of economic plenty and greater justice in its distribution within their respective national groups is not the whole of their duty in this connection; they cannot escape some measure of responsibility for those areas where for years to come there will doubtless be desperate economic need. . . .

(a) It should be reaffirmed without qualification that all human property rights are relative and contingent only, in virtue of the dependence of man upon God as the giver of all wealth and as the creator of man's capacities to develop the resources of nature. This fundamental Christian conviction must express itself both in the idea of stewardship or trusteeship and in the willingness of the Christian to examine accumulations of property in the light of their social consequences.

(b) The existing system of property rights and the existing distribution of property must be criticized in the light of the largely nonmoral processes by which they have been developed, and criticism must take account of the fact that every argument in defense of property rights which is valid for Christian thinking is also an argument for the widest possible distribution of these rights.

(c) It should further be affirmed that individual property rights must never be maintained or exercised without regard to their social consequences or without regard to the contribution which the community makes in the production of all wealth.

(d) It is very important to make clear distinction between various forms of property. The property which consists in personal possessions for use, such as the home, has behind it a clearer moral justification than property in the means of production and in land which gives the owners power over other persons. All property which represents social power stands in special need of moral scrutiny, since power to determine the lives of others is the crucial point in any scheme of justice. The question must always be asked whether this is the kind of power which can be brought under adequate social control or whether it is of the type which by its very nature escapes and evades social control. Industrial property in particular encourages the concentration of power; for it gives the owner control over both the place and the instruments of labor and thus leaves the worker powerless so far as property relations are concerned, allowing him only the organized strength of his union and his political franchise to set against the power of ownership. Property in land on a large scale may represent a similar power over those who are forced to rent it for a livelihood. There are consequently forms of feudal land ownership in Europe, in some states of America and in the Orient, which are frequent sources of social injustice. On the other hand property in land which does not extend beyond the capacity of one family to cultivate—the small freehold which determines a large part of the agriculture of the Western world—belongs to a unique category. The small freeholder may find it increasingly difficult to compete against mechanized large-scale production and to make a living without being overdriven. But on the other hand there is a special justification for this type of property, since it gives freedom to perform a social function without the interference of capricious power and without the exercise of power over others. Furthermore, there is a more organic relation between owner and property in agricultural land than in any type of industrial ownership. Small-scale property in industry and in retail trade possesses some of these same characteristics in a lesser degree. Yet there is always danger that small-scale productive property, whether in land, industry or trade, may tempt the owner, in his competition with more powerful productive units, to exploit his own family and the other workers employed, especially since in any given case the latter may be too few to organize effectively.

Excerpts from the Report of the Section on Church, Community, and State in Relation to the Economic Order. W. Beach and R. Niebuhr, *Christian Ethics*, Ronald Press, 1973 (2nd ed.).

E. Reinhold Niebuhr

No one in the twentieth century has wrestled with the relationship of Christian ethics to the political, social and economic realities more thoroughly than Reinhold Niebuhr. Recognizing that the requirements of justice call for a careful discrimination based on a sound assessment of the possibilities in the "here and now," Niebuhr spent a lifetime delineating an ethic of love workable within a world of sin. The Christian, he insists, must deal with power against power, self-interest, and choices within the context of global nuclear threat. He has been called the father of realistic politics, and his influence has been as great outside the church as within it. The architects of foreign policy in America during the cold war years have acknowledged him as their mentor.

As a young minister Niebuhr served a church in Detroit during the early years of the automobile industry. The title of his memoirs from that period reflect his experience: "Leaves from the Notebook of a Tamed Cynic." A Daniel thrown into the lions' den of urban and capitalist struggle, Niebuhr had to reckon with the colossal power of the Ford kingdom on the one hand and its effect on the laboring class on the other. "It is almost impossible to be sane and Christian at the same time," he wrote, recognizing that the adjustment between the absolute requirements of a Christian ethic and the relative demands of dealing with the forces in our society is indeed a precarious one.

Niebuhr left the parish after thirteen years to become professor of Christian ethics at Union Theological Seminary in New York where he remained until his retirement. He was a prolific writer as well as activist in many social causes. His comments on current events continued to pour out until his death in 1971.

Love and Justice

Does the Christian faith add anything significant to the concept of justice? The most immediate answer to this question is that it subordinates justice to an even higher standard, that of love. According to Christ, "all the law and the prophets" are summarized in the twofold love commandment, which enjoins both the love of God and the love of the neighbor. However, if it is assumed that the Christian contribution to economic and political life is simply contained in the purity of its ethical ideal of love (an assumption which some modern versions of the Christian faith have sought to inculcate), the relation of Christianity to man's economic and political life would seem to become even more problematic. For the question would then arise whether this ideal has any relevance to the organization of economic

85

or political society. The most ideal social possibility for man may well be so perfect an accord of life with life that each member of a community is ready to sacrifice his interests for the sake of others. But, as David Hume observed, politics (and for that matter economics too) must assume the selfishness of men.

It is certainly significant that the highest religious visions of the good life always culminate in the concept of this perfect accord. The ideal of love is not superimposed upon human history by scriptural, or any other, authority. Human existence, when profoundly analyzed, yields the law of love as the final law of human freedom. Man's unique freedom, in which he rises indeterminately above his determinate existence, requires that his life be fulfilled not within himself but in others. It also requires that this realization of himself in others should not be pursued merely from his own standpoint. That is, he cannot regard others simply as tools and instruments of his self-realization.

Yet that is precisely what he is inclined to do. Any religious faith which merely discovers the law of love but does not also make men aware of the other law, that of self-love, is a sentimental perversion of Christianity. It is a perversion which lacks true inwardness of religious experience. For in such experience men become aware, as St. Paul testified, not only of the final law of life but of another law "which wars against the law that is in my mind."

It is from the standpoint of both of these laws, from the recognition of the validity of the one and the reality of the other, that Christianity must make its contribution to the organization of man's life, whether in economic or in political terms. From the standpoint of the law of love every scheme and structure of justice will be recognized to be tentative and provisional. Not merely the positive law of particular communities but also the notions of justice, from the standpoint of which positive law is criticized, are touched by interest and passion. They always contain an ideological element, for they tend to justify a given equilibrium of power in a given historical situation.

In the relation of religion to culture it is important to distinguish sharply between the absolute and the relative. If the authority of religion is used primarily to give absolute validity to relative values, the consequence is fanaticism. It is characteristic from the standpoint of modern culture to ascribe fanaticism to religion, and not without cause. It is, however, significant that modern culture, which hoped to destroy religious fanaticism by the power of reason, did not anticipate the even more grievous fanaticisms of modern political religions which would express themselves in the name of reason and of science. Modern culture did not, in short, measure the depth of this problem, or rightly gauge the persistence with which men will use standards of justice as instruments of their interest and use religion to obscure, and thus to aggravate, the ideological taint in their reasoning about justice.

Standards of justice may be said to be (1) expressions of the law of love, insofar as the love of the neighbor requires a calculation of competitive claims when there is more than one neighbor and (2) a practical compromise between the law of love and the law of self-love. They are a compromise in the sense that norms of justice seek to arrive at an equitable adjustment of conflicting claims, assuming the selfish inclination of men to take advantage of each other. A Christian contribution to standards of justice in economic and political life must therefore not be found primarily in a precise formulation of the standard. It must be found rather in strengthening both the inclination to seek the neighbor's good and the contrite awareness that we are not inclined to do this. The inclination to seek the neighbor's good must be accompanied by an awareness that every norm of justice is but a very relative approximation of this goal. The awareness that even good men are not consistently inclined to do this will lay bare the ideological taint, the corruption of self-interest, in every historic standard.

Thus a genuine Christian contribution to the ideological conflict in democratic society must serve to mitigate, rather than aggravate, the severity of the conflict; for it will prevent men from heedlessly seeking their own interests in the name of justice and from recklessly denominating value preferences, other than their own, as evil. If Christian piety or any other kind of piety does not yield these fruits of humility and charity, it must be consistently rejected as the ''salt that has lost its savor.''

Human desires and ambitions are without natural limit. The Christian's faith can make no greater contribution to the organization of man's common life than its interpretation of the root of this inordinacy. For according to the Christian faith man is on the one hand a free spirit ''made in the image of God,'' who rises indeterminately in his consciousness over nature, history, and self. He cannot, therefore, be contained or explain the meaning of his life within the limits of any system of nature. But he is on the other hand a creature, driven by natural impulses and limited by conditions of time and place. These limitations reach into the very pinnacles of spirit, even as the freedom of spirit reaches down into every natural impulse and transmutes it into something less determinate than the impulses of other creatures. (One need only consider how the sex impulse, possessing a purely biological function in nature, is related to almost every creative and destructive force in the total human personality.) Thus from a genuinely Christian standpoint man can never be understood merely from the standpoint of his involvement in nature, on the one hand; nor can he, on the other, be regarded as a potentially discarnate spirit in whom historical development is progressively actualizing this potential. On the contrary, the evils to which human history is subject arise precisely from those forms of inordinacy which are rooted in man's vain effort to deny his creatureliness.

If we now return to the problem of the organization of economic life and to the necessity of harnessing self-interest, it will become apparent not only why it must be harnessed and not merely suppressed but also why the self-interest has a different dimension than was assumed in the theories of classical economics and in the whole of modern naturalistic thought. Self-interest must be harnessed for two reasons. It is too powerful and persistent to be simply suppressed or transmuted. Even if individual life could rise to pure disinterestedness so that no human mind would give the self, in which it is incarnate, an undue advantage, yet it would not be possible for collective man to rise to such a height. The institution of the family would alone prevent a simple substitution of "motives of service" for "motives of profit," as we have seen. For the self as "breadwinner" will seek to serve his family by seeking gain for his toil.

But self-interest must be allowed a certain free play for the additional reason that there is no one in society good or wise enough finally to determine how the individual's capacities had best be used for the common good, or his labor rewarded, or the possibilities of useful toil, to which he may be prompted by his own initiative, be anticipated.

Yet the self-interest which is thus engaged is not some harmless survival impulse as found in nature. It is not simply satisfied, as physiocratic theory assumed, when human toil yields returns adequate for man's primary needs. For human desires and needs rise indeterminately above the biological level. Self-interest expresses itself above all in what Bertrand Russell has defined as the "desire for power and glory." The two are so intermingled that we need not, for present purposes at least, distinguish them. Thomas Hobbes was able to describe this dimension of self-interest, which was obscured in the thought of his contemporaries, primarily in terms of desire for prestige. He spoke of the "constant competition for honor and prestige" among men. Yet his description yields a sense of the will-to-power lacking in the thought which lies at the foundation of liberal economics.

Because it did not recognize the unlimited nature of all human desires in general and of the desire for power and glory in particular, classical liberalism naturally underrated both the reality of the contest for power in man's social and economic life and the injustices which would result from great inequalities of power. In common with liberal thought, Marx obscured both the lust for power in the motives of men and the factor of power in social life. Self-interest is interpreted by Marxism, as by liberalism, primarily in terms of the economic motive, that is, as the desire for gain. The original state of man's innocency was, according to Engels, disturbed by "greed and covetousness." But since these inordinate desires were attributed to the corruption of the institution of property, it was possible for Marx to envisage an ideal state of society on the other side of the abolition of property. In this post-revolutionary society human needs and desires would be as limited and would achieve as simple a harmony as the liberal culture imagined possible on this side of a revolution.

Thus the foundation was laid for the tragic conflict in modern social history between two great political credos. In this conflict both creeds, in their purer form, generated monstrous contrasting evils from an essentially identical mistake. In the case of pure liberalism it was believed possible to abandon the whole economic life of man to a "natural system of liberty" because the forces in competition in the economic sphere were regarded as essentially determinate and of potentially equal strength. They were neither. Just as human freedom accentuates inequalities found in nature, so also a technical society accentuates the inequalities of more traditional societies. Marxism, on the other hand, allows the power impulses of an uncontrolled oligarchy to express themselves behind a facade of innocency, erected by the dogma that the possession of property is the only source of inordinate desire. In the one case the perils to justice arising from economic power, particularly from inequality of power, are not recognized. In the other case, the perils from the combination of economic and political power in the hands of a single oligarchy are obscured.

Thus the errors of both those who abjure every effort to control human enterprise and those who would bring it completely under a plan rest upon false estimates of the desires and ambitions of men which furnish the stuff of human history. The self-interest of men must be used, rather than merely controlled, not only because it is too variable and unpredictable to be simply controlled but also because the corruption of self-interest among the oligarchs, who would control it, is actuated by ambitions and power lusts, more dangerous than is dreamed of in either philosophy. On the other hand, the self-interest of men, when uncontrolled, does not simply create a nice harmony of competitive striving. That is why the healthier modern societies constantly experiment with social strategies in which neither creed is followed slavishly.

In arriving at this wisdom of "common sense," modern nations are revealing in the field of economics and politics insights into the character of human nature and history which belong to the Christian view of man and which both pure liberal and radical political theories have tended to obscure. This view of man recognizes that (in Pascal's phrase) the dignity and the misery of man are inextricably united. This is to say that both the creative and the destructive possibilities of man's actions in history are derived from the same uniquely human freedom. The misery (that is, man's capacity for evil) develops when he extends his power and wisdom beyond the limits of man as creature. The dignity of man implies his capacity to manage his own destiny and to create communities and social harmonies in which moral and political wisdom outwit the short-range desires and ends of man as creature. The evil in man implies the constant possibility of the corruption of this creative capacity. Therefore he is not to be trusted with too much power and his wisdom as manager of historical destiny is not to be relied on too unqualifiedly.

The Christian faith in its various historic forms has of course become involved in various errors which illustrate these corruptions. Sometimes it has championed concepts of justice or freedom which were ideologies of the strong. Sometimes it has exceeded secular culture in moralistic illusions based upon the idea of the dignity and goodness of man but lacking in understanding of man's capacity for evil. Sometimes it has fled from these errors into a quasi-Christian Marxism. In this view collectivistic economics is espoused in the name of brotherhood, but the perils of power in the collectivist organization of society are not seen.

A genuine Christian faith must always be ready to recognize the periodic involvement of its own historic forms in the various errors against which its true genius forces it to contend. It may be significant, however, that the healthiest national communities of our epoch are those in which the treasures of the Christian faith have never been completely dissipated and in which therefore the fratricidal conflict of modern technical society has been mitigated. For the cherished values of toleration, without which a democratic society would become impossible, are the fruit of a charitable understanding that all human wisdom is limited, that self-interest taints all human virtues, and that there is a similarity between our own evil and those against which we contend.

The problem is whether what Professor Heimann defines as modern "economic rationalism" has not placed so much emphasis upon the tangible ends of life, in contrast to the more intangible values, that we have in effect created a culture in which all the biblical warnings are disregarded. This is a particularly serious problem for the United States because we are being criticized by both friends and foes in Asia and Europe for having become obsessed with the tools and gadgets of life. When we speak rather idolatrously of the "American way of life," our friends and critics profess not to be certain whether we are recommending certain standards of political freedom or are extolling our living standards. The latter have reached heights of opulence beyond the dreams of avarice for most of the inhabitants of the world.

Sometimes we seem to believe that these living standards are the fruit and the proof of our virtue; at other times we suggest that they are the necessary presuppositions for a virtuous democratic national life. In the one case we follow our Puritan tradition, which did not seek after prosperity in the first instance but was nevertheless certain that since "Godliness was profitable unto all things," prosperity was a mark of divine favor and a reward of virtue. In the other case we draw upon the Jeffersonian tradition in our national heritage. The Jeffersonians believed that the superior virtues of American democracy would be guaranteed primarily by the ampler economic opportunities of our virgin continent. These would avert for America the severity of the social struggle and the subordination of man to man in the overcrowded life of Europe. The Jeffersonian interpretation has one merit of recognizing that democracy is viable only in a society in which the economic margins are sufficient to prevent a desperate struggle for the economic resources of the community.

Whatever the merit of either interpretation, it is now apparent that there is no such simple coordination between economic welfare and the moral, spiritual, and cultural life of the community as we had supposed. The criticisms which European and Asian nations make of our cultural and spiritual life may not always be just. Frequently they are prompted by envy of our good fortune, and seem to rest upon the presupposition that virtue and good fortune are completely incompatible. An impoverished world is, indeed, involved in curious inconsistencies in its relation to a wealthy and powerful preponderant nation. For on the one hand the poorer nations insist that they require our help in establishing greater economic efficiency and productivity as a basis for a healthy democratic life. On the other hand they seem to believe that our wealth is proof of our vulgarity and possibly even of our unjust exploitation of others.

The widespread criticism of American prosperity and of American culture are usually not based upon distinctively Christian presuppositions. They therefore prove the more convincingly that the issue involved is not the mere rejection of an illegitimate Christian "otherwordliness" in favor of a more unequivocal affirmation of the meaning of man's historic existence. The issue is the relation between man's immediate and ultimate ends. The question to be resolved is whether the satisfaction of immediate ends will inevitably contribute to the achievement of the more ultimate ends.

In considering this question we must note that man's economic activities are devoted in the first instance to the satisfaction of his primary needs of food, shelter, and security. Ultimately, of course, men bring economic effort into the support of every end, spiritual, cultural, and communal. It cannot be denied, however, that economic activity is always devoted in the first instance to these primary needs and that modern economic "rationalism" gives these needs a preference because they are more "tangible." The proof is furnished by the fact that a nation which indubitably has the highest living standards cannot boast of the highest achievements in the moral and spiritual quality of its culture.

Naturally any community will devote economic productivity to other than primary needs as soon as these primary needs are tolerably met. Therefore economic efficiency and increased productivity will support all higher cultural activity. Human culture depends in fact upon the ability of an economy to establish margins of welfare beyond the satisfaction of primary needs.

There are, however, two reasons why the relation of economic efficiency to culture is subject to a law of diminishing returns. The first is that human needs and desires are, as previously observed, essentially indeterminate. There is therefore no natural limit for their satisfaction. The place of the automobile in the American economy is an effective symbol of this fact. The mobility which it provides is not exactly a "primary" need. But neither is it basically a cultural one. Yet the satisfaction of this need for mobility takes precedence over many needs, some of them cultural and others actually more primary. It is a question, for instance, whether the possession of a home has not been subordinated in the American economy to the possession of an automobile. Even if there had not been such an influence as "economic rationalism," which emphasized the more tangible values, human nature, under whatever culture, would have been inclined to exploit economic margins for immediate satisfactions in preference to more ultimate ones. There is therefore no "natural" system of preferences which will guarantee that economic means will not become ends in themselves and that tangible and immediate satisfactions will not usurp the devotion of men to the exclusion of more ultimate ones. One possible wrong preference involves the "dignity of man" as a producer being violated for the sake of achieving a high degree of productivity in favor of man as consumer. Furthermore, highly efficient economies may become involved in vulgarities to which more traditional cultures are immune. For in the more traditional cultures the imagination has not been prompted to seek and to desire the unlimited on every level of human satisfactions.

The second reason for the law of diminishing returns in the relation of efficiency to culture is the fact that technical efficiency is more effective in providing the basis for cultural and spiritual values than in contributing to its heights. The invention of writing, and subsequently of printing, were fateful chapters in the cultural history of mankind. Culture depends upon communication. And these arts of communication were creative instruments for all social, as well as for more purely spiritual, achievements of mankind. But the subsequent inventions which made "mass" communication possible and which culminated in the achievement of radio and television have had the general effect of vulgarizing culture. Some of this effect will be eliminated when the instruments are brought more effectively under the control of artistic and cultural purposes. But the degrading which is due to the necessity of reaching a total audience rather than selective groups with special interests will undoubtedly remain.

These diminishing returns in the realm of culture are symbolic of the general relation between quantitative and qualitative aspects of life. The quantitative increase of the comforts and securities of life, and of the technical efficiencies which furnish the foundation for every type of human achievement, does not lead to an indeterminate increase of the highest possibilities of life, measured culturally or spiritually. No degree of economic security can finally obviate the basic insecurity of human existence, finally symbolized in the fact of death. If preoccupation with these securities creates a culture in which human beings are incapable of coming to terms with life's basic insecurity through a serenity of faith, the culture stands under Christ's condemnation of the rich fool.

No technical efficiencies can guarantee the perfection of the poet's art, and no system of card indexing can assure that the historian will have an imaginative grasp of the drama of history which he seeks to portray. While a democratic society requires both a high degree of literacy among its citizens and enough economic margins to prevent the social struggle from becoming desperate, nevertheless the problems of social justice cannot be solved indeterminately by creating so much abundance that the question of justice is less desperately argued because the goods of life need not be divided too equitably.

There are certain problems of human togetherness which we assume to have solved in America because our expanding economy has postponed them. The original expansion of the economy through an advancing frontier and the subsequent expansion through ever new achievements of technical efficiency have created the illusion of life's unlimited possibilities. Actually human existence is definitely limited, despite its apparently unlimited possibilities. The serenity of man and the sanity of his life with others finally depend upon a wisdom which knows how to come to terms with these limits. This wisdom of humility and charity must be derived from a faith which measures the ends of life in a larger context than that which the immediate desires of man supply.

For this reason the Christian faith has a very special function and challenge in a culture in which a high degree of technical efficiency has been attained. If it becomes too defensive about its alleged "otherworldliness," if it fails to call attention to the limits of the "abundance of things a man possesseth" in achieving the serenity and charity without which life becomes intolerable, if it does not define the dimensions of life which create the possibility of contradiction between the desire to survive and the desire to live in integrity of spirit, if, in short, it capitulates uncritically to the cult of technical efficiency and the culture of abundance, it must lose its uniqueness as religious faith. Perhaps this is the issue on which the Christian faith must come most directly to grips with the prevailing mood of a technical culture. Such a culture is in mortal danger of "gaining the whole world" but "losing its own soul." Certainly its idolatrous devotion to technical efficiency has accentuated a peril which Jesus perceived, even in a culture in which the tendency to seek after treasures which "moths corrupt and thieves break through and steal" had not been accentuated by the modern preoccupation with material comfort and physical security.

It would, of course, be foolish to deny the moral and spiritual significance of the "conquest" of nature in our civilization or to yearn after the poverty-stricken conditions of nontechnical societies. Man has been given a rightful dominion over the forces of nature; and the whole history of human civilization is a history of his gradual extension of that dominion. But it is also true that this dominion cannot annul nature's final triumph over man; for even the most powerful and comfortable man must finally submit to the common fate of death. The only possible triumph over death for man is a triumph of faith, which is to say a conception of the meaning of life from the standpoint of which death is not the annulment of all meaning. In the Bible the effort of man to establish the meaning of his existence upon the basis of his own power and intelligence is consistently interpreted as the root of all evil. The rich fool who builds his barns for future security has not reckoned with the fact that he may die any moment. Those who build great houses are accused by the Psalmist, with subtle psychological insight, of having the "secret thought that they will continue forever."

The nonchalance of faith's triumph over life and death is succinctly expressed in the Pauline word: "For whether we live, we live unto the Lord: and whether we die, we die unto the Lord; whether we live therefore or die, we are the Lord's" (Romans 14:8). In many ways the most basic distinction between secularism and a genuine Christian faith is at this precise point. From the standpoint of the Christian faith no achievements of culture and civilization can finally give man security. On the contrary most of the evils of life arise from the fact that man seeks frantically to establish absolute security by his power, wisdom, or virtue.

The preoccupation of a technical civilization with the external securities of life is due partly to a natural tendency of every culture to extol its unique achievements. Modern man has been remarkably successful in technics and is naturally prone to overestimate the significance of his success in this enterprise for the total problem of human existence. But there is also a deeper religious issue in this idolatry. The frantic pursuit of the immediate goals of life is partly occasioned by an uneasy awareness that this pursuit has not resulted in its promised happiness and by a consequent final and desperate effort to reach the illusive goal of happiness by a more consistent application of principles of efficiency.

If there is such motivation in the current preoccupations of a technical society, particularly in America, they may well be regarded as abortive, but also dangerous, efforts of the spirit of "secularism" in unconscious and therefore purer form to bring human destiny under the control of human power.

This problem is the most serious challenge to the Christian faith. It is the more serious because it cannot be solved by a simple denial of the significance of man's conquest of nature. It can be solved only by recognizing the moral and spiritual resources in the technical achievements on the one hand and by recognizing their limits on the other. The final limits remain the same for the most advanced as well as for the most primitive society.

"The Christian Faith and the Economic Life of Liberal Society," in his *Faith and Politics*, ed. Ronald H. Stone. New York, Braziller, 1968.

F. Liberation Theology

Liberation theology comes from Latin America where Catholic laymen and priests have joined in protest against the economic and political oppression of military and dictatorial governments, and where the condition of the poor has remained unimproved and unchanged for centuries. The movement is relatively recent, germinating in the 1960's and steadily growing in numbers and visibility. Although the theologians of this camp appear "radical" in the eyes of the middle class and affluent world, they have attempted to found their teachings on Scripture and tradition, putting new emphasis upon aspects that have been pushed aside or neglected. The association of Jesus with the poor, his attack on the Jewish establishment, his Palm Sunday march into Jerusalem, his identification with the oppressed and vindication of the social rejects, and his insistence upon a Kingdom of the meek and lowly are all themes that lend credence to this view.

Both of the writers whose selections appear below reflect the tension that the active Christian must embody, that between historical involvement in causes and movements of reform and the recognition that their cause is not final or absolute. It is a tension between the present and the eschatological. The final Kingdom is not of this world, but that does not annul human responsibility for social justice and freedom in the world today. How far should the Christian go in his activism? Should he resist existing law and government if it is unjust? What about committing acts of violence, or organizing the oppressed into an army of resistance? Should the Christian call for the overthrow of existing governments that commit terror, or merely their reform? Such are a few of the questions raised by the liberation theologians.

Enrique Dussel is a political refugee from Argentina and now teaches in Mexico. He earned his doctorate in philosophy and presently is working on a ten-volume history of the church in Latin America. Denis Goulet, a native of Fall River, Mass., did graduate work in philosophy at Catholic University in Washington, D.C. and worked in factories in France and Spain. After receiving his doctorate from the University of Sao Paulo in Brazil, he was visiting professor at several universities in Canada, France and the United States, and has continued extensive research and writing. He also spent some time living among the nomadic tribes in Algeria. Both Dussel and Goulet are eloquent spokesmen for the new movement in Catholic theology.

Enrique Dussel

The violence that killed Jesus was the violence of the conquistador, repressive violence designed to nullify the authentic gesture of liberation. There is, on the other hand, the liberating violence of the liberator, for example, San Martín and his army of the Andes. Furthermore, there is the pedagogical violence of the prophet, the kind we see in Jesus. He organized a church and not a state. The function of the church will always be that of pedagogue and prophet, and not one of armed violence, not even in the cause of liberation. As a prophetic institution its function is eschatological—preaching what is to come. It takes a critical look at the fixation and anti-historicity of the totalized system, which is sin. The system would have wished that the Word of God had never come to this world. Nothing arouses greater anger in it than that God would have become man and placed himself *within* the system. Jesus Christ is now present until the end of time, continuously supplying Christians with the vocation of commitment to the poor. Having done away with the old order, these Christians work toward a new order. But they will have to do this over and over again. The function of the Christian is to deinstitutionalize the institutions of sin and, like Jesus in his identification with the poor, turn history toward eschatology.

"Being-in-the-Money"

At one point in their history people said that being rich was all that mattered. Then the Christians came along and said that people have a natural right to private property. And this is true if we are talking about what a person needs according to individual human nature: a car, a house, clothing, food. But a piece of land measuring a thousand square miles cannot be *natural* private property, but only juridically so. That kind of property has a social function. If I am able to make institutions work for the good of the poor, I am complying with the demands of the gospel. Excessive private property leads to an economic system of subjugation. In the time of the monarchy there were Christians who fought for democracy and they made out badly. Now, in a time of capitalist democracy and private enterprise, there are Christians who are fighting for a more perfect society that would be socialized. They are faring badly, too. It frequently happens also that the church aligns itself with the subjugators, and this is its sin. Only by identifying itself with the poor can the church liberate the world from an unjust system.

Natural private property is not contrary to socialistic principles because I have a natural right to whatever I need to live—things like calories, protein, clothing, housing, etc. There is no socialist system that quarrels with this. But the excessive and unjust accumulation of juridical private property is an offshoot of original sin, of the death of Abel, of the disobedience of Adam. It is at the root of the subjugation of peoples in Latin America.

If Jesus had respected the law, the Jewish "constitution" of the Sanhedrin, the reigning order and the socially acceptable virtues, he would have died an old man within the confines of the city. But he died *outside* the city—crucified.

On Palm Sunday the people celebrated the arrival of their king; the poor were quick to recognize his kingship. One week later, the great ones, the subjugators killed him. Jesus is the proclamation of the Parousia and the only ones who see him as king are the poor because he is one of them. The frenzy of Palm Sunday is the last straw; "he" will have to be killed because of the ugly situation brewing—*the people are following him.* His death a week later is a foregone conclusion.

His resurrection is the re-creation, the birth of the new person; it is death that has died and that which is born is new life, a new order. It is the new order that rises up unmerited in Christian history, a bonanza, the walking again of the paralytic. Jesus said, "You believe; well then, walk." The Christian today in Latin America says, "You, do you believe in Christ?" The other answers, "We'll wait and see." The prophets must risk themselves for the liberation of Latin America. It will believe if the paralytics walk again, if the people become free. Only in this way can we today give meaning to the kingdom of heaven.

We can no longer say, "We have no use for economics or politics; we believe only in the kingdom and nothing else because we reckon only with things of the spirit." What we would be doing in this instance, without realizing it, would be to consecrate the order, sin. Others can say, "We are betting everything on the historical kingdom." They do so with such enthusiasm that history becomes a new religion. When the new order takes over, the poor end up being subjugated all over again and we have a new divinization of the order.

Christians, however, assert that there is an eschatological order and a historical order; working toward the historical future which they know is not absolute, they witness to the eschatological kingdom. The doctrine of the Incarnation allows us to say that we have to commit ourselves to a historical, pedagogical, political level, but only as a sign of the eschatological.

This is so very obvious, yet how often are there misunderstandings! How often do people say, "Watch out for Latin American messianism!" Messianism in the temporal order that becomes absolutized is bad; but if we temper it with a view to the eschatological, it is perfect. If we do nothing more than cry out against messianism in the temporal order, we eviscerate the Christian's critical contribution; we put ourselves on the side of the prevailing order and we make Christianity the opium of the people.

If we say, "Bear with your suffering because the king will come!" we are saying, "Accept the Devil!" In this case the kingdom of God will not come; the kingdom to come will be the kingdom of this world.

It is wrong to preach "resignation." On the contrary, we should preach a holy liberating Christian restlessness for the coming of the kingdom. Be resigned, yes, when it comes our turn to shoulder the cross. But in an active way. In the moment of our inevitable crucifixion, we shall have to resign ourselves. There is a difference.

Ethics and the Theology of Liberation. **Maryknoll, N.Y.: Orbis Books, 1978.**

Denis Goulet

. . . even revolutionary Christians are less sanguine than most Marxists as to the likelihood that new relations of production will destroy all alienation. Christians continue to believe that, at the deepest level, alienation means the sinful self-isolation of the human ego from divinizing influences which are proferred, but never imposed, by God. Human beings must be converted, even if their institutions are good, to prevent their reverting to the vilest forms of oppression or mystification.

Even theologians of liberation aspire after grace. Gustavo Gutierrez reminds us, in a recent essay:

> Jesus is opposed to all politico-religious messianism which does not respect either the depth of the religious realm or the autonomy of political action. Messianism can be efficacious in the short run, but the ambiguities and confusions which it entails frustrate the ends it attempts to accomplish.

In other words, Christians can never place unbridled hope in the reform of institutions. Even when they accept class struggle as necessary, they must have no illusions that the proletariat has been vested, in any absolute sense, with the historic mission of redeeming humanity. The proletariat is also heir to human passions and vices. Because faith summons Christians to refuse to make idols of anything other than God himself, they cannot accept, in unqualified terms, the notion that any social class is the messiah of all mankind. Marx's claim that the oppressed classes carry *universal* human values within themselves is ambiguous. To the extent that these classes are oppressed, negatively speaking, his statement is true. But to the degree that the proletariat asserts itself positively by concrete historical choices, its members cannot incarnate universal human values. Like members of any other class, they are particularistic, they are able to exploit others, they can get carried away by their own self-conferred grandeur. Marx's image of the proletariat is very romantic at root. He almost sounds like one of the nineteenth-century Russians Solzhenitsyn describes, a man who had "to change his clothes and feel his way down the staircase to go to the people." But those who are themselves members of the proletariat do not idealize the companions who share their misery: like all men or women, they can be selfish or stupid, lazy or aggressive, bitter or treacherous.

From this observation conservatives draw the conclusion that government can safely be placed only in the hands of qualified elites. But critical Marxists and revolutionary Christians conclude, instead, that even the people must have institutional barriers to prevent them from lording it over others once they accede to power.

Inherent in Christianity is the belief that no one can ever be fully converted to goodness. As Claudel once put it facetiously, "There are parts of me which have not yet been evangelized!" Nevertheless, the evil which a person commits is not irreversible, and it can be minimized. Above all, it is worth the effort to struggle to eliminate it. Hence the question, "Is it better to work at converting people or at changing institutions?" can only be answered by saying, "One must do both." Christian progressives, like Marxists, give priority to altering oppressive institutions, without neglecting to emphasize the essential corruptibility of men, even in socialist institutions. They acknowledge that socialism can generate its own special forms of alienation. Yet, on balance, they prefer to run this risk than to support an oppressive status quo. The only alternatives they rule out are passive complicity with present injustice and a naive belief in the redemptive power of liberating institutions. In a critical spirit, they see liberation as a dialectical task: an endless process whose gains are always fragile, but whose promise justifies all sacrifices.

These Christian "makers of history" have an uphill battle to wage against the distrust of institutions innate in their acceptance of sin being firmly rooted in human life. One is not surprised, therefore, when some theologians of liberation seem to fall into a simplistic Rousseauism as they preach the merits of new institutions. It is as though they naively believed that men wielding power in those institutions could not err or could no longer be seduced by temptations to private wealth or ego-satisfying power over others. In most cases, however, such language is mere rhetorical overkill. Many use it because they deem it necessary to refute the abiding conservative bias of the traditional Christian insistence on human sinfulness.

There are further tensions faced by Christian moralists as they reflect on the development debate. Many progressive Christians feel uneasy over what appears to be the logical outcome of the Marxist tendency to deemphasize sinfulness and to emphasize liberating structures. New interpretations of biblical original sin will doubtless become necessary. Perhaps Adam's sin was hubris only in the sense that he did not recognize the perfections he enjoyed as gifts. Instead, he clung to them as coming from himself. Accordingly, he could view the "knowledge of good and evil" which the tempter placed before his eyes under two aspects: as a missing perfection he must have (since all perfection must be his); and as evidence that God had "cheated" him by denying him something valuable, to wit, full knowledge. As it turned out, "knowledge of good and evil" was not a further cognitive perfection, but the *experience of misery.*

At the cosmic level, the human race rightly aspires after its own redemption. And such redemption *must come in time, it must come within history.* Any redemption which is outside time, therefore, is alienating to men. But perhaps the human race, like Adam, is summoned by destiny to display a modicum of ontological humility, to recognize its finiteness by admitting that perhaps it may be radically unable to achieve total redemption in time. If the human race collectively interprets this radical impotence as an unjust deprivation of its due by jealous gods or absurd existential forces, it will reject any form of transcendence which would keep history open to fulfillment partially outside history. For mankind, therefore, to erect its own historical efforts as an absolute idol constitutes collective hubris analogous to Adam's personal sin.

Revolutionary Christians fully committed to history are beginning to sense that they may need to reinterpret their theology of history in some such light. They are encouraged by the pleas of such heretical Marxists as Ernst Bloch, Ernst Fischer, Leszek Kolakowski, and Roger Garaudy to help them incorporate even transhistorical transcendence into the human struggle. Garaudy's reflections are especially germane here. He declares that "Christians do not know how to live in a revolution," and explains that sin is not the revolt against authority, or pride, but the failure to fight against injustice, the "desertion of the creative human task." Nevertheless, he adds, Christians have two tasks: to contribute their resources of faith and vision to the transformation of this world so as to fulfill human beings; and "never to forget to ordain this renovation of life on earth to a finality which is ever higher. Faith, in this perspective, is no longer an opium, but the ferment of the continuous creation of the world by man, and the opening of human history onto an horizon that has no end."

Hugo Assmann, a Brazilian theologian and sociologist, outlines the possible Christian contribution to liberation in even more precise terms:

It is clear that a rereading of the Bible, especially of the words of Christ, in the context of history raises for us a series of radical questions to which Marxism is unable to give the necessary attention. Perhaps the culmination of these questions is the Christian affirmation about conquering death, that radical alienation about whose overcoming Marx had nothing important or satisfactory to say.

The historical aspect of the problem of death is not the affirmation of our faith in a "hereafter" (which, as we know, does not eliminate temptations to egotism), but rather this: that the God who raised up Jesus is not a God of the Dead but of the living and that because life is the "milieu" of God he wants it to be also the "environment" of men. When we understand this in a historical and trans-historical way, in terms of a Christian eschatology whose ultimate questions are necessarily mediated to us through questions posed by our immediate situation in history, we are able to penetrate to the heart of that mystery of love which is giving one's life for others. Marxism in fact asks the same of all revolutionaries.

Christians have no trouble agreeing that the greatest sin today is omission: absenteeism from the liberating struggle. Yet liberation itself must be given its full dimensions; it cannot be enclosed within purely finite borders.

A New Moral Order: Development Ethics and Liberation Theology. **Maryknoll, N.Y.: Orbis Books, 1974.**

IV. Contemporary Theories of Justice

Life is unfair," it is often said, and human experience tends to support that observation. By nature we are given different starts in life, different endowments of talents and strengths, different environments with their opportunities and incentives for education and roles in society. The accident of birth plays a substantial part in shaping our destiny to succeed or to suffer, to sit in high places or low ones.

Are these natural inequalities "just"? Some would argue that they are to be accepted. Not everyone can be quarterback of the team, and therefore not everyone should aspire to that position. Let each live and work according to his or her assigned station in life, and the result will be a social harmony according to appropriate rank. Furthermore, some will transcend their own humble backgrounds by sheer effort and persistence to emerge as leaders, thinkers, and doers. Even within nature some unexpected qualities emerge that enable individuals to excel in spite of the circumstances of their birth. The less we interfere with nature and allow the individual the freedom to pursue his or her own good, the better the outcome will be for all.

On the other hand, comes the rejoinder, it does not make much sense to say that a person deserves his or her birth. Some people are born with deficiencies and handicaps. Some may work hard at their jobs and remain at the same menial level of life. There are elements of chance or luck involved, knowing the right person, or knowing where to be at the right time. How shall we deal with these elements? Distributive justice attempts to deal with the question of fairness in the face of the natural inequalities which are in themselves oblivious to questions of human justice. It begins by asking what individuals deserve.

We assume that achievements, labors, talents, and services rendered to others or to the society as a whole deserve to be rewarded. Thus it is the possession of some relevant property that serves as the title to reward: it is earned or merited. But what about need? Does need also qualify persons to receive benefits? Even in the absence of the properties mentioned? It is here that controversy begins.

The question is especially urgent in a society such as ours that includes great disparities of wealth. Is it fair to take through taxation from those who have earned their incomes and benefits by hard work and intelligence and redistribute the revenues collected through social welfare? Are the poor "entitled" to unearned compensation? On the other hand we encounter another set of questions. Have the poor deserved their fate if it is due to factors beyond their control? Does society have some obligation to see that they are fed, clothed, educated and provided jobs? From this point of view, do the corporations and individuals who reap mighty profits, dividends and salaries deserve all that they receive? Should they be given a completely free hand to spend all of their money as they please, even foolishly, if there are human beings who cannot afford the bare necessities?

Distributive justice deals with how much freedom we should have in earning and spending our incomes, and how much equalizing of the wealth through redistribution should take place on the basis of need. If there is to be redistribution, how extensive should it be? What commodities and services are to be included? Individual freedom tends to create increasing inequality since the members of the society have unequal assets. To achieve equality, however, means some compromising of our liberties by limiting our choices.

The theories we shall be studying will place themselves somewhere on a spectrum between the two norms. Rawls' design of the just society aims at avoiding extreme inequalities at the outset and protecting the individual by making the privileges and offices open to all and by guaranteeing fundamental benefits. Nozick presents a justification of liberty as the ultimate norm and argues that its infringement leads to results that are unjust. Bowie and Simon, addressing the issue of economic justice in particular, bid us to look at the question contextually, and introduce the norm of well-being alongside that of freedom. The prevailing economic conditions and availability of resources provide the boundaries within which a society must structure its institutions and processes. The more wealth there is, the greater the obligation to provide for the well-being of all members of the society.

A. John Rawls

John Rawls' position is probably the most important contemporary restatement of the social contract theory of which John Locke is the classic exponent. The essential problem of justice, as Rawls sees it, is that of developing the proper procedure by which to draw up principles for a just society. These principles in turn would function as norms for constructing and evaluating the various social and political institutions of that society.

Let us begin, he says, by supposing that we are parties engaged in drawing up the fundamental design of a just society. In order to insure fairness Rawls posits that none of us would know in advance just what our position in that society would be. One may be a rich mogul, another a beggar; one may be a chief executive or end up as a janitor. In such a case we would want to design a society which will extend its benefits to everyone including the worst-off. Liberty will be granted across the board, but how shall we deal with the inequalities that liberty brings? Rawls insists that as rational beings we would want to arrange them so that the inequalities of rank and fortune will be to the advantage of all. We will at least want to insure ourselves of minimum benefits and minimum opportunities to secure well-being. Thus the just society will include some mechanism to maintain a fair distribution of the wealth.

The concept of justice that Rawls presents is one of fairness which means for him that "men agree to share one another's fate." Inequalities can be accepted by rational beings only if they work to the advantage of the least well-off. And this can be accomplished only when all the members of the society subscribe to the fundamental procedures to achieve a fair equilibrium and mitigate the harsh inequalities of nature.

Rawls' theory can be better understood if we separate its three subdivisions and identify them clearly. One has to do with the actual practices, institutions and laws that are created and evaluated by members of the society in question. The second deals with the principles that serve as norms to evaluate the practices, institutions and laws that have been put into effect. The third concerns the hypothetical procedure by which the social contract is drawn up behind the "veil of ignorance," that is, without knowing what our position in society will be beforehand. Each level rests on the preceding one.

Rawls is a fierce opponent of utilitarianism as a basis for designing a society, measuring justice according to the consequences for the greatest number. Such calculation might lead to the enslaving of one portion of the population for the enjoyment and well-being of another. The miseries of the downtrodden could be justified by the happiness of the prosperous. A social contract built upon the principles of reason would protect individuals against such an eventuality.

The theory of John Rawls is a very complex one. It has provoked a wide range of responses. College courses and seminars devote themselves exclusively to analysis and comment on its features. In the brief space that we can devote to it here we *shall raise one of the most common questions asked, namely, whether the "veil of ignorance" behind which members of the proposed society would draw up its basic principles would guarantee fairness to all and extend advantages to the least well-off. Is it possible that some parties to the contract might want to run the risk of sacrificing the good of some for the good of others? If there were some individuals who would have the opportunity to make an income in six figures and hold the reins of power, might you not take the chance that you would be among them despite an alternative risk of having virtually nothing at all? Would not the decision rest largely upon the type of society possible, whether it was one in which a large proportion of its members would be well off or one in which the peasantry was vast and the elite very few in number? It is difficult for us to conceive of making decisions behind a veil of ignorance so complete that no experiential factors based on previous knowledge enter in.*

The essential features of Rawls' theory are fertile grounds for reflection, and they will serve to bring out the contrast between Rawls and the second theory to be considered, that of Robert Nozick.

A Theory of Justice

The Role of Justice

Justice is the first virtue of social institutions, as truth is of systems of thought. A theory however elegant and economical must be rejected or revised if it is untrue; likewise laws and institutions no matter how efficient and well-arranged must be reformed or abolished if they are unjust. Each person possesses an inviolability founded on justice that even the welfare of society as a whole cannot override. For this reason justice denies that the loss of freedom for some is made right by a greater good shared by others. It does not allow that the sacrifices imposed on a few are outweighed by the larger sum of advantages enjoyed by many. Therefore in a just society the liberties of equal citizenship are taken as settled; the rights secured by justice are not subject to political bargaining or to the calculus of social interests. The only thing that permits us to acquiesce in an erroneous theory is the lack of a better one; analogously, an injustice is tolerable only when it is necessary to avoid an even greater injustice. Being first virtues of human activities, truth and justice are uncompromising.

These propositions seem to express our intuitive conviction of the primacy of justice. No doubt they are expressed too strongly. In any event I wish to inquire whether these contentions or others similar to them are sound, and if so how they can be accounted for. To this end it is necessary to work out a theory of justice in the light of which these assertions can be interpreted and assessed. I shall begin by considering the role of the principles of justice. Let us assume, to fix ideas, that a society is a more or less self-sufficient association of persons who in their relations to one another recognize certain rules of conduct as binding and who for the most part act in accordance with them. Suppose further that these rules specify a system of cooperation designed to advance the good of those taking part in it. Then, although a society is a cooperative venture for mutual advantage, it is typically marked by a conflict as well as by an identity of interests. There is an identity of interests since social cooperation makes possible a better life for all than any would have if each were to live solely by his own efforts. There is a conflict of interests since persons are not indifferent as to how the greater benefits produced by their collaboration are distributed, for in order to pursue their ends they each prefer a larger to a lesser share. A set of principles is required for choosing among the various social arrangements which determine this division of advantages and for underwriting an agreement on the proper distributive shares. These principles are the principles of social justice: they provide a way of assigning rights and duties in the basic institutions of society and they define the appropriate distribution of the benefits and burdens of social cooperation. . . .

The Main Idea of the Theory of Justice

My aim is to present a conception of justice which generalizes and carries to a higher level of abstraction the familiar theory of the social contract as found, say, in Locke, Rousseau, and Kant. In order to do this we are not to think of the original contract as one to enter a particular society or to set up a particular form of government. Rather, the guiding idea is that the principles of justice for the basic structure of society are the object of the original agreement. They are the principles that free and rational persons concerned to further their own interests would accept in an initial position of equality as defining the fundamental terms of their association. These principles are to regulate all further agreements; they specify the kinds of social cooperation that can be entered into and the forms of government that can be established. This way of regarding the principles of justice I shall call justice as fairness.

Thus we are to imagine that those who engage in social cooperation choose together, in one joint act, the principles which are to assign basic rights and duties and to determine the division of social benefits. Men are to decide in advance how they are to regulate their claims against one another and what is to be the foundation charter of their society. Just as each person must decide by rational reflection what constitutes his good, that is, the system of ends which it is rational for him to pursue, so a group of persons must decide once and for all what is to count among them as just and unjust. The choice which rational men would make in this hypothetical situation of equal liberty, assuming for the present that this choice problem has a solution, determines the principles of justice.

In justice as fairness the original position of equality corresponds to the state of nature in the traditional theory of the social contract. This original position is not, of course, thought of as an actual historical state of affairs, much less as a primitive condition of culture. It is understood as a purely hypothetical situation characterized so as to lead to a certain conception of justice. Among the essential features of this situation is that no one knows his place in society, his class position or social status, nor does any one know his fortune in the distribution of natural assets and abilities, his intelligence, strength, and the like. I shall even assume that the parties do not know their conceptions of the good or their special psychological propensities. The principles of justice are chosen behind a veil of ignorance. This ensures that no one is advantaged or disadvantaged in the choice of principles by the outcome of natural chance or the contingency of social circumstances. Since all are similarly situated and no one is able to design principles to favor his particular condition, the principles of justice are the result of a fair agreement or bargain. For given the circumstances of the original position, the symmetry of everyone's relations to each other, this initial situation is fair between individuals as moral persons, that is, as rational beings with their own ends and capable, I shall assume, of a sense of justice. The original position is, one might say, the appropriate initial status quo, and thus the fundamental agreements reached in it are fair. This explains the propriety of the name "justice as fairness": it conveys the idea that the principles of justice are agreed to in an initial situation that is fair. The name does not mean that the concepts of justice and fairness are the same, any more than the phrase "poetry as metaphor" means that the concepts of poetry and metaphor are the same.

Justice as fairness begins, as I have said, with one of the most general of all choices which persons might make together, namely, with the choice of the first principles of a conception of justice which is to regulate all subsequent criticism and reform of institutions. Then, having chosen a conception of justice, we can suppose that they are to choose a constitution and a legislature to enact laws, and so on, all in accordance with the principles of justice initially agreed upon. Our social situation is just if it is such that by this sequence of hypothetical agreements we would have contracted into the general system of rules which defines it. Moreover, assuming that the original position does determine a set of principles (that is, that a particular conception of justice would be chosen), it will then be true that whenever social institutions satisfy these principles those engaged in them can say to one another that they are cooperating on terms to which they would agree if they were free and equal persons whose relations with respect to one another were fair. They could all view their arrangements as meeting the stipulations which they would acknowledge in an initial situation that embodies widely accepted and reasonable constraints on the choice of principles. The general recognition of this fact would provide the basis for a public acceptance of the corresponding principles of justice. No society can, of course, be a scheme of cooperation which men enter voluntarily in a literal sense; each person finds himself placed at birth in some particular position in some particular society, and the nature of this position materially affects his life prospects. Yet a society satisfying the principles of justice as fairness comes as close as a society can to being a voluntary scheme, for it meets the principles which free and equal persons would assent to under circumstances that are fair. In this sense its members are autonomous and the obligations they recognize self-imposed.

One feature of justice as fairness is to think of the parties in the initial situation as rational and mutually disinterested. This does not mean that the parties are egoists, that is, individuals with only certain kinds of interests, say in wealth, prestige, and domination. But they are conceived as not taking an interest in one another's interests. They are to presume that even their spiritual aims may be opposed, in the way that the aims of those of different religions may be opposed. Moreover, the concept of rationality must be interpreted as far as possible in the narrow sense, standard in economic theory, of taking the most effective means to given ends. I shall modify this concept to some extent, but one must try to avoid introducing into it any controversial ethical elements. The initial situation must be characterized by stipulations that are widely accepted. . . .

It may be observed, however, that once the principles of justice are thought of as arising from an original agreement in a situation of equality, it is an open question whether the principle of utility would be acknowledged. Offhand it hardly seems likely that persons who view themselves as equals, entitled to press their claims upon one another, would agree to a principle which may require lesser life prospects for some simply for the sake of a greater sum of advantages enjoyed by others. Since each desires to protect his interests, his capacity to advance his conception of the good, no one has a reason to acquiesce in an enduring loss for himself in order to bring about a greater net balance of satisfaction. In the absence of strong and lasting benevolent impulses, a rational man would not accept a basic structure merely because it maximized the algebraic sum of advantages irrespective of its permanent effects on his own basic rights and interests. Thus it seems that the principle of utility is incompatible with the conception of social cooperation among equals for mutual advantage. It appears to be inconsistent with the idea of reciprocity implicit in the notion of a well-ordered society. Or, at any rate, so I shall argue.

I shall maintain instead that the persons in the initial situation would choose two rather different principles: the first requires equality in the assignment of basic rights and duties, while the second holds that social and economic inequalities, for example inequalities of wealth and authority, are just only if they result in compensating benefits for everyone, and in particular for the least advantaged members of society. These principles rule out justifying institutions on the grounds that the hardships of some are offset by a greater good in the aggregate. It may be expedient but it is not just that some should have less in order that others may prosper. But there is no injustice in the greater benefits earned by a few provided that the situation of persons not so fortunate is thereby improved. The intuitive idea is that since everyone's well-being depends upon a scheme of cooperation without which no one could have a satisfactory life, the division of advantages should be such as to draw forth the willing cooperation of everyone taking part in it, including those less well situated. Yet this can be expected only if reasonable terms are proposed. The two principles mentioned seem to be a fair agreement on the basis of which those better endowed, or more fortunate in their social position, neither of which we can be said to deserve, could expect the willing cooperation of others when some workable scheme is a necessary condition of the welfare of all. Once we decide to look for a conception of justice that nullifies the accidents of natural endowment and the contingencies of social circumstance as counters in quest for political and economic advantage, we are led to these principles. They express the result of leaving aside those aspects of the social world that seem arbitrary from a moral point of view.

The problem of the choice of principles, however, is extremely difficult. I do not expect the answer I shall suggest to be convincing to everyone. It is, therefore, worth noting from the outset that justice as fairness, like other contract views, consists of two parts: (1) an interpretation of the initial situation and of the problem of choice posed there, and (2) a set of principles which, it is argued, would be agreed to. One may accept the first part of the theory (or some variant thereof), but not the other, and conversely. The concept of the initial contractual situation may seem reasonable although the particular principles proposed are rejected. To be sure, I want to maintain that the most appropriate conception of this situation does lead to principles of justice contrary to utilitarianism and perfectionism, and therefore that the contract doctrine provides an alternative to these views. Still, one may dispute this contention even though one grants that the contractarian method is a useful way of studying ethical theories and of setting forth their underlying assumptions.

The merit of the contract terminology is that it conveys the idea that principles of justice may be conceived as principles that would be chosen by rational persons, and that in this way conceptions of justice may be explained and justified. The theory of justice is a part, perhaps the most significant part, of the theory of rational choice. Furthermore, principles of justice deal with conflicting claims upon the advantages won by social cooperation; they apply to the relations among several persons or groups. The word "contract" suggests this plurality as well as the condition that the appropriate division of advantages must be in accordance with principles acceptable to all parties. The condition of publicity for principles of justice is also connoted by the contract phraseology. Thus, if these principles are the outcome of an agreement, citizens have a knowledge of the principles that others follow. It is characteristic of contract theories to stress the public nature of political principles. Finally there is the long tradition of the contract doctrine. Expressing the tie with this line of thought helps to define ideas and accords with natural piety. There are then several advantages in the use of the term "contract." With due precautions taken, it should not be misleading. . . .

The Original Position and Justification

I have said that the original position is the appropriate initial status quo which insures that the fundamental agreements reached in it are fair. This fact yields the name "justice as fairness." It is clear, then, that I want to say that one conception of justice is more reasonable than another, or justifiable with respect to it, if rational persons in the initial situation would choose its principles over those of the other for the role of justice. Conceptions of justice are to be ranked by their acceptability to persons so circumstanced. Understood in this way the question of justification is settled by working out a problem of deliberation: we have to ascertain which principles it would be rational to adopt given the contractual situation. This connects the theory of justice with the theory of rational choice.

If this view of the problem of justification is to succeed, we must, of course, describe in some detail the nature of this choice problem. A problem of rational decision has a definite answer only if we know the beliefs and interests of the parties, their relations with respect to one another, the alternatives between which they are to choose, the procedure whereby they make up their minds, and so on. As the circumstances are presented in different ways, correspondingly different principles are accepted. The concept of the original position, as I shall refer to it, is that of the most philosophically favored interpretation of this initial choice situation for the purposes of a theory of justice.

But how are we to decide what is the most favored interpretation? I assume, for one thing, that there is a broad measure of agreement that principles of justice should be chosen under certain conditions. To justify a particular description of the initial situation one shows that it incorporates these commonly shared presumptions. One argues from widely accepted but weak premises to more specific conclusions. Each of the presumptions should by itself be natural and plausible; some of them may seem innocuous or even trivial. The aim of the contract approach is to establish that taken together they impose significant bounds on acceptable principles; of justice. The ideal outcome would be that these conditions determine a unique set of principles; but I shall be satisfied if they suffice to rank the main traditional conceptions of social justice.

One should not be misled, then, by the somewhat unusual conditions which characterize the original position. The idea here is simply to make vivid to ourselves the restrictions that it seems reasonable to impose on arguments for principles of justice, and therefore on these principles themselves. Thus it seems reasonable and generally acceptable that no one should be advantaged or disadvantaged by natural fortune or social circumstances in the choice of principles. It also seems widely agreed that it should be impossible to tailor principles to the circumstances of one's own case. We should insure further that particular inclinations and aspirations, and persons' conceptions of their good do not affect the principles adopted. The aim is to rule out those principles that it would be rational to propose for acceptance, however little the chance of success, only if one knew certain things that are irrelevant from the standpoint of justice. For example, if a man knew that he was wealthy, he might find it rational to advance the principle that various taxes for welfare measures be counted unjust; if he knew that he was poor, he would most likely propose the contrary principle. To represent the desired restrictions one imagines a situation in which everyone is deprived of this sort of information. One excludes the knowledge of those contingencies which sets men at odds and allows them to be guided by their prejudices. In this manner the veil of ignorance is arrived at in a natural way. This concept should cause no difficulty if we keep in mind the constraints on arguments that it is meant to express. At any time we can enter the original position, so to speak, simply by following a certain procedure, namely, by arguing for principles of justice in accordance with these restrictions.

It seems reasonable to suppose that the parties in the original position are equal. That is, all have the same rights in the procedure for choosing principles; each can make proposals, submit reasons for their acceptance, and so on. Obviously the purpose of these conditions is to represent equality between human beings as moral persons, as creatures having a conception of their good and capable of a sense of justice. The basis of equality is taken to be similarity in these two respects. Systems of ends are not ranked in value; and each man is presumed to have the requisite ability to understand and to act upon whatever principles are adopted. Together with the veil of ignorance, these conditions define the principles of justice as those which rational persons concerned to advance their interests would consent to as equals when none are known to be advantaged or disadvantaged by social and natural contingencies.

Two Principles of Justice

I shall now state in a provisional form the two principles of justice that I believe would be chosen in the original position.

First: each person is to have an equal right to the most extensive basic liberty compatible with a similar liberty for others.

Second: social and economic inequalities are to be arranged so that they are both (a) reasonably expected to be to everyone's advantage, and (b) attached to positions and offices open to all. . . .

By way of general comment, these principles primarily apply, as I have said, to the basic structure of society. They are to govern the assignment of rights and duties and to regulate the distribution of social and economic advantages. As their formulation suggests, these principles presuppose that the social structure can be divided into two more or less distinct parts, the first principle applying to the one, the second to the other. They distinguish between those aspects of the social system that define and secure the equal liberties of citizenship and those that specify and establish social and economic inequalities. The basic liberties of citizens are, roughly speaking, political liberty (the right to vote and to be eligible for public office) together with freedom of speech and assembly; liberty of conscience and freedom of thought; freedom of the person along with the right to hold (personal) property; and freedom from arbitrary arrest and seizure as defined by the concept of the rule of law. These liberties are all required to be equal by the first principle, since citizens of a just society are to have the same basic rights.

The second principle applies, in the first approximation, to the distribution of income and wealth and to the design of organizations that make use of differences in authority and responsibility, or chains of command. While the distribution of wealth and income need not be equal, it must be to everyone's advantage, and at the same time, positions of authority and offices of command must be accessible to all. One applies the second principle by holding positions open, and then, subject to this constraint, arranges social and economic inequalities so that everyone benefits.

These principles are to be arranged in a serial order with the first principle prior to the second. This ordering means that a departure from the institutions of equal liberty required by the first principle cannot be justified by, or compensated for, by greater social and economic advantages. The distribution of wealth and income, and the hierarchies of authority, must be consistent with both the liberties of equal citizenship and equality of opportunity.

It is clear that these principles are rather specific in their content, and their acceptance rests on certain assumptions that I must eventually try to explain and justify. A theory of justice depends upon a theory of society in ways that will become evident as we proceed. For the present, it should be observed that the two principles (and this holds for all formulations) are a special case of a more general conception of justice that can be expressed as follows.

> All social values—liberty and opportunity, income and wealth, and the bases of self-respect—are to be distributed equally unless an unequal distribution of any, or all, of these values is to everyone's advantage.

Injustice, then, is simply inequalities that are not to the benefit of all. Of course, this conception is extremely vague and requires interpretation.

As a first step, suppose that the basic structure of society distributes certain primary goods, that is, things that every rational man is presumed to want. These goods normally have a use whatever a person's rational plan of life. For simplicity, assume that the chief primary goods at the disposition of society are rights and liberties, powers and opportunities, income and wealth. (Later on in Part Three the primary good of self-respect has a central place.) These are the social primary goods. Other primary goods such as health and vigor, intelligence and imagination, are natural goods; although their possession is influenced by the basic structure, they are not so directly under its control. Imagine, then, a hypothetical initial arrangement in which all the social primary goods are equally distributed: everyone has similar rights and duties, and income and wealth are evenly shared. This state of affairs provides a benchmark for judging improvements. If certain inequalities of wealth and organizational powers would make everyone better off than in this hypothetical starting situation, then they accord with the general conception.

Now it is possible, at least theoretically, that by giving up some of their fundamental liberties men are sufficiently compensated by the resulting social and economic gains. The general conception of justice imposes no restrictions on what sort of inequalities are permissible; it only requires that everyone's position be improved. . . .

Now the second principle insists that each person benefit from permissible inequalities in the basic structure. This means that it must be reasonable for each relevant representative man defined by this structure, when he views it as a going concern, to prefer his prospects with the inequality to his prospects without it. One is not allowed to justify differences in income or organizational powers on the ground that the disadvantages of those in one position are outweighed by the greater advantages of those in another. Much less can infringements of liberty be counterbalanced in this way. Applied to the basic structure, the principle of utility would have us maximize the sum of expectations of representative men (weighted by the number of persons they represent, on the classic view); and this would permit us to compensate for the losses of some by the gains of others. Instead, the two principles require that everyone benefit from economic and social inequalities. . . .

The Tendency to Equality

I wish to conclude this discussion of the two principles by explaining the sense in which they express an egalitarian conception of justice. Also I should like to forestall the objection to the principle of fair opportunity that it leads to a callous meritocratic society. In order to prepare the way for doing this, I note several aspects of the conception of justice that I have set out.

First we may observe that the difference principle gives some weight to the considerations singled out by the principle of redress. This is the principle that undeserved inequalities call for redress; and since inequalities of birth and natural endowment are undeserved, these inequalities are to be somehow compensated for. Thus the principle holds that in order to treat all persons equally, to provide genuine equality of opportunity, society must give more attention to those with fewer native assets and to those born into the less favorable social positions. The idea is to redress the bias of contingencies in the direction of equality. In pursuit of this principle greater resources might be spent on the education of the less rather than the more intelligent, at least over a certain time of life, say the earlier years of school.

Now the principle of redress has not to my knowledge been proposed as the sole criterion of justice, as the single aim of the social order. It is plausible as most such principles are only as a prima facie principle, one that is to be weighed in the balance with others. For example, we are to weigh it against the principle to improve the average standard of life, or to advance the common good. But whatever other principles we hold, the claims of redress are to be taken into account. It is thought to represent one of the elements in our conception of justice. Now the difference principle is not of course the principle of redress. It does not require society to try to even out handicaps as if all were expected to compete on a fair basis in the same race. But the difference principle would allocate resources in education, say, so as to improve the long-term expectation of the least favored. If this end is attained by giving more attention to the better endowed, it is permissible; otherwise not. And in making this decision, the value of education should not be assessed only in terms of economic efficiency and social welfare. Equally if not more important is the role of education in enabling a person to enjoy the culture of his society and to take part in its affairs, and in this way to provide for each individual a secure sense of his own worth.

Thus although the difference principle is not the same as that of redress, it does achieve some of the intent of the latter principle. It transforms the aims of the basic structure so that the total scheme of institutions no longer emphasizes social efficiency and technocratic values. We see then that the difference principle represents, in effect, an agreement to regard the distribution of natural talents as a common asset and to share in the benefits of this distribution whatever it turns out to be. Those who have been favored by nature, whoever they are, may gain from their good fortune only on terms that improve the situation of those who have lost out. The naturally advantaged are not to gain merely because they are more gifted, but only to cover the costs of training and education and for using their endowments in ways that help the less fortunate as well. No one deserves his greater natural capacity nor merits a more favorable starting place in society. But it does not follow that one should eliminate these distinctions. There is another way to deal with them. The basic structure can be arranged so that these contingencies work for the good of the least fortunate. Thus we are led to the difference principle if we wish to set up the social system so that no one gains or loses from his arbitrary place in the distribution of natural assets or his initial position in society without giving or receiving compensating advantages in return.

In view of these remarks we may reject the contention that the ordering of institutions is always defective because the distribution of natural talents and the contingencies of social circumstance are unjust, and this injustice must inevitably carry over to human arrangements. Occasionally this reflection is offered as an excuse for ignoring injustice, as if the refusal to acquiesce in injustice is on a par with being unable to accept death. The natural distribution is neither just nor unjust; nor is it unjust that men are born into society at some particular position. These are simply natural facts. What is just and unjust is the way that institutions deal with these facts. Aristocratic and caste societies are unjust because they make these contingencies the ascriptive basis for belonging to more or less enclosed and privileged social classes. The basic structure of these societies incorporates the arbitrariness found in nature. But there is no necessity for men to resign themselves to these contingencies. The social system is not an unchangeable order beyond human control but a pattern of human action. In justice as fairness men agree to share one another's fate. In designing institutions they undertake to avail themselves of the accidents of nature and social circumstance only when doing so is for the common benefit. The two principles are a fair way of meeting the arbitrariness of fortune; and while no doubt imperfect in other ways, the institutions which satisfy these principles are just. . . .

There is a natural inclination to object that those better situated deserve their greater advantages whether or not they are to the benefit of others. At this point it is necessary to be clear about the notion of desert. It is perfectly true that given a just system of cooperation as a scheme of public rules and the expectations set up by it, those who, with the prospect of improving their condition, have done what the system announces that it will reward are entitled to their advantages. In this sense the more fortunate have a claim to their better situation; their claims are legitimate expectations established by social institutions, and the community is obligated to meet them. But this sense of desert presupposes the existence of the cooperative scheme; it is irrelevant to the question whether in the first place the scheme is to be designed in accordance with the difference principle or some other criterion.

Perhaps some will think that the person with greater natural endowments deserves those assets and the superior character that made their development possible. Because he is more worthy in this sense, he deserves the greater advantages that he could achieve with them. This view, however, is surely incorrect. It seems to be one of the fixed points of our considered judgments that no one deserves his place in the distribution of native endowments, any more than one deserves one's initial starting place in society. The assertion that a man deserves the superior character that enables him to make the effort to cultivate his abilities is equally problematic; for his character depends in large part upon fortunate family and social circumstances for which he can claim no credit. The notion of desert seems not to apply to these cases. Thus the more advantaged representative man cannot say that he deserves and therefore has a right to a scheme of cooperation in which he is permitted to acquire benefits in ways that do not contribute to the welfare of others. There is no basis for his making this claim. From the standpoint of common sense, then, the difference principle appears to be acceptable both to the more advantaged and to the less advantaged individual.

A Theory of Justice, Cambridge: Harvard University Press, 1971, pp. 3–4. 11–15, 18–19, 60–62, 64–65, 100–104.

B. Robert Nozick

The theory of justice offered by Nozick is in the classical libertarian tradition. He holds that individuals should be left alone to pursue their own interests, to acquire, possess and transfer property, and accumulate wealth without interference on the part of any person or institution without expressed consent. Justice consists in the widest possible latitude of freedom possible granted to each member of society across the board.

When it comes to the question of how goods are to be distributed, the theory argues that no pattern of justice can be truly just. A pattern would impose a formula or rule to which all members of a society are bound to adhere for the purpose of redistributing the wealth. This invariably entails the curbing of the individual's freedom of acquiring, possessing and disposing of his goods as he sees fit.

The key notion in Nozick's philosophy is that of acquisition. So long as wealth has been gained lawfully and honestly, then everyone is entitled to his holdings. Persons may rightfully acquire and transfer property and other assets in any way desirable short of outright theft, and so long as they do not "worsen the situation of others." Just what does this qualification mean? The only interpretation Nozick makes of this principle is by way of an example in which it appears to mean owning something which someone knows about and without which that other person would die. If Smith owns the only water supply and Jones knows that Smith owns it and, further, Jones will die without access to Smith's water, then the sole possession of the only water source on the part of Smith is not just. But Nozick does not mean by "worsening the situation of others" causing someone to fall below a minimum standard of living, or going without necessities such as health care, housing, education, and the like. These would require interference with the free market and involve violation of the prior right to liberty.

What about taxes: are these an unjust imposition? If it is for the purpose of providing others with minimum benefits or well-being, they are unjust. For they are like forcing a person to work so many hours to earn wealth that is to be taken away and given to someone else. They are a compulsory gift.

Three issues emerge for our consideration. Earlier we noted that the freedom of individuals to pursue their own interests without constraint increases disparities in wealth and opportunity and tends to establish patterns of inequality, leading to poverty and want. This may be of little concern to the individual, but is it a concern of society as a whole? What effects will it have on the general population? Suppose it creates massive unemployment, social conflict, urban rot, increased crime and delinquency. What should be done about these ills in a libertarian environment? Is there any way the libertarian can address these issues without infringing on the right to liberty?

The second issue has to do with the means of acquisition which, says Nozick, should be legal, honest, and not worsen the situation of others. Is this a sufficient definition for what counts as fraudulent gain? What about deceptive and subliminal

121

*kinds of advertising? What of preying on the powerlessness of the poor or the gul-
libility of the inexperienced? Are there to be any standards of safety for products—
for example, untested drugs, flammable clothing, and automobiles that are death-
traps in collision? And finally, just what does one own? Can a property owner protect himself against atmospheric pollution, noise from jets flying over residential
areas, the invasion of industry into housing developments? What about the public
domain? How establish who owns the wilderness, or the wealth of minerals on the
oceans' floors?*

*The last and most fundamental of all questions concerns the notion of liberty
itself. Nozick uses it as a normative term; in fact, it is the one right that cannot be
violated. He does not offer grounds for doing so. Nor does he explain why we must
exclude other norms for justice or make them conditional upon liberty. Are there
other ethical principles of justice that might be posited as having a claim upon us
equally important to that of liberty? Are any moral considerations besides liberty
entailed by the very existence of other persons in society?*

Anarchy, State and Utopia: Distributive Justice

The minimal state is the most extensive state that can be justified. Any
state more extensive violates people's rights. Yet many persons have put
forth reasons purporting to justify a more extensive state. It is impossible
within the compass of this book to examine all the reasons that have been
put forth. Therefore, I shall focus upon those generally acknowledged to be
most weighty and influential, to see precisely wherein they fail. In this
chapter we consider the claim that a more extensive state is justified, because necessary (or the best instrument) to achieve distributive justice.

The term "distributive justice" is not a neutral one. Hearing the term
"distribution," most people presume that some thing or mechanism uses
some principle or criterion to give out a supply of things. Into this process
of distributing shares some error may have crept. So it is an open question,
at least, whether *re*distribution should take place; whether we should do
again what has already been done once, though poorly. However, we are
not in the position of children who have been given portions of pie by someone who now makes last minute adjustments to rectify careless cutting.
There is no *central* distribution, no person or group entitled to control all
the resources, jointly deciding how they are to be doled out. What each person gets, he gets from others who give to him in exchange for something,
or as a gift. In a free society, diverse persons control different resources,
and new holdings arise out of the voluntary exchanges and actions of per-

sons. There is no more a distributing or distribution of shares than there is a distributing of mates in a society in which persons choose whom they shall marry. The total result is the product of many individual decisions which the different individuals involved are entitled to make. Some uses of the term "distribution," it is true, do not imply a previous distributing appropriately judged by some criterion (for example, "probability distribution"); nevertheless, despite the title of this chapter, it would be best to use a terminology that clearly is neutral. We shall speak of people's holdings; a principle of justice in holdings describes (part of) what justice tells us (requires) about holdings.

Section I
The Entitlement Theory

The subject of justice in holdings consists of three major topics. The first is the *original acquisition of holdings,* the appropriation of unheld things. This includes the issues of how unheld things may come to be held, the process, or processes, by which unheld things may come to be held, the things that may come to be held by these processes, the extent of what comes to be held by a particular process, and so on. We shall refer to the complicated truth about this topic, which we shall not formulate here, as the principle of justice in acquisition. The second topic concerns the *transfer of holdings* from one person to another. By what processes may a person transfer holdings to another? How may a person acquire a holding from another who holds it? Under this topic come general descriptions of voluntary exchange, and gift and (on the other hand) fraud, as well as reference to particular conventional details fixed upon in a given society. The complicated truth about this subject (with placeholders for conventional details) we shall call the principle of justice in transfer. (And we shall suppose it also includes principles governing how a person may divest himself of a holding, passing it into an unheld state.)

If the world were wholly just, the following inductive definition would exhaustively cover the subject of justice in holdings.

1. A person who acquires a holding in accordance with the principle of justice in acquisition is entitled to that holding.
2. A person who acquires a holding in accordance with the principle of justice in transfer, from someone else entitled to the holding, is entitled to the holding.
3. No one is entitled to a holding except by (repeated) applications of 1 and 2.

The complete principle of distributive justice would say simply that a distribution is just if everyone is entitled to the holdings they possess under the distribution.

A distribution is just if it arises from another just distribution by legitimate means. The legitimate means of moving from one distribution to another are specified by the principle of justice in transfer. The legitimate first "moves" are specified by the principle of justice in acquisition. Whatever arises from a just situation by just steps is itself just. The means of change specified by the principle of justice in transfer preserve justice. As correct rules of inference are truth-preserving, and any conclusion deduced via repeated application of such rules from only true premises is itself true, so the means of transition from one situation to another specified by the principle of justice in transfer are justice-preserving, and any situation actually arising from repeated transitions in accordance with the principle from a just situation is itself just. The parallel between justice-preserving transformations and truth-preserving transformations illuminates where it fails as well as where it holds. That a conclusion could have been deduced by truth-preserving means from premises that are true suffices to show its truth. That from a just situation a situation *could* have arisen via justice-preserving means does *not* suffice to show its justice. The fact that a thief's victims voluntarily *could* have presented him with gifts does not entitle the thief to his ill-gotten gains. Justice in holdings is historical; it depends upon what actually has happened. We shall return to this point later.

Not all actual situations are generated in accordance with the two principles of justice in holdings: the principle of justice in acquisition and the principle of justice in transfer. Some people steal from others, or defraud them, or enslave them, seizing their product and preventing them from living as they choose, or forcibly exclude others from competing in exchanges. None of these are permissible modes of transition from one situation to another. And some persons acquire holdings by means not sanctioned by the principle of justice in acquisition. The existence of past injustice (previous violations of the first two principles of justice in holdings) raises the third major topic under justice in holdings: the rectification of injustice in holdings. If past injustice has shaped present holdings in various ways, some identifiable and some not, what now, if anything, ought to be done to rectify these injustices? What obligations do the performers of injustice have toward those whose position is worse than it would have been had the injustice not been done? Or, than it would have been had compensation been paid promptly? How, if at all, do things change if the beneficiaries and those made worse off are not the direct parties in the act of injustice, but, for example, their descendants? Is an injustice done to someone whose holding was itself based upon an unrectified injustice? How far back must one go in wiping clean the historical slate of injustices? What may victims of injustice permissibly do in order to rectify the injustices being done to them, including the many injustices done by persons acting through their government? I do not know of a thorough or theoretically sophisticated treatment of such issues. Idealizing greatly, let us suppose theoretical investigation will produce a principle of rectification. This principle uses historical information about previous situations and injustices done in them (as defined by the first two principles of justice and rights against interference), and information about the actual course of events that flowed from these injustices, until the present, and it yields a description (or descriptions) of holdings in the society. The principle of rectification presumably will make use of its best estimate of subjunctive information about what would have occurred (or a probability distribution over what might have occurred, using the expected value) if the injustice had not taken place. If the actual description of holdings turns out not to be one of the descriptions yielded by the principle, then one of the descriptions yielded must be realized.

The general outlines of the theory of justice in holdings are that the holdings of a person are just if he is entitled to them by the principles of justice in acquisition and transfer, or by the principle of rectification of injustice (as specified by the first two principles). If each person's holdings are just, then the total set (distribution) of holdings is just. To turn these general outlines into a specific theory we would have to specify the details of each of the three principles of justice in holdings: the principle of acquisition of holdings, the principle of transfer of holdings, and the principle of rectification of violations of the first two principles. I shall not attempt that task here. (Locke's principle of justice in acquisition is discussed below.)

Historical Principles and End-Result Principles

The general outlines of the entitlement theory illuminate the nature and defects of other conceptions of distributive justice. The entitlement theory of justice in distribution is *historical;* whether a distribution is just depends upon how it came about. In contrast, *current time-slice principles* of justice hold that the justice of a distribution is determined by how things are distributed (who has what) as judged by some *structural* principle(s) of just distribution. A utilitarian who judges between any two distributions by seeing which has the greater sum of utility and, if the sums tie, applies some fixed equality criterion to choose the more equal distribution, would hold a current time-slice principle of justice. As would someone who had a fixed schedule of trade-offs between the sum of happiness and equality.

According to a current time-slice principle, all that needs to be looked at, in judging the justice of a distribution, is who ends up with what; in comparing any two distributions one need look only at the matrix presenting the distributions. No further information need be fed into a principle of justice. It is a consequence of such principles of justice that any two structurally identical distributions are equally just. (Two distributions are structurally identical if they present the same profile, but perhaps have different persons occupying the particular slots. My having ten and your having five, and my having five and your having ten are structurally identical distributions.) Welfare economics is the theory of current time-slice principles of justice. The subject is conceived as operating on matrices representing only current information about distribution. This, as well as some of the usual conditions (for example, the choice of distribution is invariant under relabeling of columns), guarantees that welfare economics will be a current time-slice theory, with all of its inadequacies.

Most persons do not accept current time-slice principles as constituting the whole story about distributive shares. They think it relevant in assessing the justice of a situation to consider not only the distribution it embodies, but also how that distribution came about. If some persons are in prison for murder or war crimes, we do not say that to assess the justice of the distribution in the society we must look only at what this person has, and that person has, and that person has, . . . at the current time. We think it relevant to ask whether someone did something so that he *deserved* to be punished, deserved to have a lower share. . . .

Almost every suggested principle of distributive justice is patterned: to each according to his moral merit, or needs, or marginal product, or how hard he tries, or the weighted sum of the foregoing, and so on. The principle of entitlement we have sketched is *not* patterned. There is no one natural dimension or weighted sum or combination of a small number of natural dimensions that yields the distributions generated in accordance with the principle of entitlement. The set of holdings that results when some persons receive their marginal products, others win at gambling, others receive a share of their mate's income, others receive gifts from foundations, others receive interest on loans, others receive gifts from admirers, others receive returns on investment, others make for themselves much of what they have, others find things, and so on, will not be patterned. . . .

To think that the task of a theory of distributive justice is to fill in the blank in ''to each according to his _____ '' is to be predisposed to search for a pattern; and the separate treatment of ''from each according to his _____'' treats production and distribution as two separate and independent issues. On an entitlement view these are *not* two separate questions. Whoever makes something, having bought or contracted for all other held resources used in the process (transferring some of his holdings for these cooperating factors), is entitled to it. The situation is *not* one of something's getting made, and there being an open question of who is to get it. Things come into the world already attached to people having entitlements over them. From the point of view of the historical entitlement conception of justice in holdings, those who start afresh to complete "to each according to his _____ " treat objects as if they appeared from nowhere, out of nothing. A complete theory of justice might cover this limit case as well; perhaps here is a use for the usual conceptions of distributive justice.

So entrenched are maxims of the usual form that perhaps we should present the entitlement conception as a competitor. Ignoring acquisition and rectification, we might say:

> From each according to what he chooses to do, to each according to what he makes for himself (perhaps with the contracted aid of others) and what others choose to do for him and choose to give him of what they've been given previously (under this maxim) and haven't yet expended or transferred.

This, the discerning reader will have noticed, has its defects as a slogan. So as a summary and great simplification (and not as a maxim with any independent meaning) we have:

> *From each as they choose, to each as they are chosen.*

How Liberty Upsets Patterns

It is not clear how those holding alternative conceptions of distributive justice can reject the entitlement conception of justice in holdings. For suppose a distribution favored by one of these non-entitlement conceptions is realized. Let us suppose it is your favorite one and let us call this distribution D_1; perhaps everyone has an equal share, perhaps shares vary in accordance with some dimension you treasure. Now suppose that Wilt Chamberlain is greatly in demand by basketball teams, being a great gate attraction. (Also suppose contracts run only for a year, with players being free agents.) He signs the following sort of contract with a team: In each home game, twenty-five cents from the price of each ticket of admission goes to him. (We ignore the question of whether he is "gouging" the owners, letting them look out for themselves.) The season starts, and people cheerfully attend his team's games; they buy their tickets, each time dropping a separate twenty-five cents of their admission price into a special box with Chamberlain's name on it. They are excited about seeing him play; it is worth the total admission price to them. Let us suppose that in one season one million persons attend his home games, and Wilt Chamberlain winds up with $250,000, a much larger sum than the average income and larger even than anyone else has. Is he entitled to this income? Is this new distribution D_2, unjust? If so, why? There is *no* question about whether each of the people was entitled to the control over the resources they held in D_1; because that was the distribution (your favorite) that (for the purposes of argument) we assumed was acceptable. Each of these persons *chose* to give twenty-five cents of their money to Chamberlain. They could have spent it on going to the movies, or on candy bars, or on copies of *Dissent* magazine, or of *Monthly Review*. But they all, at least one million of them, converged on giving it to Wilt Chamberlain in exchange for watching him play basketball. If D_1 was a just distribution, and people voluntarily moved from it to D_2, transferring parts of their shares they were given under D_2 (what was it for if not to do something with?), isn't D_2 also just? If the people were entitled to dispose of the resources to which they were entitled (under D_1), didn't this include their being entitled to give it to, or exchange it with, Wilt Chamberlain? Can anyone else complain on grounds of justice? Each other person already has his legitimate share under D_1. Under D_1, there is nothing that anyone has that anyone else has a claim of justice against. After someone transfers something to Wilt Chamberlain, third parties *still* have their legitimate shares; *their* shares are not changed. By what process could such a transfer among two persons give rise to a legitimate claim of distributive justice on a portion of what was transferred, by a third party who had no claim of justice on any holding of the others *before* the transfer? To cut off objections irrelevant here, we might imagine the exchanges occurring in a socialist society, after hours. After playing whatever basketball he does in his daily work, or doing whatever other daily work he does, Wilt Chamberlain decides to put in *overtime* to earn additional money. (First his work quota is set; he works time over that.) Or imagine it is a skilled juggler people like to see, who puts on shows after hours. . . .

The general point illustrated by the Wilt Chamberlain example and the example of the entrepreneur in a socialist society is that no end-state principle or distributional patterned principle of justice can be continuously realized without continuous interference with people's lives. Any favored pattern would be transformed into one unfavored by the principle, by people choosing to act in various ways; for example, by people exchanging goods and services with other people, or giving things to other people, things the transferrers are entitled to under the favored distributional pattern. To maintain a pattern one must either continually interfere to stop people from transferring resources as they wish to, or continually (or periodically) interfere to take from some persons resources that others for some reason chose to transfer to them. . . .

Patterned principles of distributive justice necessitate *re*distributive activities. The likelihood is small that any actual freely-arrived-at set of holdings fits a given pattern; and the likelihood is nil that it will continue to fit the pattern as people exchange and give. From the point of view of an entitlement theory, redistribution is a serious matter indeed, involving, as it does, the violation of people's rights. (An exception is those takings that fall under the principle of the rectification of injustices.) From other points of view, also, it is serious.

Taxation of earnings from labor is on a par with forced labor. Some persons find this claim obviously true: taking the earnings of *n* hours labor is like taking *n* hours from the person; it is like forcing the person to work *n* hours for another's purpose. Others find the claim absurd. But even these, *if* they object to forced labor, would oppose forcing unemployed hippies to work for the benefit of the needy. And they would also object to forcing each person to work five extra hours each week for the benefit of the needy. But a system that takes five hours' wages in taxes does not seem to them like one that forces someone to work five hours, since it offers the person forced a wider range of choice in activities than does taxation in kind with the particular labor specified. . . .

Whether it is done through taxation on wages or on wages over a certain amount, or through seizure of profits, or through there being a big *social pot* so that it's not clear what's coming from where and what's going where, patterned principles of distributive justice involve appropriating the actions of other persons. Seizing the results of someone's labor is equivalent to seizing hours from him and directing him to carry on various activities. If people force you to do certain work, or unrewarded work, for a certain period of time, they decide what you are to do and what purposes your work is to serve apart from your decisions. This process whereby they take this decision from you makes them a *part-owner* of you; it gives them a property right in you. Just as having such partial control and power of decision, by right, over an animal or inanimate object would be to have a property right in it. . . .

Locke's Theory of Acquisition

Before we turn to consider other theories of justice in detail, we must introduce an additional bit of complexity into the structure of the entitlement theory. This is best approached by considering Locke's attempt to specify a principle of justice in acquisition. Locke views property rights in an unowned object as originating through someone's mixing his labor with it. This gives rise to many questions. What are the boundaries of what labor is mixed with? If a private astronaut clears a place on Mars, has he mixed his labor with (so that he comes to own) the whole planet, the whole uninhabited universe, or just a particular plot? Which plot does an act bring under ownership?

I assume that any adequate theory of justice in acquisition will contain a proviso similar to the weaker of the ones we have attributed to Locke. A process normally giving rise to a permanent bequeathable property right in a previously unowned thing will not do so if the position of others no longer at liberty to use the thing is thereby worsened. It is important to specify *this* particular mode of worsening the situation of others, for the proviso does not encompass other modes. It does not include the worsening due to more limited opportunities to appropriate and it does not include how I "worsen" a seller's position if I appropriate materials to make some of what he is selling, and then enter into competition with him. Someone whose appropriation otherwise would violate the proviso still may appropriate provided he compensates the others so that their situation is not thereby worsened; unless he does compensate these others, his appropriation will violate the proviso of the principle of justice in acquisition and will be an illegitimate one. A theory of appropriation incorporating this Lockean proviso will handle correctly the cases (objections to the theory lacking the proviso) where someone appropriates the total supply of something necessary for life.

A theory which includes this proviso in its principle of justice in acquisition must also contain a more complex principle of justice in transfer. Some reflection of the proviso about appropriation constrains later actions. If my appropriating all of a certain substance violates the Lockean proviso, then so does my appropriating some and purchasing all the rest from others who obtained it without otherwise violating the Lockean proviso. If the proviso excludes someone's appropriating all the drinkable water in the world, it also excludes his purchasing it all. (More weakly, and messily, it may exclude his charging certain prices for some of his supply.) This proviso (almost?) never will come into effect; the more someone acquires of a scarce substance which others want, the higher the price of the rest will go, and the more difficult it will become for him to acquire it all. But still, we can imagine, at least, that something like this occurs: someone makes simultaneous secret bids to the separate owners of a substance, each of whom sells assuming he can easily purchase more from the other owners; or some natural catastrophe destroys all of the supply of something except that in one person's possession. The total supply could not be permissibly appropriated by one person at the beginning. His later acquisition of it all does not show that the original appropriation violated the proviso (even by a reverse argument similar to the one above that tried to zip back from Z to A). Rather, it is the combination of the original appropriation *plus* all the later transfers and actions that violates the Lockean proviso.

Each owner's title to his holding includes the historical shadow of the Lockean proviso on appropriation. This excludes his transferring it into an agglomeration that does violate the Lockean proviso and excludes his using it in a way, in coordination with others or independently of them, so as to violate the proviso by making the situation of others worse than their baseline situation. Once it is known that someone's ownership runs afoul of the Lockean proviso, there are stringent limits on what he may do with (what it is difficult any longer unreservedly to call) "his property." Thus a person may not appropriate the only water hole in a desert and charge what he will. Nor may he charge what he will if he possesses one, and unfortunately it happens that all the water holes in the desert dry up, except for his. This unfortunate circumstance, admittedly no fault of his, brings into operation the Lockean proviso and limits his property rights. Similarly, an owner's property right in the only island in an area does not allow him to order a castaway from a shipwreck off his island as a trespasser, for this would violate the Lockean proviso.

Notice that the theory does not say that owners do have these rights, but that the rights are overridden to avoid some catastrophe. (Overridden rights do not disappear; they leave a trace of a sort absent in the cases under discussion.) There is no such external (and *ad hoc?*) overriding. Considerations internal to the theory of property itself, to its theory of acquisition and appropriation, provide the means for handling such cases. . . .

I believe that the free operation of a market system will not actually run afoul of the Lockean proviso. If this is correct, the proviso will not play a very important role in the activities of protective agencies and will not provide a significant opportunity for future state action. Indeed, were it not for the effects of previous *illegitimate* state action, people would not think the possibility of the proviso's being violated as of more interest than any other logical possibility.

Anarchy, State and Utopia, **New York: Basic Books, 1974, pp. 149–163, 169, 172, 178–182.**

C. Norman E. Bowie and Robert L. Simon

Bowie and Simon offer some thought-provoking criticisms of both the classical laissez-faire position and its egalitarian alternatives. The substance of their argument, however, lies in its offering a contextual theory of distributive justice, one that takes into account different economies. A key formulation is that of well-being as a natural right. The more affluent the society, the greater obligation there is for society to fulfill that right. This will mean a greater need to curtail the individual's freedom to dispose of income as he or she pleases. But, at the same time, we are reminded that the greater the affluence, the greater increase in freedom as well, since higher standards of living and the possession of wealth produce wider ranges of choice. Well-being entails a minimum standard of decency for all.

The authors suggest that such a minimum standard includes at least food, health care, housing and education. Are there other components that should be included? What about employment? Protection from exploitation? Then there is the question of how this right is to be enforced and implemented. Are there ways in which the public and private sectors of the economy can work together?

Economic Justice

After a period of relative optimism concerning the conquest of scarcity and the elimination of poverty, the recent years of endemic inflation and a growing energy crisis have caused the pressing problems of economic justice to regain prominence. Indeed, a number of economic crises have sharpened debate about issues of economic justice. Overpopulation, famine, the Arab oil embargo, the gap in living standards between industrial and nonindustrial societies, the costs of pollution, the consumption of energy, and the rising costs of health care and education all raise issues of economic justice, and these issues are so complex that even enlightened, well-intentioned persons frequently have sharp disagreement over them.

To a great extent, the solution of these problems depends on a better empirical determination of the facts. Technology and scientific experimentation are two of the necessary keys of unlocking solutions. The philosophers' task is to clarify the issues and to formulate some defensible principles of economic justice that would provide a moral framework within which the solution would take place.

132

For purposes of this text we shall say that any question of the following type is a question of distributive justice:

> Given: some situation in which the goods and services produced are inadequate to satisfy everyone's desire for them. On what basis or according to what principles can these goods and services be distributed justly?

The moral philosopher demands that any answer to this question be a moral one. This perspective is different from that of the pure economist or positive political scientist. Their analyses are descriptive; ours are normative. We are indicating how an economic system ought to work, not how it does work. Our analysis is constrained in two ways. First, the only solutions to the problem are moral ones. To solve the population problem by killing every third child or to eliminate the overcrowding of public facilities by denying their use to members of minority, ethnic, or religious groups is morally unacceptable. Our analysis is also constrained by factual statements about the capabilities of economic systems. It does no good to argue that everyone ought to have a minimum income of $10,000 if that simply is impossible given the available resources and other facts about productive resources. The difficult task of moral philosophy is to steer a middle course between an impossible ideal and a rationalization of the status quo. It is this middle course that we will try to steer in our discussion. In this chapter we analyze traditional theories of distributive justice and conclude the chapter with our own theory.

The Market Solution to Economic Justice

Classical Laissez-Faire

In classical laissez-faire economics, the problem of distributive justice was to be resolved by the automatic working of the marketplace. Distributive justice was not to be achieved by conscious striving. Rather it was to be achieved by the self-regulating device of the market place. Interference with the market mechanism, no matter how well-intentioned, created inefficiency and thwarted achievement. In other words, under a market system our rights to well-being and to liberty are not in conflict; the market system satisfies both of them.

The recognition that the operation of the laissez-faire market supports our right to individual liberty has not only been the thesis of the libertarian

economists, Milton Friedman and Friedrich von Hayek, but has been pas-
sionately argued in Robert Nozick's *Anarchy, State, and Utopia*. Milton
Friedman argues that the market mechanism enables us to exercise our natural right to liberty in the following ways. First, it guarantees freedom of
property including the right to spend our income as we see fit. Second, it
guarantees freedom of occupation. Each person chooses the occupation he
most desires consistent with his ability to get hired. Third, it enhances freedom of development. Each person chooses his own life style and is free to
go as far as possible consistent with one's abilities. Fourth, it enhances
freedom of expression. Friedman argues that the competitive market pro-
tects the basic freedoms of communication by separating economic and political power and by decentralizing economic power. One's freedom of
speech is more meaningful so long as alternative opportunities for employment exist, a condition that cannot exist if the government owns and operates the economy. One's freedom of expression, especially freedom of the
press, is also enhanced since ideas inconsistent with those of the government or one's editorial board may still get published. The fear that a competitor may publish the work often overcomes the distaste of certain ideas.
For this reason, contemporary libertarians decry the increasing centralization of industry, the growth of government influence, and the establishment
of the business-government-university alliance that Galbraith has characterized as the New Industrial State.

Friedman's appeal to our natural right to liberty is also a useful device
to combat contemporary critics of the market in general, and of American
capitalism in particular. Consider the kinds of criticisms we hear of American life these days. First, many groups believe that their salaries are too
low, especially in light of salaries in other professions. In the market, salary
depends, at least to a considerable degree, on the extent to which the product or services produced is in demand. Under market conditions, social
workers and teachers may get paid less than bartenders and prostitutes. It
does not seem adequate to inform the former group that their lower salaries
are justified since their service is less in demand. What about the artist who
is ahead of his time and finds that his creations are not in demand? Just how
serious should the economic consequences be for those who find the goods
and services they have to offer unpopular?

Other critics focus on product quality. They argue that the major corporations do not have adequate concern for the durability or even the safety
of their products. The developers of nuclear power plants are criticized for
failing to have developed adequate fail-safe devices. Nearly every month,
another product is added to the growing list of suspected causes of cancer.
The aerosol spray can allegedly threatens the earth's protective ozone layer.

Surely the market is incapable of policing itself; outside regulation is needed. Or so the critics argue.

Against such critics, Friedman delivers a stern lecture. He thinks the notion of passing judgment on the quality or social desirability of goods is a dangerous one. Who is to decide whether or not a good is socially desirable? Certainly we would not want government officials, or psychologists, or even philosopher kings making that decision. What the market place provides is a democratic vote; the supply-and-demand procedure is really a voting procedure for determining quality. What the critic of libertarianism is really attacking is the democratic determination of the market place and he is trying to substitute the voices of a few for the voices of all. Such an elitist attitude is (*a*) unjustified because there are no experts on matters of value; and (*b*) dangerous because expert determination of product quality undermines the individual freedom of consumer choice, which the market place is designed to protect. The fact that bartenders are paid more than social workers is the price we must pay for our individual freedom. Hence the market solution, which rewards producers on the basis of demand, is the best method of distributing goods and services.

In addition to protecting our natural right to liberty the market enhances our natural right to well-being. Since the workings of the market place provide for maximum efficiency, the greatest amount of economic good for the greatest number is produced. To tamper with the market interferes with its efficiency and the end result is a smaller aggregate amount of goods and services. Hence, the unfettered market provides the greatest gross national product from which rights to well-being can be implemented.

The critics of the market mechanism condemn it since it allows distributive patterns that would be intolerable from the moral point of view. On *pure* classical theory, one receives economic reward if and only if (*a*) he has contributed to the productive process; or (*b*) he is voluntarily supported by a producer, either as a member of a family or by gifts through charity. Clearly, to the extent that individuals are unable to contribute to the productive process through no fault of their own and to the extent that voluntary charity is unable to meet their basic needs, the distributive pattern is unjust. It does seem to be a fact that the innocent nonproductive, e.g., the aged, the ill, the mentally defective, receive marginal treatment at best. Exposés regarding these groups in our society are a commonplace. Other groups easily could be added to the list.

The defenders of the market solution to the problem of distribution are quick to point out the dangers of any other approach, however. The distribution of goods and services is related to and dependent upon the production of them. Any distribution scheme that interferes with the optimal conditions of production is at least inefficient in the sense that less goods and services will be produced than could have been produced. If the interference is especially severe, the total amount of goods and services will actually decline. There are technical reasons why certain distributive schemes, e.g., taxes, interfere with the optimal conditions for production. Unsophisticated but popular expressions of this argument abound:

> "Why should I work so hard if 30 percent of my income is taken up in taxes?"
> "Why bother with overtime? Most of the money I make goes to welfare."
> "Hell, why should I work at all? I can do better on welfare."

As sentiments such as these become more and more pervasive, economic growth slows and in severe cases the absolute amount of goods and services decline. Well-intentioned guarantees for living standards do more harm than good.

Rather than interfere with incentives, the defender of the market mechanism argues that one should let the rapidly rising living standards that result from an efficient economic system bury the distributive problem in a cornucopia of goods. . . .

The classical laissez-faire theory of distributive justice is one of the most famous examples of procedural justice. One is not concerned with determining the justice of each individual situation. Rather, one is concerned with a just procedure such that whatever the actual distribution, so long as the procedure is followed, the distribution is ipso facto just. Moreover, this implementation occurs without human moral effort. In fact, such conscious effort would only work to the detriment of the implementation. Instead, the driving force is egoism. As persons try to maximize their own selfish good, the greatest good for all is achieved. In a strange paradox, selfishness produces beneficence: a private vice produces public benefits. The classical laissez-faire theory is most persuasive, especially if it is viewed as a moral theory of what should be and not a descriptive theory of how the economic world really operates. To see the deficiencies of the theory we must take its unified argument apart piece by piece.

Critique

A more careful analysis of this theory destroys its utopian result. Abruptly we return to a world where the pursuit of one's selfish economic goals inevitably interferes with the pursuit of others' selfish goals. The success of one diminishes the success of another. The market solution to the problem of distributive justice can be attacked both on economic grounds and on the grounds that it provides an inadequate answer to the problem of economic justice. Our chief concern is with the moral criticisms of the theory. We will just sketch the economic criticisms.

Economic Criticisms

The laissez-faire view that the market mechanism provides for optimal efficiency has been challenged on three economic grounds. First, the analysis of John Maynard Keynes showed how the mechanism could be stuck on a lower rung of the economic ladder. The ideal is to have equilibrium at or near full employment. However, Keynes showed that the self-regulating features of the market were not sufficient to guarantee equilibrium at this ideal position. The market can be in equilibrium at any level of employment.

Secondly, the classical theory rests on a number of assumptions that are not empirically correct descriptions of the world. The chief assumption for the theory to work is that the business environment be one of perfect competition. A perfect competitor is by definition ". . . one who can sell all he wishes at the going market price but is unable in any appreciable degree to raise or depress that market price." In today's world of giant corporations and conglomerates, perfect competition applies to an ever diminishing number of industries. Two other economic assumptions that appear highly unrealistic are the assumptions about the individual consumer and about the absence of diseconomies of production and consumption. In the classical view, each consumer is a satisfaction maximizer, i.e., he is a rational egoist concerned with achieving as many goals as he can in the correct order of priorities at the least cost. This assumption is so obviously contrary to fact that economists have turned it into a tautology. Any consumer behavior is by definition an attempt to maximize satisfaction. Although this move makes criticism of the axiom impossible, a price is paid for this maneuver. We no longer have an empirical theory about consumer behavior in the world. This is because once a consumer is defined as a satisfaction maximizer, the claim "all consumers are satisfaction maximizers" reduces to the utterly trivial "all satisfaction maximizers are satisfaction maximizers." Second, the classical theory usually has assumed that there are no side effects (good or bad) that result from the consumption and production of goods and services. The environmental crisis has changed all that. Of course, what the classical theory really meant to say was that there were no side effects that could not be figured into the cost. Many economists are currently trying to devise accounting schemes that determine and assign costs for such side effects of production as air and water pollution, excessive noise, and the congestion of public facilities near industrial plants.

This discussion leads directly to a third economic criticism. The market mechanism does not apply to certain goods—most of them in the public sector. For private goods, my consumption affects your consumption. You cannot eat the apple that I have eaten. For this reason each of us will express our true desires for the apple in the market place. The price one is willing to pay is a measurement of that desire. Hence, the pricing mechanism rations scarce goods according to one's willingness to pay. Regrettably, this rationing scheme does not work for public goods. You can drive on the same road that I drive on. Hence, when it comes time to fix the road, you will understate the price you are willing to pay, hoping that I will pick up the burden. Of course, as rational egoists we all think this way, and the real value of the road to us is not reflected in the market place as is the real value of apples. . . .

The Market Mechanism and Justice

Our chief objection to the market approach to economic justice is that it fails to resolve adequately conflicts between our natural right to liberty and our natural right to well-being. Our first objection is that Friedman's notion of "freedom" is inadequate.

Although we have accepted Friedman's argument that private property is supportive of the traditional freedoms of press, speech, and so on, we do not find all his analysis of "freedom" satisfactory. For example, we believe that his analogy between a democratic voting procedure and consumer purchasing power is inappropriate. In the democratic voting procedure each person has only one vote. In the market place voting strength is a function of income strength. Since income is unequal, the analogy between political voting and consumer-purchasing voting breaks down. In fact the analogy is further weakened when one considers the ability of advertising to mold and influence wants.

There are also problems with Friedman's analysis of the market as the enhancer of individualism in matters of taste and expression. Although he has a point when he argues that centralization creates dangers, the market mechanism creates problems as well. Some welfare economists argue that the market itself leads to uniformity and mediocrity. The following is a concise statement of the argument by the economist Tibor Scitovsky:

1. Economic conditions require that most companies operate at a high volume.

2. Since most companies operate at a high volume, it is the tastes of the vast majority which are more important.

3. The tastes of the minority are either omitted or molded into the majority through advertising.

4. In any case, the minority tastes have little influence in the market place.

5. The informed and cultivated are in the minority.

6. Therefore the informed and cultivated have little influence in the market place.

7. This loss of influence is reflected in substandard products of a uniform nature designed for mass mediocrity.

This argument can be illustrated by a consideration of music. Classical recordings hold only a small percentage of the market. Many symphony orchestras are threatened with extinction and even the major symphonies are in the throes of financial difficulties. However, certain rock stars can and do command over $100,000 for a single performance. With respect to radio broadcasting, the lack of classical FM stations is appalling.

Moreover, the market place does not adequately protect freedom of employment. In the classical model there are no unions to protect the individual employee against his employers. Even with unions in the picture, many employers can and do constrain their employees in matters of dress, political and religious affiliation, and even personal life style. Constraints of other types work against employee mobility. Training, family ties, and social affiliations make it difficult, and in some cases impossible, for employees to leave present occupations for better conditions elsewhere. In these respects the market place fails to provide conditions for genuine job alternatives.

Finally, it is frequently rational to choose to be coerced. It is not uncommon for people to choose to impose deadlines upon themselves in order to provide the necessary discipline to reach their goals. Modern game theory provides many illustrations of instances where it is rational to be coerced. Consider a landlord in a decaying neighborhood trying to decide whether he should repair his property. Suppose his position with respect to any other landlord can be represented in the following game matrix:

		OWNER A			
		Column 1 Invest		Column 2 Do Not Invest	
OWNER B	Row 1 Invest	.07	.07	.03	.10
	Row 2 Do Not Invest	.10	.03	.04	.04

Clearly the best joint result is that they both invest (Column I, row 1). However, to achieve this result both Owner A and Owner B must be coerced to cooperate. Otherwise, so long as Owner A and Owner B act independently, Owner A will choose Column 2 no matter what Owner B does and Owner B will choose Row 2 no matter what Owner A does. The result Column 2, Row 2 is in the best interest of neither. Since both Owners want the best result, they will agree to coercion. On this occasion, agreement to coercion is an expression of freedom.

In general our point is this. Although laissez-faire capitalism supports the value of freedom in many instances, it also ignores or even inhibits that value in many other instances. Freedom from external constraints is not always enough. A just society must frequently provide genuine alternatives, e.g., something more than a choice among ten rock stations. Moreover, we indicated that not all coercion is bad; indeed certain types of coercion may be supportive of freedom itself.

Capitalism and Well-Being

The classical response to the egalitarian critique of the market place is to bury the objection in a cornucopia of economic gods. The long-range growth of the economic system makes everyone better off in the long run. The moral problem centers around the expression "long run." As John Maynard Keynes so cheerfully reminded us, "In the long run we are all dead." It may be just to distribute eight units of economic welfare to one man and two units to another in order that tomorrow we can distribute twenty units to the one and fifteen to the other. However, it seems unjust to distribute eight units to one man and two units to another so that their great-grandchildren may receive twenty and fifteen units respectively. The philosophical point is a simple one. It is simply not true that all unjust distributions can be rectified in the long run. Certain basic economic necessities ought to be provided now, not later. Thus, the future can only justify the past if the individuals are the same in both cases. For certain groups in our society, particularly blacks, the long run has become very long indeed.

This inability of the market place to guarantee the basic needs of some citizens has been conceded by nearly everyone. As a result, the concept of a welfare floor or minimum standard of living is rather widely accepted. Of course, there remains much disagreement as to the scope of the minimum standard and the means of implementing it. However, it is important to realize that the acceptance of the concept marks a departure from the laissez-faire theory. We believe that the criticisms of the classical market place are strong enough to deprive the market mechanism from providing either a necessary or sufficient condition of distributive justice. What role the market should play and the extent to which the market should be supplemented are questions discussed at the conclusion of this chapter. We now turn to more egalitarian alternatives for economic justice.

Egalitarian Alternatives

The defenders of the market approach to economic justice have been impressed with the ability of the market to provide an increasing standard of living for a large number of citizens. The egalitarian critics, however, focus on the needs of those the market has overlooked. Indeed, one of the problems in an affluent society is the relative invisibility of those whom the market has bypassed. . . .

Although the poor may be largely invisible, they number in the millions and the extent of their needs is very great. The poor have inadequate diet, inadequate housing, inadequate medical care. They are undereducated and if they are fortunate enough to be employed they hold marginal dead-end jobs. The lack of education makes the poor easy prey to exploitation. Soon a depressing cycle is under way and a culture of poverty develops. The critics of the market find the existence of such a culture of poverty a gross violation of economic justice. The thrust of egalitarian theories is to redistribute economic goods and services so that the cycle of poverty might be ended.

We shall now discuss several egalitarian theories of distributive justice. Although most of us would agree with the sentiments expressed by Harrington and others, it has been difficult to formulate an egalitarian alternative to the market mechanism that is not free of difficulties of its own.

Equal Distribution

In one interpretation, the French egalitarian Babeuf endorses the most uncompromising egalitarian position—the equal distribution of all goods and services:

. . . . [To establish justice requires] a simple *administration of needs* which keeping a record of all individuals and all the things that are available to them will distribute these available goods with the most scrupulous equality. . . . But the general Reformer would like to obtain for all individuals without distinction, an absolutely equal portion of all the goods and advantages that can be enjoyed in this mean world.

It seems obvious, however, that most commodities ought not to be distributed equally. Medicine should go to the sick, food to the hungry, and so on. The distribution of particular commodities depends upon needs. Since needs are unequal, equal distribution would often be immoral. It is considerations of need, not considerations of equality that are relevant.

Perhaps it is income rather than goods and services that should be distributed equally. People then could buy whatever goods and services they need or want with their equal incomes. The popular criticism of an equal distribution of income is that it would cripple incentives. Excellence of performance would not receive monetary recognition. The proposal has also been charged with being immoral since both the lazy and the industrious would receive the same reward. However, alternative accounts of human motivation and incentives might mitigate this popular difficulty.

Perhaps more serious is the fact that to distribute income equally does not meet the original difficulty concerning needs. Those with certain acute needs could be treated unjustly. Suppose that Jones is suffering from a serious illness that requires an expensive operation and a lengthy postoperative recovery. In the event of this personal catastrophe, Jones would not only have to spend his share of the total income but would have to go into debt as well. In such a situation the requirements of justice demand that Jones receive a greater rather than an equal share of the total income. Social insurance works on the principle of equal risk sharing rather than on equal receipt of benefits. For these reasons the equal distribution of income is not a moral imperative of distributive justice. At most it is a practical imperative. When relevant grounds for discrimination cannot be applied, equal distribution seems to be the appropriate method. The egalitarian principle of equal distribution is adequate only in these limited practical cases.

When confronted with the objections above, egalitarians frequently introduce the notion of equal treatment. Sometimes the appeal of equal treatment is purely formal, e.g., when the appeal is made to the principle that equals be treated equally. These principles have been previously discussed at length. The chief difficulty is to find the appropriate criteria for treating equals equally.

Other egalitarians build content into their equal treatment formulas. There are many variations of the substantive equal-treatment position, but the major one is to appeal to equal rights. In the language of this book it could be argued that distribution patterns be consistent with everyone's rights to well-being and freedom. This formulation of the egalitarian position in no way entails the equal distribution of commodities or income. The principle commits us to 100 units of a good to Smith and 200 units of a good to Jones if those unequal amounts are necessary for the achievement of the equal rights of Smith and Jones.

This formula only provides a necessary condition for justice, however. It cannot be a sufficient condition since the conflicts between rights that give rise to so many of the problems of justice have not been eliminated. Sometimes it is necessary to deny Smith's right to liberty, e.g., by taxing him, to provide for Jones's right to well-being, e.g., to provide Jones with medical care. This problem becomes more acute when we realize that as a practical matter the extent of well-being to which we have a natural right must be elucidated. However, the more we expand the notion of well-being, the greater the likelihood of conflicts between rights to liberty and rights to well-being.

Equal distribution of commodities or incomes can serve only as a practical principle in rather rare cases. Formal principles of equal treatment are empty. Substantive principles of equal treatment need to be modified by nonegalitarian considerations.

From Each According to His Ability; to Each According to His Need

One formula for equal treatment deserves special discussion. It is the so-called socialist formula "From each according to his ability; to each according to his need."

In point of fact, this formula cannot be referred to as the socialist formula without considerable qualifications. "Socialism" is given such a wide-ranging application that there is no one formula of distributive justice common to all so-called socialist positions. Moreover, one seldom finds one socialist position that adheres to one formula in all situations. Hence, historically speaking there is no warrant for speaking of the socialist position.

Actually, the socialist formula requires immediate qualification. If it is to apply in conditions of scarcity, needs must be ranked so that meaningful distributions can be made. The revised socialist formula may be stated as follows: A just distributive system is one in which everyone produces according to his ability and receives according to his need where the claim to need is proportional to urgency.

One of the chief difficulties with this socialist formula is a conceptual one; it is difficult to provide an acceptable analysis of the key terms "ability" and "need." With respect to ability, is someone working according to his ability when he (a) meets the standards for his job, or (b) when he is doing as well as he can? When we speak of standards how are they to be determined? Do some occupations, e.g., art, have any standards at all? Questions such as these, which must receive some answer if the socialist formula is to be plausible, have received surprisingly little attention.

With respect to "need," some analysis has been provided. We have the familiar distinction between basic and nonbasic needs. In general a need is considered basic if it is a biological need necessary for survival or physical health. The fulfillment of basic needs is a necessary condition for the satisfaction of other needs. This notion of a basic need is widely accepted in all theories of distributive justice. Basic needs determine the welfare floor of modified libertarian theories, the minimum standard of living in egalitarian theories, and are central in socialist theory as well. We too accept this notion by insisting that a necessary condition for fulfillment of our natural rights to conditions of at least minimal well-being is the fulfillment of our basic needs.

The socialist, however, cannot stop with basic needs. Since the sole criterion for distribution is need, even the nonbasic needs must be ranked according to urgency. This is because many societies can provide for all basic needs; however, no society can provide for all nonbasic needs. Since not all nonbasic needs can be satisfied, some criterion must be provided so that we know which nonbasic needs should be satisfied first.

However, the ranking of nonbasic needs is a difficult task. Statements about nonbasic needs may not be objective in the way that statements about basic needs are. Consider the statements below:

1. Smith needs the blood plasma more than Jones.

2. Smith needs the medicine more than Jones needs food.

3. Smith needs a holiday in Florida more than Jones.

4. Smith needs a holiday in Florida more than Jones needs to see the symphony.

Statements 1 and 2 are about basic needs and are objective in the sense that they are not equivalent to statements about the psychological desires of Jones and Smith and the truth of the statements is subject to empirical verification. For the socialist formula to work, statements 3 and 4 must be objective in the same way. However, there are good reasons to think that 3 and 4 are not objective in this way. For example, we cannot rank nonbasic needs by saying that some are necessary for the fulfillment of others. What nonbasic needs are necessary for satisfying our aesthetic needs? What non-basic need is necessary for satisfying some other nonbasic need? Unlike basic needs, the urgency of nonbasic needs appears to be more a matter of taste; neither science nor convention enables us to rank them uniformly. For these reasons, it could not be a fundamental principle of distributive justice that dine-and-dance clubs are more important than symphony concerts or that additional public parks are more important than the undisturbed wilds of nature.

A popular criticism of the socialist formula is its failure to guarantee a reward to the efficient. In fact, traditional critics of socialism emphasize the point that those with the greatest need are often those who contribute least to the economic system. The distribution required on the socialist account would stifle incentive and lead to distortions in the market place. Whether this criticism is correct depends to a large extent on the truth of the empirical claims about human motivation. Economic rewards seem less important in certain countries, e.g., Sweden, and psychological investigations might show other ways of inciting high productive capacity. We already know that job satisfaction is extremely important as a motivating device. The question of which empirical theories of human motivation are correct goes far beyond the scope of our present inquiry. For now, it is sufficient to note that the claim that socialism stifles incentive rests on controversial and contested empirical assumptions.

Whether or not incentive could be generated by nonmonetary means, many wish to argue that productive capacity *merits* some kind of reward on moral grounds. Consider the following proposed distribution:

	I		II	
	% PRODUCED	% RECEIVED	% PRODUCED	% RECEIVED
JONES	90	50	90	60
SMITH	10	50	10	40

Assume that Jones and Smith have equal needs and that in both proposed distributions Jones's and Smith's basic needs are fulfilled. Also assume that Smith has no physical incapacity. Which of the proposed distributions is the just one? Although the socialist must be committed to I, it is at least controversial whether or not that distribution is the just one. Philosophers in the classical or neoclassical tradition would certainly choose distribution II. For such philosophers, productive capacity, at least after basic needs have been fulfilled, does seem to make a *moral* claim on us. However, the socialist is unable to recognize that claim. This is a serious gap in the socialist account.

Yet another traditional criticism of the socialist formula is that the im
plementation of it presents a danger to negative liberty. Consider the two
central concepts of need and ability. What should be done with the person
who does not wish to work at the jobs for which he or she is most able? It
is not at all clear how freedom of occupation could be adequately protected
by the socialist formula. A similar problem occurs when we consider
needs. Our previous analysis has indicated the necessity of an elaborate
classification of needs according to urgency if the socialist formula is to be
implemented. Who determines this classification, however? If a democratic voting procedure is used, it is to each person's advantage to overstate
his case so that he will receive more. Just how these inflated claims would
be handled is far from clear. Sooner or later the decision must be left to an
authority. It is exactly this inevitability of such a powerful authority that
most frightens the libertarians.

If the libertarian critique is to be avoided it must be supplemented by
an analysis of a legitimate democratic voting procedure. Knowing it would
be to the advantage of each citizen to overstate his case, some procedure for
canceling out this tendency would have to be found. Although this might
meet the theoretical objection of the libertarian, the practical difficulties of
finding any objective means for obtaining the necessary priority ratings for
needs remain.

Certainly the socialists are right in emphasizing needs as an important
consideration in matters of distributive justice. However, other considerations are also relevant and the socialist formula requires considerable sup-
plementation.

Before presenting our own theory of distributive justice, it is important
to note that there is far more to the egalitarian socialist program than commitment to a formula. For the socialist, economic justice involves the re-
organization of economic institutions; his concerns go far beyond the issue
of the distribution of goods and services that has been discussed here. Some
of the planks found in a typical socialist's platform include:

1. The collective ownership of the means of production and of capital.

2. The substitution of worker participatory democracy for hierarchical
   decision making.

3. A disinclination to use wage differentials as incentives for efficiency,
   or as a method for allocating labor to different jobs.

4. A commitment to a meaningful work experience.

5. A planned economy.

The adequacy of the socialist blueprint for the reform of economic in stitutions is a matter of great controversy—a controversy that requires a book of its own for proper discussion. It should be noted, however, that few socialists subscribe to all the points just listed and that an intense debate rages inside the socialist camp on the importance of various planks. Since none of the socialist points given above are in contradiction to our own theory, let us move to that directly.

The Contextual Theory of Distributive Justice

The common difficulty with the traditional theories is that each emphasizes one principle that is meant to apply in all situations. We, however, think this is a mistake and agree with Walter Kaufmann's analysis that justice is highly dependent on particular circumstances. Hence, we agree with him that no one formula can be applied universally. However we do not accept his negative conclusions regarding the possibility of a theory of distributive justice. To provide a realistic theory of economic justice, we will formulate principles of distributive justice for types of societies according to their economic capabilities. In doing this we are accepting the view that different economic situations require different principles of distributive justice. These principles will then function as moral constraints on the democratic process as it resolves specific economic issues. In all cases, the principles of distributive justice either implement one's rights to well-being and liberty or resolve conflicts between them.

We arrive at these principles in the following way. From within each of the societies we have classified, we ask how the individual's natural rights to liberty and well-being should be implemented by the organization of the economic institution. We also decide how conflicts between the natural rights should be resolved within each society. Remaining issues of economic justice will be resolved by the institutions of democratic government.

Critics surely will ask how these particular principles are to be justified. Our answer is two-fold. We arrive at our principles from within the natural-rights perspective and our understanding of the proper function of the state. To those critics who do not accept our starting point, we can only refer them to the arguments of our earlier chapters. To those who accept our starting points, our argument is that extended discussion would show that these particular principles are indeed the ones that would be adopted by those taking the point of view expressed here. Of course, it is likely that we have erred at some point and our principles would need to be modified in the light of criticism. Keeping that in mind, let us consider the particular principles.

In summary, we will argue that an economic system is just if and only if:

1. it is organized so that individual rights are implemented and rights conflicts in the economic realm are resolved;

2. the structure of the economic system and the rules of its operation are in conformity with the particular principles of economic justice appropriate for that society; and

3. the structure of the economic system and the rules for its operation have been endorsed by democratic institutions.

Extreme Scarcity

The first society we consider is one of extreme scarcity. In a situation of extreme scarcity, the supply of commodities is such that it is impossible to meet all the basic needs of its members. That is, it is impossible to prevent some from dying of starvation, exposure, and other hardships. This situation is called a triage situation, and the overcrowded lifeboat is the popular image for it. Until recently, triage situations were considered rare. However, the worldwide 1973 crop failures and the serious famines in portions of Africa and Asia made the triage situation a frightening possibility, with planet Earth the understocked lifeboat. Whether or not the earth is in imminent danger of running out of food is an empirical question that transcends the scope of this book. However, as a precaution, both the heavy-energy use of the industrialized countries and the rapid population growth of developing countries must be curtailed. If a triage situation develops on the planet, it will be localized and temporary and our account of justice for triage situations is made with that in mind.

In a society of extreme scarcity, production should be as efficient as possible since the number of those who perish should be kept as small as possible. The goods produced will then be distributed so that the producers are provided a minimum standard of living. Any goods over and above those required for the minimum standard of living of the producers should be distributed to as many nonproducers as possible according to some criterion. This criterion would be established by democratic principles. In such a situation, a universal right to well-being or to liberty cannot be honored. At most a producer is entitled to a minimum standard of living. However, after the minimum standard for producers has been achieved, the rights of others take priority over property claims of the producers.

Subsistence

A society is in a subsistence situation whenever its resources can just provide a minimum standard of living for all its members. The concept of a minimum standard of living is a biological and physiological one. Hence, it can be determined with considerable objectivity. A family has a minimum standard of living when it has the resources to stay alive and to remain sufficiently healthy for contribution to the productive effort. Life is certainly not pleasant in such a society but everyone can exist there. The family resources are limited to minimum amounts of food, clothing, shelter, and medical care. In this society no one is entitled to more than a minimum standard of living, since a greater share for some would effect the loss of life for others. Here the right to a minimum standard of living has priority over property claims. It is assumed that this priority determination will not adversely affect incentives to produce. This assumption is not a large one provided it is clear that the situation is so serious that an extra share for some would cause the death of another.

Relative Comfort

A society may be described as comfortable whenever its productive resources are such that a minimum standard of decency is available for all. The concept of a minimum standard of decency is different in kind from that of a minimum standard of living. Whereas the latter is biological in nature, the former is psychological and political in nature. In trying to specify the concept, one must avoid the fruitless attempt at an exhaustive definition and ranking of nonbasic needs. An understanding of the concept of a minimum standard of decency cannot be achieved in that way.

To provide a description of what constitutes a minimum standard of decency, we will focus on a concept recently developed by a number of social scientists. This concept is called the the social-indicator approach to economic welfare. Social indicators are normative indicators rather than descriptive ones. This normative understanding is not surprising given our analysis of a subsistence society and our acceptance of the distinction between basic and nonbasic needs. What is significant about the social-indicators approach and what makes it a departure from common ways of looking at welfare is the recognition that income is an inadequate measure of human welfare. Perhaps the following passage might provide a sense of what the social indicators approach is trying to achieve:

> In the last third of this century, we need new approaches to the quality of life in every country. We suggest a minimum approach by government

in any society with significant inequalities must provide for rising minimum levels not only of incomes, assets, and basic services, but also of self-respect and opportunities for social mobility and participation in many forms of decision making. . . . The general position which we espouse in this paper is that income alone is an inadequate indicator of level of living.

The concern of the advocates of the social indicators approach is with the welfare of the whole person. Social scientists, including psychologists committed to the social-indicators approach, would consider the constitution of a minimum standard of decency by attempting to answer the following questions: What goods and services are required if citizens are to lead happy and well-adjusted lives? What provisions for economic security contribute to the productive capacity of citizens? What arrangements should be made to protect people from adversity and the fear of adversity? What states of affairs that interfere with self-realization can be eliminated or mitigated by economic institutions?

In terms of the language of this book, we would express their concerns as follows. The minimum standard of decency exists when the individuals in a society have those natural conditions that enable them to participate with a sense of purpose and self-respect in a democratic society and to enjoy some of the pleasures and conveniences of living in such a society. We have argued that natural-rights claims are genuine moral claims because they protect the integrity and self-respect of individual rational persons. Our natural right to well-being constitutes a legitimate moral claim to a minimum standard of decency in any society above the subsistence level. Each society above the subsistence level should develop a series of indicators that set standards for the achievement of a minimum standard of decency. Different societies will develop slightly different lists. The focal point, however, is provision of such material conditions as are necessary to enable people to develop their human capacities, especially reason, to make a contribution to democratic society and, as a result, to maintain a sense of self-respect and to achieve a sense of happiness or fulfillment. One might expect social indicators to include housing, consumers' durables, savings, insurance, basic services, health, neighborhood amenities, public transportation, legal services, education, mobility, political power, status, and satisfaction. A society that has the resources to provide a sufficient amount of the goods and services above so that each citizen has an opportunity to develop into a well-integrated rational citizen is a society that can provide a minimum standard of decency.

In a society with a minimum standard of decency, the productive capacity is such that our natural right to liberty can be implemented. In this society everyone has a right to choose his occupation. What makes this right significant, however, are the principles of distribution in such a society. In such a society, the right to well-being is expanded from a minimum standard of living to a minimum standard of decency. This situation enhances freedom of occupation because the job applicant is not primarily concerned with salary differentials. Freedom of occupational choice is constrained only by natural ability. Everyone is entitled to the prerequisites of an at least minimally decent human existence whatever occupational choice a person makes.

This analysis would come under immediate attack from the traditional laissez-faire libertarians. They would charge that any attempt to provide a minimum standard of decency for all is completely impractical and would violate one's natural right to liberty. It is impractical because it seems to undermine the pricing system that allocates scarce resources and it seriously seems to affect incentives. The natural right to liberty is violated if the goods and services that provide a minimum standard of decency are not the ones most desired by consumers. Let us consider the libertarian critique in some detail.

The question of incentives is really out of place here, since if we are constrained by morality and the principles of justice, incentives are not a problem. We are committed to taking the moral point of view. The traditional problem of incentives in no way undermines the conceptual or moral adequacy of the suggested principle. However, if the practical point is pressed, important responses can be made.

The concept of a minimum standard of decency may provide some escape from this practical difficulty. First, there are a number of constituents of decency; a minimum standard of decency can be achieved piecemeal. For example, education, social security, medical insurance, and unemployment insurance are all elements of a minimum standard of decency. Moreover, any one element of a minimum standard of decency will usually not be available to everyone all at once. Hence, each new element could be introduced on incentive grounds; i.e., the most efficient producers would benefit first. Moreover, according to this principle we can assume that most people enjoy their job and that is an extremely important boost to incentive. Finally, nonmonetary incentives can be effective as the cooperative programs of Scandinavian countries illustrate. Nonmonetary incentives may play an even larger role in the future. For these reasons, it is not clear that our principle for a comfortable society is subject to serious practical difficulties.

A more serious problem is the impact of this analysis on labor allocation. Traditionally, price differentials are the device used to accomplish this task. To avoid serious overcrowding in some occupations and great scarcity in others, any plausible analysis of distributive justice in a society of comfort must take this allocation problem into account. Actually the difficulty may not be as great as it seems since wage differentials are not the only means of allocation. In the first place, job qualifications and differences in natural ability will provide considerable natural allocation. One must be qualified to be a surgeon. Secondly, differences in taste will provide further natural allocation. In fact, this aspect of natural allocation will be strengthened because choice of occupation will not depend so heavily on salary considerations. One need not maintain, however, that these two devices can completely replace the pricing system. But as we saw above, the concept of a minimum standard of decency does allow for wage differentials. Moreover, since each new element cannot be given to all, it will first be provided in those occupations where shortages exist in order to induce laborers into that occupation. As any element of the decency standard is provided, it will first be distributed on the basis of efficiency and act as a pricing mechanism. Gradually this element will be provided to all and a new element will be introduced on efficiency grounds. An example illustrates this procedure. Let us assume that a high-school education and medical insurance are currently available to all. Everyone has an equal right to these commodities. However, those occupations that need more laborers might offer such features as paid vacations and college education for employee children in order to attract employees. The point is that the right to a minimum standard of decency is not something that can be implemented in all societies or all at once. One has an equal right to part of it; the remainder is introduced on the basis of efficiency, i.e., on the basis of the market.

The final difficulty concerns a possible conflict between the desires of consumers and the requirements for a minimum standard of decency. For example, suppose a consumer prefers to buy a color television set before health and accident insurance. If there is a divergence here, a dilemma results. Either the right to liberty must be violated or the right to a minimum standard of decency will not be achieved. In general, it is a variation of the problem. Can persons be coerced to do what is in their best interest? Should people be forced to make Social Security payments rather than being allowed to use their money for color television sets and snowmobiles?

Again our problem can be mitigated. Many of the constituents of a minimum standard of decency are public goods and hence the actual demand for them is not reflected in the market place. If we take as our model of freedom, consumer choice, we do not get a true picture. The actual production of these public goods is not in line with what people really desire.

Some mechanism other than the market must be used here. We also have the further distortion created by noninformational advertising, which has induced desires for luxuries before the minimum standard of decency has been provided for all. Both these distorting effects should be eliminated. When they are eliminated, the conflict can be eliminated as well.

Once the imperfections of the market and the effect of advertising have been overcome, we can get a more accurate reading of consumer desire. At this point we are committed to majority choice. Having removed the impediments to rational choice, the government is not justified in imposing its own views on the wishes of its citizens. A democratic voting procedure is the one that should be adopted. Hence, with respect to the majority, there can no longer be a conflict between what is desired and the requirements of a minimum standard of decency. What is desired has priority. The responsibility of the state is to insure that this desire is uncoerced and well-informed. In certain cases, the minority is compelled to follow the wishes of the majority. This coercion is only justified, however, if minority support is required to make the project work and if democratic procedures are followed. Compulsory participation in Social Security is frequently justified on these grounds. Finally, it should be noted that nothing in our analysis eliminates the possibility for great variety. The consumer may choose from a variety of educational, recreational, and cultural goods and services. To say that a person is coerced into participating in some insurance scheme does not entail that he be coerced to participate in any particular insurance scheme, especially a government one. Compulsory health insurance is not necessarily government health insurance.

We believe that we have met the chief objections of libertarians to our analysis of distributive justice in the comfortable society. We believe that on the basis of our discussion, this analysis is the analysis that would be accepted through using a natural-rights framework in this society.

The Affluent Society

The last society to be considered is the affluent society. In the affluent society, the level of production far exceeds the requirements for a minimum standard of decency. Food, clothing, housing, education, medical facilities, and recreational facilities are available in great abundance and variety. In addition, large numbers of goods and services are available for newly discovered consumer wants. All citizens possess some of the new household gadgets, attend places of recreation, enjoy at least an occasional dinner out at a restaurant, and engage themselves productively with increased leisure time.

In the affluent society we can be less concerned with efficiency. The productive output of the affluent society is so great that a large amount of inefficiency can be sustained. Even after a minimum standard of decency is provided for all, a substantial amount of goods and services remains available for distribution. This excess should be distributed according to laissez-faire libertarian principles. It is at this point that the principle "to each according to what the market provides" seems correct. No finer principles are available. In this way we avoid the error of the socialists who broaden the concept of need so much that the theory becomes unworkable. After the provision of a minimum standard of decency, the right to spend one's income as one sees fit becomes morally acceptable. If the inequality should become too great, then those at the bottom would become frustrated and their self-respect would suffer. At that point, not every citizen would have a minimum standard of decency and justice would require the inequality to be lessened. In this way, the concept of a minimum standard of decency acts as a self-correcting device to prevent excessive inequality in an affluent society.

It is plausible to think that the implementation of our right to liberty is best implemented as living standards rise. For example, as living standards rise, freedom of occupational choice is possible. As living standards rise still further, occupational choice is given some security by the right to a minimum standard of living. Finally, in the affluent society, the right to spend one's income as one sees fit becomes a significant right and no longer simply a concession of efficiency.

However, the freedom to spend one's income as one sees fit is not a natural right. A democratic society in which some property, e.g., major industries, is owned communally rather than privately does not necessarily run afoul of any principles of good government. Moreover, freedom to spend one's income may sometimes have to be restricted in order to better implement basic rights of others.

It should also be noted that the requirements of justice become stricter as societies make material progress. In societies with severe economic problems, the goal is to produce more and efficiency is of great importance. As living standards rise, however, rights to liberty and well-being are *enhanced* because they can be implemented.

Summary

This completes our analysis of distributive justice. The problems that remain must be resolved by processes of political democracy. The goal of this chapter has been to provide some analysis of what a democracy ought to accomplish in this area of economic organization, given various states of the economy. Given our classification of societies, we believe our analysis would be acceptable to those taking the natural-rights perspective. Finally, our analysis is not otiose. The United States is clearly an affluent society and hence the existence here of hunger, inadequate health care, inadequate housing, and inadequate education are clearly unjust. If we are to be a just society, these conditions must be corrected at once.

The Individual and the Political Order, Englewood Cliffs, N.J.: Prentice-Hall, 1977, pp. 189–215.

V. How We View the Poor in Our Society: The Structure of Our Perspective

Philosophizing about human beings and their complex social organizations is risky business. For in attempting to define the general or essential characteristics of any group, or to explain and justify differences in class, race, culture and rank, the philosopher is likely to express the biases of his own time and place. Aristotle declared that by nature there are masters and slaves, implying that this state of affairs is to be accepted, that inequality is created by forces beyond human control and responsibility, and that even though the slave should aspire to purchase his freedom if possible, he should go about his proper duties so long as he remains a slave. Even the enlightened Thomas Jefferson who attempted to study human nature scientifically regarded the Negro race as inherently deficient because it was ordained to be so by biological inheritance. In his *Notes on the State of Virginia* Jefferson lists the characteristics which he thought were permanent attributes of the race and made the black unfit for white civilized society. Plato, Locke, Hume, Spencer, Hegel and Marx, to add a few more to the list, all betrayed certain prejudices in their writings despite their efforts to follow the dictates of dispassioned reason and observation.

The goal of philosophy, however, remains a valid one, namely, to think within as wide and objective a framework as is humanly possible. The Socratic method and spirit presses us on to ask the question again and again, confess our ignorance, see truth afresh. It calls for self-examination as well as inquiry into the world about us. In social and economic matters there are personal and non-rational factors that need to be brought to light and reflected upon since the issues have a bearing upon our own existence.

In the introductory chapter we referred to Hanson's analysis of perception as a "seeing as" and "seeing that," underscoring the fact that all perception is perspectival from its very inception. Assumptions are present, familiar patterns prevail, and experience tends to reinforce what we already accept as true. A change in perspective is difficult and often painful. At the same time such a change has been taking place recently because many of the old stereotypes and commonly accepted beliefs concerning persons and their roles in society have been severely shaken by the research of the last quarter century or so. We have come to realize, for example, how much of what we call "intelligence" is as much a product of the environment as it is of nature. Standardized tests such as the SAT and IQ measurements have been shown to include an inherent cultural and class bias. The line between genetic inheritance and the vast range of social factors and forces at work upon the individual has become more and more difficult to draw. It has led us to reconsider even the fundamental notion of "nature."

The purpose of this chapter is to examine some of the implicit assumptions, beliefs and values that provide the basis for the way in which we see and think about the poor in American society. It will entail a questioning of some of our social "myths." A myth in this context refers to the ways in which we generalize about people or groups by ascribing to them general determining characteristics without regard to individual differences. To say that professors are dull, businessmen are unprincipled, athletes are dumb, is to echo the stereotypes that govern the way in which we look at a group as a whole and individuals within that group. Myths exaggerate certain characteristics out of proportion and context and extend them to all members of a class or group, ignoring individual differences.

The myths concerning the poor are familiar to most of us already: lacking in motivation, deficient in personal traits that make for success, having a different (inferior) set of values than the non-poor, void of self-discipline. The readings in this chapter, however, ask us to suspend our judgment, examine the various assumptions that we commonly make about the poor, and be willing to reconsider our view in light of the arguments, evidences, and criticisms that the authors provide.

A. Lee Rainwater

Lee Rainwater, professor of sociology at Harvard, points out that even among professionals there are perspectives that contain "discerned beliefs concerning the humanness or personality of disinherited persons and also beliefs having to do with their way of life somewhat apart from their individual personalities" (italics mine). In philosophical terms these beliefs operate as a priori truths which predetermine who the poor are. From them certain things follow in terms of how the poor are to be treated and what is to be done even before actual investigation of the facts gets under way. Even the term "poor" is objectionable to Rainwater since it carries derogatory connotations; he prefers "disinherited."

The perspectives that Rainwater describes are not sheer distortions of reality; they are more like half-truths that highlight some of the features of some of the poor some of the time, but elevated to the status of defining characteristics of the poor generally under most or all conditions. Thus a perspective comes to operate as a fixed model or type. It usually emerges from subconscious levels of awareness, is seldom articulated, and remains exempt from critical scrutiny. Although the origin of such perspectives is largely a psychological question, their presence has a direct bearing upon the more philosophical question of theory formulation. They raise the question of how to prevent our theories about the poor from becoming little more than rationalizations of subconscious outlooks reflecting our own fears and prejudices.

Rainwater comments that "each one of these perspectives has something to offer in coming to a balanced appreciation of the life of the disinherited." What is the authentic element in each of them and what are the blind-spots that each incorporates?

Neutralizing the Disinherited

Introduction

The central existential fact of life for the lower class, the poor, the deprived, and discriminated-against ethnic groups, is that their members are not included in the collectivity that makes up the "real" society of "real" people. They are not considered, and often do not consider themselves, quite part of the regular moral system taken in common as ordinary and regular society. They may not be allowed, or may not be able, to participate in those activities, or with those people, who are defined as integral to regular society. For this reason such groups can quite legitimately be considered "disinherited" in the sense that no valued and taken-for-granted place is made for them and their children in the society; they are on the outside looking in. Yet, at the same time, their activities are subject to surveillance and control by society in such a way that they are not truly autonomous, not free to make a way of life of their own.

All of this is known, in a vague way, by everybody—the man in the street knows it as well as the social scientist. To the extent that members of regular society confront the reality of a disinherited group, they must develop some understanding that "explains" the fact that there are people among us who are not part of us. Social science views of these phenomena are more elaborated, logically organized, and sophisticated versions of the different common-sense understandings that develop about disinherited groups. At the same time, to the extent that social science views derive from reasonably adequate theory and empirical research, they are not merely more elaborated, logically organized, and sophisticated versions, but do indeed have a higher level of truth content than common-sense views, even though they are not fully independent of these views.

When we seek to examine the various common-sense/social science understandings of poverty, we are engaged in a study of what deviance experts call the *labeling process* (Lemert, 1967). In order to cope with the presence of individuals who are not a regular part of a society, its members develop labels that signify the moral status of the deviant and carry within them a folk etiology and diagnosis, and often a folk therapy. The social scientist inevitably imports these folk understandings into his own work. They yield both understanding and misunderstanding for him.

David Matza (1966) has neatly summarized the wide range of conceptions of the "disreputable poor" which social commentators have brought to bear historically in their recurrent discovery of the poor. These labels—be they *hard-to-reach, problem family, multiproblem family, lower-lower class, lumpenproletariat, spurious leisure class,* or *paupers*—all can and do exercise tremendous influence on the intellectual's grasp of the problems of poverty, and by extension also influence the kinds of policies that are imagined whenever a "war on poverty" comes into being. . . .

From the popular literature dealing with problems of the disinherited and from the social science literature, as well as from inevitable participant observation during discussions of these matters by lay people and by social scientists, I think it is possible to identify five different perspectives that are brought to bear on understanding the situation of the disinherited. In each perspective there can be discerned beliefs concerning the humanness or personality of disinherited persons and also beliefs having to do with their way of life somewhat apart from their individual personalities.

Before discussing in detail these five perspectives, I want to note that

Figure 1: Five Perspectives on the Poor

The poor are evaluated as:	The poor are characterized as:	
	Weak	Potent
Virtuous	Normalizing	Apotheosizing
	Naturalizing	
Evil	Medicalizing	Moralizing

with one possible exception there are highly convincing portraits of each one of these points of view in both the popular and the social science literature. This suggests that each perspective may capture a certain amount of truth of the condition of the disinherited. But, by the same token, portraits hewing closely to any one of these views are often unsatisfactory both because it is easy to think of exceptions and because the characterizations tend to have the quality of making their subjects seem to be, in Harold Garfinkel's phrase, "conceptual boobs."

These five conceptions I will call the *moralizing*, the *naturalizing*, the *medicalizing*, the *apotheosizing*, and the *normalizing* perspectives. Four of them seem to me to represent combinations of two basic dichotomies about the situation of the disinherited, and one represents instead an effort to rise above these dichotomies. The relationship between these two dichotomous variables and the five perspectives is indicated in Figure 1. I suggest that the poor can be characterized as either weak or potent, and that they can be evaluated as either virtuous or lacking in virtue—as evil, if you will. The combination of a perception of the disinherited as evil and potent leads to what I will call the *moralizing* perspective; of virtuous and potent to the *apotheosizing* perspective; of evil and weak to the *medicalizing* perspective; of virtuous and weak to the *normalizing* perspective. The fifth—the *naturalizing* perspective—comes about as a result of an effort to rise above these value judgments of virtuousness versus evil and weakness versus potency, and to develop a value-free conception that leans heavily on an impersonal, natural science perspective. (Of course, in this latter case, we are often able to see ample evidence that the explanation is neither value-free nor impersonal.) . . .

The Moralizing Perspective

This is perhaps the oldest approach to understanding the disinherited. In this perspective a moral flaw is perceived in the disinherited or in their environment which explains the fact that they live unlivable lives—that is, they are able to live this way because they are morally different from regular people. The focus of the moralizing perspective can be on the individual disinherited person or on a quality of his environment (although, of course, the two are generally very much linked).

The Sinners. In the moralizing view the disinherited are afflicted with the mark of Cain. They are meant to suffer, indeed must suffer, because of their moral failings. They live in a deserved hell on earth. As long as they do not renounce their immorality and allow themselves to be saved they must continue in the status of the disinherited. If they do renounce their immorality they may come into God's inheritance as members of the regular community.

An Environment of Sin. Regardless of the moral status of particular individuals, the disinherited live in a world in which immorality is the rule. Though innocent at birth, they do not stay this way long because of the seductions and temptations around them.

Therapy. Perhaps the most pressing claims for social action that stem from the moralizing perspective have to do with demands for punishment and control of the immorality lest it "infect" and "attack" the rest of the community. Beyond punishment and control the therapies that go most naturally with this view emphasize efforts to redeem and "save" the disinherited sinners through evangelistic movements which may start either spontaneously within the community of the disinherited or be imposed from outside.

It would be difficult to overemphasize the extent to which the moralizing perspective undergirds seemingly more sophisticated views of poverty. It would also be difficult to exaggerate the extent to which the views of a great many of the disinherited themselves, about their own conditions and about the conditions of those around them, are informed by a moralizing perspective. Manifestations of this point of view are readily apparent at the popular level in the characterizations by lower-class people of themselves and their peers, more officially in the ideologies of fundamentalist churches, and particularly of movements such as the Black Muslims.

The Medicalizing Perspective

The medicalizing perspective is perhaps the most direct descendant of the moralizing one in the sense that it is relatively simple to replace the con-

dition of "sin" with that of "sickness." In the medicalizing perspective
the explanation of how the disinherited live unlivable lives lies in the understanding that normal people and normal social patterns have somehow
been subjected to pathological processes. The disinherited and their way of
life may be human, but sick. As before, various commentators will place
primary emphasis either on the sickness of individuals or on the sickness of
the environment.

Psychopathologizing. This perspective predicates that the disinherited
live the way they do because their psyches are pathologically formed. This
pathology can be taken to refer most directly to the personality: there will
be emphasis on mental illness, sociopathic behavior, apathetic or depres-
sive orientations, disturbed child-rearing practices, etc. More recently, as
psychology has become increasingly intrigued with mental processes rather
than with personality processes in general, emphasis has shifted to the pathological character of cognitive development, to trained incapacities, to the
absence of certain kinds of experiences that leave the child cognitively
underdeveloped, and the like. In both cases the disinherited live as they do
because of the way things are put together inside their heads. The human
material from which they sprang has in the course of life been blunted and
malformed; from this pathology results behavior that is destructive both to
the individuals involved and to people around them. In this way, although
it started out the same, the human material of the disinherited ends up different from that of the rest of us.

The Pathological Environment. Here the emphasis is on the sickness
of the social environment. In contrast to the psychological emphasis on individual personality and mental processes, there is a sociological emphasis
on social disorganization and pathology. Participation in this sick world,
though in the extreme sociological view it may be considered not to rub off
on the individual personality, nevertheless leads to unhappy and disorganized lives. The disinherited are seen as falling in, not with bad company,
but with sick company. No matter how hard the individual tries he is constantly interfered with by a disorganized community which frustrates his
constructive goals, and tends to replace them with deviant ones.

Therapy. In terms of therapy the implications of the first, more psychological, view are fairly straightforward. There is emphasis on psycho-
therapy and counseling for the disturbed personalities involved, or on the
development of compensatory education and training programs that somehow repair cognitive damage. The choices this perspective leads to tend

systematically to highlight the importance of clinical approaches and individual diagnosis.

With respect to the pathological environment, therapy will emphasize the building of a less pathological community of the disinherited. There will be emphasis on developing an organized, as opposed to a disorganized, community "infrastructure," and on generating community involvement in new institutions of various kinds which direct energies in a constructive, as opposed to a destructive, direction.

At the more extreme levels, however, where the perception is of a community that is hopelessly disorganized, the suggested solution may instead be to remove at least the children from the disorganizing environment as in the underground suggestion one hears repeatedly from unself-conscious, usually nonprofessional, commentators on the War on Poverty that all poor children should be removed from their families and communities and put into government-run *kibbutzim* where they will learn proper ways.

The Naturalizing Perspective

Here there is a great effort to gain evaluative distance from the situation of the disinherited. The emphasis is on discovering a "natural" explanation of how the disinherited live as they seem to. Science is to provide the answer in an impersonal, value-free way by the application of scientific knowledge about humans and their behavior.

Biological Determinism. Thirty to forty years ago the emphasis on biological differences was probably the major alternative to the moralizing perspective. Great efforts were expended in demonstrating that the disinherited, particularly the darker racial groups but also the white disreputable poor, were biologically different and inferior to regular people. This inferiority was said to explain the fact that the disinherited are able to live in a way that regular folk cannot live. The disinherited were biologically below standard, were genetically inferior in one way or another. This was indeed unfortunate, and one should deal humanely with such people as one might with domestic animals, but it was believed unnatural to expect them to perform in regular ways and it was unwise (because of the stress on their inferior constitutions) to provide them with the regular rewards that society had to offer.

The major thrust of biological determinism as an explanatory perspective in this area had to do with intelligence—an effort was made to demonstrate inferior brains in those who are not part of regular society—but there were also congeries of other presumed traits that were believed to be genetically based: greater insensitivity to pain, greater ability to tolerate manual labor, lesser control of the emotions, etc. Biological determinism has not been very respectable intellectually for at least thirty years, but that should not lead us to underestimate its influence as a lay perspective.

The therapy that goes most naturally with biological determinism might be characterized as benign totalitarianism. Here a heavy emphasis is placed both on control of the activities of those who are biologically inferior since they obviously cannot judge best for themselves, and on a castelike social structure in which those who are marked as inferior are not allowed to weaken regular society by mating with it. From this perspective, eugenics is an important applied therapy in the progressive weeding out of the inferior.

The Cultural-Relativistic Perspective. The other ''natural'' explanation of the situation of the disinherited is quite different. Not only is there a disinterest in biological determinism, but it is asserted that the way of life of the disinherited is perfectly valid, equally as functional as that of regular society. While the disinherited may have troubles from their way of life, just as every way has its characteristic difficulties, they are socialized into appropriate behavior for their world just as regular persons are socialized into appropriate behavior for theirs. The disinherited can be, and are, reasonably well-adjusted and happy within their world. They are neither inferior nor superior to regular society; they are just different. Their way of life has the same degree of organization and adaptiveness as has that of regular society. We are right in our initial perception that they are human, but we are wrong in our perception of the disinherited way of life, because we miss its inner coherence and validity.

The implications for action that flow from this view are less straightforward than in other cases because of the emphasis of cultural relativism on the inherent validity of each way of life. ''Cultural pluralism'' tends to be the main thrust, a request that regular society recognize the imperatives and the values of the culture of the disinherited, that it not be stigmatized, that regular society ''get off their backs.'' In the conservative version of this view it may be argued that very little should be done in the way of special therapy, but that natural events should be allowed to run their course—if the disinherited want to buy into the regular society, they eventually will. A leftist view will hold that, despite the validity of the way of life of the disinherited, they do need resources of various kinds. This view will suggest a kind of ''foreign aid'' approach which turns over to the disinherited *as a group* certain kinds of resources that it will then use in whatever way seems appropriate given its cultural priorities rather than those of regular society. In its purest form, however, cultural relativism probably reinforces an emphasis on simply studying the disinherited, and tends to play down both the desirability and the possibility of regular society's doing anything about the situation in which the disinherited find themselves. The cultural relativist who also holds strong activist views will probably tend to be pushed in the direction of the next perspective, that of apotheosizing.

The Apotheosizing Perspective

This substitutes a perception of heroic adaptation for the initial perception of disinheritance—a kind of standing the initial perception on its head. The central myth that informs this perspective is that of the "natural man" in a "natural world." The villain is civilization which has deprived and alienated members of regular society while leaving the disinherited free to be natural. In a more moderate version apotheosizing asserts that "we're just as bad as they are, maybe worse."

The Natural Man. From this perspective the disinherited are perceived as stronger, as a kind of supermen who have developed special capacities (e.g., rhythm!), special philosophies, a special quality of existential humanity that eschews the artificiality of regular society. In a somewhat less complimentary, though still highly romantic version, the disinherited are seen as fortunately insensitive to pain and possessed of a natural self-assurance which allows them to endure the insult and derogation to which regular society subjects them. There are many representations of natural man among the disinherited (indeed, the myth of the "natural man" seems difficult to sustain except where the hero is among the disinherited). The ballad of John Henry, the hustler and the blues singer, the cowboy, the stoic sharecropper, the *macho* Latin, the newly conscious black man—all of these provide convenient symbolic representations of such a perspective.

Heroic Culture. When the emphasis shifts from the individuals involved to the social life of the group, the perspective tends to emphasize the heroic quality of the life of the disinherited. Heroic, not just in the sense of being able to cope with adversity and still maintain life, but in the sense that as a result of adversity the disinherited have been able to create a way of life that has beauty and virtue. The disinherited are seen as having a good thing going for them. Despite the fact that they are exploited, despite the punishment regular society dishes out, they have succeeded in constructing a way of life that actually has *more* validity, is *less* alienated, than regular middle-class society. Contrast to middle-class society becomes important for this perspective—"look at the pathology of the suburbs!" "Look at the disintegration of the sense of community in middle-class society!" In short, civilization dilutes the sense of both community and human individuality in regular society, but this sense is alive in the community of the despised.

Therapy. The most direct implication of these views involves the adoption by regular folk of natural man and heroic culture as symbols and the enjoyment of the superior inventions of the disinherited, whether these inventions be pizza, the hully gully, or the cool way of life. Beyond consumption, the apotheosizing perspective is tailor-made for use in attacking the rest of society. The disinherited are held up to the rest of society not as an example of its destructiveness and barbarity, but rather of its self-destructiveness, its artificiality, and its unreal and alienated ways. Beyond these relatively passive uses of the apotheosizing perspective, it can become the core for an effort to create a new revolutionary man, to provide new hope for the old leftism and inspiration for a new radicalism. The apotheosized disinherited provide a source of human energy and creativity which can be organized to revitalize the total society, because only among them do human meaning and vitality persist. There is no more *lumpenproletariat,* for among the disinherited lie the real proletariat who have not been coopted and bought off by materialistic society. It is only necessary that the insightful members of regular society who perceive this throw in their lot with the disinherited and organize and manipulate them to provide a power base and an ideology for achieving the new society.

The Normalizing Perspective

Finally, there is the perspective that resolves the initial perplexity and anxiety by the simplest mechanism possible—denial. Following Fred Davis (1964), I mean by the normalizing perspective a process by which the individual who seeks to understand the situation of the disinherited "comes to view as normal and morally acceptable that which initially strikes him as odd, unnatural, 'crazy,' deviant, etc., irrespective of whether his perception was in the first instance reasonable, accurate, or justifiable." In the normalizing perspective the initial perception of disinherited individuals and their way of life as unlivable is simply denied, treated as the result of processes of middle-class projection and stereotyping. The disinherited are really just like you and me except perhaps that they are mistreated and poor, but these latter conditions do not result in other than superficial differences.

Ordinary People. In the normalizing perspective it is asserted that the disinherited have essentially the same hopes, wishes, goals, interests, joys, and sorrows that everybody else does and that they express these in the same way. Furthermore, they are just as law-abiding, self-controlled, sensitive, sensible, and intelligent as you and I. They are no more and no less than ordinary human beings, and their condition of disinheritance has only superficial impact on their personalities. They are deprived of the means to live in superficially conventional ways, that is, to have the same material goods, to participate socially in the same ways as the members of regular society. But these deprivations do not have any fundamental impact on their personalities and their world views, or on their values. From this perspective, then, the null hypothesis reigns—that is, except for behavior and attitudes that are simple, direct, and immediate responses to deprivation or prejudice, their views of life and their behavior are indistinguishable from those of others in the society.

An Adequately Coping Way of Life. With respect to the social life of the disinherited, as opposed to their individual characters, the normalizing perspective suggests that while it is true that they have a great many troubles and the rest of society imposes many penalties and punishments on them, nevertheless they somehow manage their situation in such a way that their interpersonal relations and their ways of coping with the world are not deeply affected. Thus, in this perspective the disinherited love their children and their kin; help each other out (perhaps more than members of regular society because it is necessary to do so); and are reasonably well-adjusted and happy in their social relations, except that they have a realistic awareness of the problems that society makes for them. The anger that they may feel at their lot is simply healthy anger; it does not repercuss on their personalities or on the informal institutions of their day-to-day lives. In short, their lives are eminently livable, if somewhat restricted by lack of resources and barriers artificially imposed by the outside world.

Therapy. In many ways the major effect of the normalizing perspective is to debunk other perspectives by denying the validity of their various conceptualizations of the disinherited life. This is often done to ward off or argue against the policy implications of the other perspectives, either out of a sense of identification with the essential humanity of the disinherited, or (probably equally common) out of a wish to do nothing and to underemphasize the deprivation and destruction that rejection from the conventional system involves.

In a more sophisticated way the normalizing perspective suggests therapies that emphasize "opportunity" rather than more radical alterations in the system. That is, it is argued that since the disinherited are really ordinary people who happen to be caught in an unfavorable situation for achieving their ordinary desires, it is necessary only to provide them with the ordinary means to the achievement of these desires. For example, such things as job-training programs, more thoughtfully and seriously under-taken education programs to replace the poorly equipped and poorly staffed schools that are available to them, and perhaps some counseling to make them aware of the opportunities that exist in the larger world should be pro-vided. In other words, the intervention that is required is basically the fairly superficial one of providing realistic access to means of achieving the level of income and other kinds of functioning that are necessary to be a part of regular society. To a great extent this involves not stereotyping the disin-herited or in any way emphasizing what little may be different about their way of life and their personal techniques for coping with their situation. In short, one wants to accentuate the positive both at the verbal level of the semantics of poverty and at the action level of making better-coordinated and -supported services and opportunities available.

Conclusion

. . . One attractive solution to the problem of discovering that some poor people fit one perspective while others fit another is to develop a ty-pology that apportions poor people to one or another type—in my schema we could have the immoral, the sick, the mentally retarded, the subcultural practitioner, the hero, and the normal. There may indeed be individuals who fit one of these perspectives not only at a given time but throughout their lives. However, I am much more impressed by the alterations in be-havior and psychological state that poor people can experience as their sit-uations change. The same individual can at one period of his life to all intents and purposes behave and feel like a conventional member of soci-ety, at another period seem the perfect example of the psychopathologically afflicted, and at another period seem content with a subculturally different existence. And, as Robert Coles has so sensitively shown, given particu-larly challenging circumstances, the disinherited child or adult can be truly heroic in ways that surprise and appall conventional people. For these rea-sons I suspect that the "typological solution" inevitably breaks down when we add a longitudinal dimension to our usual cross-sectional perspective.

Finally, adherence to these perspectives either singly or in combina-tion can very readily be found not only among social scientists and middle-class and stable working-class onlookers, but also among lower-class peo-ple themselves. Indeed, a very interesting study could examine the question of the ethnodiagnosis of the condition of poverty by people who themselves are afflicted with that condition.

More broadly, it should be noted that these five perspectives are prob-ably fundamental explanatory categories for any problem in the way of life of a particular group. With some modifications this kind of schema could probably be applied to studying folk diagnoses of the situations of groups as different from the disinherited as business executives, the power elite, the artistically creative, and the government bureaucrat. We are probably always going to be confronted with the basic psychological issue of perplexity and anxiety which arises from trying to understand and account for the human condition. This issue comes to the fore when one concentrates on any particular group of human beings and discovers that his conception of what is human is so heavily personalized that he finds it difficult to empathize with the behavior of persons who are in notably different situations. It certainly would be true that the more conventional the group being studied, the more attractive will be the normalizing perspective unless one has a particular axe to grind. Nevertheless, I think it is also true that if one systematically surveyed the literature on exceptional groups in the society, whether they be exceptional by virtue of unusual achievement or (as in the case of the disinherited) lack of achievement, the issue of ''they can't possibly be human in the way I am human'' would come to the fore.

Neutralizing the Disinherited: Some Psychological Aspects of Understanding the Poor in Vernon L. Allen, ed., *Psychological Factors in Poverty*. Chicago: Markham Publishing Company, 1970, pp. 9–27.

B. William Ryan

Studies of young people's attitudes during the Depression of the 1930's have shown that a great many of them blamed themselves rather than the economic system for their jobless plight, even though very few employment opportunities were available. Again, during the late 1940's, a study of the unskilled and semi-skilled workers in an automobile plant showed that the workers blamed themselves for their lack of promotion in rank during their working life rather than the system within which they operated, even though there was opportunity for advancement for only a handful out of the total number of workers, and even though factories are generally places of very limited chance for personal advancement. Both of these instances illustrate the power of social myths and ideologies. So firmly does the myth of success by individual efforts rule over our minds that we pay tribute to it even in the face of facts over which we have little or no control.

The "blaming the victim" syndrome that William Ryan, professor of psychology at Boston College, describes offers further evidence of myth's power. It is difficult for members of our society who have "made it" by hard work, use of opportunity, intelligent planning and preparation to understand how others cannot do so as well. The unsuccessful are held to be at fault in some way. Even among trained social workers who deal with the poor on a daily basis this attitude is often evident. Blaming the victim occurs as much among intelligent, sensitive people whose altruistic motives are sincere as it does among their counterparts. Can you identify some of the subtle ways in which people you know or have observed blame the victim? How much of it would you consider to be a form of self-justification or defense of one's own position?

Blaming the Victim

I

Twenty years ago, Zero Mostel used to do a sketch in which he impersonated a Dixiecrat Senator conducting an investigation of the origins of World War II. At the climax of the sketch, the Senator boomed out, in an excruciating mixture of triumph and suspicion, "What was Pearl Harbor *doing* in the Pacific?" This is an extreme example of Blaming the Victim.

Twenty years ago, we could laugh at Zero Mostel's caricature. In recent years, however, the same process has been going on every day in the arena of social problems, public health, anti-poverty programs, and social welfare. A philosopher might analyze this process and prove that, technically, it is comic. But it is hardly ever funny.

Consider some victims. One is the miseducated child in the slum school. He is blamed for his own miseducation. He is said to contain within himself the causes of his inability to read and write well. The shorthand phrase is "cultural deprivation," which, to those in the know, conveys what they allege to be inside information: that the poor child carries a scanty pack of cultural baggage as he enters school. He doesn't know about books and magazines and newspapers, they say. (No books in the home: the mother fails to subscribe to *Reader's Digest*.) They say that if he talks at all—an unlikely event since slum parents don't talk to their children—he certainly doesn't talk correctly. (Lower-class dialect spoken here, or even—God forbid!—Southern Negro. *Ici on parle nigra*.) If you can manage to get him to sit in a chair, they say, he squirms and looks out the window. (Impulse-ridden, these kids, motoric rather than verbal.) In a word he is "disadvantaged" and "socially deprived," they say, and this, of course, accounts for his failure (*his* failure, they say) to learn much in school.

Note the similarity to the logic of Zero Mostel's Dixiecrat Senator. What is the culturally deprived child *doing* in the school? What is wrong with the victim? In pursuing this logic, no one remembers to ask questions about the collapsing buildings and torn textbooks, the frightened, insensitive teachers, the six additional desks in the room, the blustering, frightened principals, the relentless segregation, the callous administrator, the irrelevant curriculum, the bigoted or cowardly members of the school board, the insulting history book, the stingy taxpayers, the fairy-tale readers, or the self-serving faculty of the local teachers' college. We are encouraged to confine our attention to the child and to dwell on all his alleged defects. Cultural deprivation becomes an omnibus explanation for the educational disaster area known as the inner-city school. This is Blaming the Victim.

Pointing to the supposedly deviant Negro family as the "fundamental weakness of the Negro community" is another way to blame the victim. Like "cultural deprivation," "Negro family" has become a shorthand phrase with stereotyped connotations of matriarchy, fatherlessness, and pervasive illegitimacy. Growing up in the "crumbling" Negro family is supposed to account for most of the racial evils in America. Insiders have the word, of course, and know that this phrase is supposed to evoke images of growing up with a long-absent or never-present father (replaced from time to time perhaps by a series of transient lovers) and with bossy women ruling the roost, so that the children are irreparably damaged. This refers particularly to the poor, bewildered male children, whose psyches are fatally wounded and who are never, alas, to learn the trick of becoming upright, downright, forthright all-American boys. Is it any wonder the Negros cannot achieve equality? From such families! And, again, by focusing our attention on the Negro family as the apparent *cause* of racial inequality, our eye is diverted. Racism, discrimination, segregation, and the powerlessness of the ghetto are subtly, but thoroughly, downgraded in importance.

The generic process of Blaming the Victim is applied to almost every American problem. The miserable health care of the poor is explained away on the grounds that the victim has poor motivation and lacks health information. The problems of slum housing are traced to the characteristics of tenants who are labeled as "Southern rural migrants" not yet "acculturated" to life in the big city. The "multiproblem" poor, it is claimed, suffer the psychological effects of impoverishment, the "culture of poverty," and the deviant value system of the lower classes; consequently, though unwittingly, they cause their own troubles. From such a viewpoint, the obvious fact that poverty is primarily an absence of money is easily overlooked or set aside.

The growing number of families receiving welfare are fallaciously linked together with the increased number of illegitimate children as twin results of promiscuity and sexual abandon among members of the lower orders. Every important social problem—crime, mental illness, civil disorder, unemployment—has been analyzed within the framework of the victim-blaming ideology. In the following pages, I shall present in detail nine examples that relate to social problems and human services in urban areas.

It would be possible for me to venture into other areas—one finds a perfect example in literature about the underdeveloped countries of the Third World, in which the lack of prosperity and technological progress is attributed to some aspect of the national character of the people, such as lack of "achievement motivation"—but I plan to stay within the confines of my own personal and professional experience, which is, generally, with racial injustice, social welfare, and human services in the city.

I have been listening to the victim-blamers and pondering their thought processes for a number of years. That process is often very subtle. Victim-blaming is cloaked in kindness and concern, and bears all the trappings and statistical furbelows of scientism; it is obscured by a perfumed haze of humanitarianism. In observing the process of Blaming the Victim, one tends to be confused and disoriented because those who practice this art display a deep concern for the victims that is quite genuine. In this way, the new ideology is very different from the open prejudice and reactionary tactics of the old days. Its adherents include sympathetic social scientists with social consciences in good working order, and liberal politicians with a genuine commitment to reform. They are very careful to dissociate themselves from vulgar Calvinism or crude racism; they indignantly condemn any notions of innate wickedness or genetic defect. "The Negro is *not born* inferior," they shout apoplectically. "Force of circumstance," they explain in reasonable tones, "has *made* him inferior." And they dismiss with self-righteous contempt any claims that the poor man in America is plainly unworthy or shiftless or enamored of idleness. No, they say, he is "caught in the cycle of poverty." He is trained to be poor by his culture and his family life, endowed by his environment (perhaps by his ignorant mother's outdated style of toilet training) with those unfortunately unpleasant characteristics that make him ineligible for a passport into the affluent society.

Blaming the Victim is, of course, quite different from old-fashioned conservative ideologies. The latter simply dismissed victims as inferior, genetically defective, or morally unfit; the emphasis is on the intrinsic, even hereditary, defect. The former shifts its emphasis to the environmental causation. The old-fashioned conservative could hold firmly to the belief that the oppressed and the victimized were born that way—"that way" being defective or inadequate in character or ability. The new ideology attributes defect and inadequacy to the malignant nature of poverty, injustice, slum life, and racial difficulties. The stigma that marks the victim and accounts for his victimization is an acquired stigma, a stigma of social, rather than genetic, origin. But the stigma, the defect, the fatal difference—though derived in the past from environmental forces—is still located *within* the victim, inside his skin. With such an elegant formulation, the humanitarian can have it both ways. He can, all at the same time, concentrate his charitable interest on the defects of the victim, condemn the vague social and environmental stresses that produced the defect (some time ago), and ignore the continuing effect of victimizing social forces (right now). It is a brilliant ideology for justifying a perverse form of social action designed to change, not society, as one might expect, but rather society's victim.

As a result, there is a terrifying sameness in the programs that arise from this kind of analysis. In education, we have programs of "compensatory education" to build up the skills and attitudes of the ghetto child, rather than structural changes in the schools. In race relations, we have social engineers who think up ways of "strengthening" the Negro family, rather than methods of eradicating racism. In health care, we develop new programs to provide health information (to correct the supposed ignorance of the poor) and to reach out and discover cases of untreated illness and disability (to compensate for their supposed unwillingness to seek treatment). Meanwhile, the gross inequities of our medical care delivery systems are left completely unchanged. As we might expect, the logical outcome of analyzing social problems in terms of the deficiences of the victim is the development of programs aimed at correcting those deficiencies. The formula for action becomes extraordinarily simple: change the victim.

All of this happens so smoothly that it seems downright rational. First, identify a social problem. Second, study those affected by the problem and discover in what ways they are different from the rest of us as a consequence of deprivation and injustice. Third, define the differences as the cause of the social problem itself. Finally, of course, assign a government bureaucrat to invent a humanitarian action program to correct the differences.

Now no one in his right mind would quarrel with the assertion that social problems are present in abundance and are readily identifiable. God knows it is true that when hundreds of thousands of poor children drop out of school—or even graduate from school—they are barely literate. After spending some ten thousand hours in the company of professional educators, these children appear to have learned very little. The fact of failure in their education is undisputed. And the racial situation in America is usually acknowledged to be a number one item on the nation's agenda. Despite years of marches, commissions, judicial decisions, and endless legislative remedies, we are confronted with unchanging or even widening racial differences in achievement. In addition, despite our assertions that Americans get the best health care in the world, the poor stubbornly remain unhealthy. They lose more work because of illness, have more carious teeth, lose more babies as a result of both miscarriage and infant death, and die considerably younger than the well-to-do.

The problems are there, and there in great quantities. They make us uneasy. Added together, these disturbing signs reflect inequality and a puzzlingly high level of unalleviated distress in America totally inconsistent with our proclaimed ideals and our enormous wealth. This thread—this rope—of inconsistency stands out so visibly in the fabric of American life, that it is jarring to the eye. And this must be explained, to the satisfaction of our conscience as well as our patriotism. Blaming the Victim is an ideal, almost painless, evasion.

The second step in applying this explanation is to look sympathetically at those who "have" the problem in question, to separate them out and define them in some way as a special group, a group that is *different* from the population in general. This is a crucial and essential step in the process, for that difference is in itself hampering and maladaptive. The Different Ones are seen as less competent, less skilled, less knowing—in short, less human. The ancient Greeks deduced from a single characteristic, a difference in language, that the barbarians—that is, the "babblers" who spoke a

strange tongue—were wild, uncivilized, dangerous, rapacious, uneducated, lawless, and, indeed, scarcely more than animals. Automatically labeling strangers as savages, weird and inhuman creatures (thus explaining
difference by exaggerating difference) not infrequently justifies mistreat-
ment, enslavement, or even extermination of the Different Ones.

Blaming the Victim depends on a very similar process of identification
(carried out, to be sure, in the most kindly, philanthropic and intellectual
manner) whereby the victim of social problems is identified as strange, different—in other words, as a barbarian, a savage. Discovering savages,
then, is an essential component of, and prerequisite to, Blaming the Victim, and the art of Savage Discovery is a core skill that must be acquired by
all aspiring Victim Blamers. They must learn how to demonstrate that the
poor, the black, the ill, the jobless, the slum tenants, are different and
strange. They must learn to conduct or interpret the research that shows
how "these people" think in different forms, act in different patterns, cling
to different values, seek different goals, and learn different truths. Which is
to say that they are strangers, barbarians, savages. This is how the distressed and disinherited are redefined in order to make it possible for us to
look at society's problems and to attribute their causation to the individuals
affected.

II

Blaming the Victim is an ideological process, which is to say that it is
a set of ideas and concepts deriving from systematically motivated, but *un-
intended,* distortions of reality. In the sense that Karl Mannheim used the
term, an ideology develops from the "collective unconscious" of a group
or class and is rooted in a class-based interest in maintaining the *status quo*
(as contrasted with what he calls a *utopia,* a set of ideas rooted in a class-
based interest in *changing* the *status quo*). An ideology, then, has several
components: First, there is the belief system itself, the way of looking at the
world, the set of ideas and concepts. Second, there is the systematic distortion of reality reflected in those ideas. Third is the condition that the distortion must not be a conscious, intentional process. Finally, though they are
not intentional, the ideas must serve a specific function: maintaining the
status quo in the interest of a specific group. Blaming the Victim fits this
definition on all counts, as I will attempt to show in detail in the following
chapters. Most particularly, it is important to realize that Blaming the Victim is not a process of *intentional* distortion although it does serve the class
interests of those who practice it. And it has a rich ancestry in American
thought about social problems and how to deal with them.

Thinking about social problems is especially susceptible to ideological influences since, as John Seeley has pointed out, defining a social problem is not so simple. "What is a social problem?" may seem an ingenuous question until one turns to confront its opposite: "What human problem is *not* a social problem?" Since any problem in which people are involved is social, why do we reserve the label for some problems in which people are involved and withhold it from others? To use Seeley's example, why is crime called a social problem when university administration is not? The phenomena we look at are bounded by the act of definition. They become social problems only by being so considered. In Seeley's words, "*naming* it as a problem, after naming it as a *problem.*"

It is only recently, for example, that we have begun to *name* the rather large quantity of people on earth as the *problem* of overpopulation, or the population explosion. Such phenomena often become proper predicaments for certain solutions, certain treatments. Before the 1930's, the most anti-Semitic German was unaware that Germany had a "Jewish problem." It took the Nazis to *name* the simple existence of Jews in the Third Reich as a "social problem," and that act of definition helped to shape the final solution.

We have removed "immigration" from our list of social problems (after executing a solution—choking off the flow of immigrants) and have added "urbanization." Nowadays, we define the situation of men out of work as the social problem of "unemployment" rather than, as in Elizabethan times, that of "idleness." (The McCone Commission, investigating the Watts Riot of 1966, showed how hard old ideologies die; it specified both unemployment *and* idleness as causes of the disorder.) In the near future, if we are to credit the prophets of automation, the label "unemployment" will fade away and "idleness," now renamed the "leisure-time problem," will begin again to raise its lazy head. We have been comfortable for years with the "Negro problem," a term that clearly implies that the existence of Negroes is somehow a problematic fact. *Ebony* Magazine turned the tables recently and renamed the phenomenon as "The White Problem in America," which may be a good deal more accurate.

We must particularly ask, "To whom are social problems a problem?" And usually, if truth were to be told, we would have to admit that we mean they are a problem to those of us who are outside the boundaries of what we have defined as the problem. Negroes are a problem to racist whites, welfare is a problem to stingy taxpayers, delinquency is a problem to nervous property owners.

Now, if this is the quality of our assumptions about social problems, we are led unerringly to certain beliefs about the causes of these problems. We cannot comfortably believe that *we* are the cause of that which is problematic to us; therefore, we are almost compelled to believe that *they*—the problematic ones—are the cause and this immediately prompts us to search for deviance. Identification of the deviance as the cause of the problem is a simple step that ordinarily does not even require evidence.

C. Wright Mills analyzed the ideology of those who write about social problems and demonstrated the relationship of their texts to class interest and to the preservation of the existent social order. In sifting the material in thirty-one widely used textbooks in "social problems," "social pathology," and "social disorganization," Mills found a pervasive, coherent ideology with a number of common characteristics.

First, the textbooks present material about these problems, he says, in simple, descriptive terms, with each problem unrelated to the others and none related in any meaningful way to other aspects of the social environment. Second, the problems are selected and described largely according to predetermined norms. Poverty is a problem in that it deviates from the standard of economic self-sufficiency; divorce is a problem because the family is supposed to remain intact; crime and delinquency are problematic insofar as they depart from the accepted moral and legal standards of the community. The norms themselves are taken as givens, and no effort is made to examine them. Nor is there any thought given to the manner in which norms might themselves contribute to the development of the problems. (In a society in which everyone is assumed and expected to be economically self-sufficient, as an example, doesn't economic dependency almost automatically mean poverty? No attention is given to such issues.)

Within such a framework, then, deviation from norms and standards comes to be defined as failed or incomplete socialization—failure to learn the rules or the inability to learn how to keep to them. Those with social problems are then viewed as unable or unwilling to adjust to society's standards, which are narrowly conceived by what Mills calls "independent middle class persons verbally living out Protestant ideas in small town America." This, obviously, is a precise description of the social origins and status of almost every one of the authors.

In defining social problems in this way, the social pathologists are, of course, ignoring a whole set of factors that ordinarily might be considered relevant—for instance, unequal distribution of income, social stratification, political struggle, ethnic and racial group conflict, and inequality of power. Their ideology concentrates almost exclusively on the failure of the deviant. To the extent that society plays any part in social problems, it is said to have somehow failed to socialize the individual, to teach him how to adjust to circumstances, which, though far from perfect, are gradually changing for the better. Mills' essay provides a solid foundation for understanding the concept of Blaming the Victim. . . .

Blaming the Victim can take its place in a long series of American ideologies that have rationalized cruelty and injustice.

Slavery, for example, was justified—even praised—on the basis of a complex ideology that showed quite conclusively how useful slavery was to society and how uplifting it was for the slaves. Eminent physicians could be relied upon to provide the biological justification for slavery since after all, they said, the slaves were a separate species—as, for example, cattle are a separate species. No one in his right mind would dream of freeing the cows and fighting to abolish the ownership of cattle. In the view of the average American of 1825, it was important to preserve slavery, not simply because it was in accord with his own group interests (he was not fully aware of that), but because reason and logic showed clearly to the reasonable and intelligent man that slavery was good. In order to persuade a good and moral man to *do* evil, then, it is not necessary first to persuade him to *become* evil. It is only necessary to teach him that he is doing good. No one, in the words of a legendary newspaperman, thinks of himself as a son of a bitch.

In late-nineteenth-century America there flowered another ideology of injustice that seemed rational and just to the decent, progressive person. But Richard Hofstadter's analysis of the phenomenon of Social Darwinism shows clearly its functional role in the preservation of the *status quo*. One can scarcely imagine a better fit than the one between this ideology and the purposes and actions of the robber barons, who descended like piranha fish on the America of this era and picked its bones clean. Their extraordinarily unethical operations netted them not only hundreds of millions of dollars but also, perversely, the adoration of the nation. Behavior that would be, in any more rational land (including today's America), more than enough to have landed them all in jail, was praised as the very model of a captain of modern industry. And the philosophy that justified their thievery was such that John D. Rockefeller could actually stand up and preach it in church. Listen as he speaks in, of all places, Sunday school:

> The growth of a large business is merely a survival of the fittest. . . .
> The American Beauty rose can be produced in the splendor and fragrance which bring cheer to its beholder only by sacrificing the early buds which grow up around it. This is not an evil tendency in business. It is merely the working-out of a law of nature and a law of God.

This was the core of the gospel, adapted analogically from Darwin's writings on evolution. Herbert Spencer and, later, William Graham Sumner and other beginners in the social sciences considered Darwin's work to be directly applicable to social processes: ultimately as a guarantee that life was progressing toward perfection but, in the short run, as a justification for an absolutely uncontrolled laissez-faire economic system. The central concepts of "survival of the fittest," "natural selection," and "gradualism" were exalted in Rockefeller's preaching to the status of laws of God and Nature. Not only did this ideology justify the criminal rapacity of those who rose to the top of the industrial heap, defining them automatically as naturally superior (this was bad enough), but at the same time it also required that those at the bottom of the heap be labeled as patently *unfit*—a label based solely on their position in society. According to the law of natural selection, they should be, in Spencer's judgment, eliminated. "The whole effort of nature is to get rid of such, to clear the world of them and make room for better."

For a generation, Social Darwinism was the orthodox doctrine in the social sciences, such as they were at that time. Opponents of this ideology were shut out of respectable intellectual life. The philosophy that enabled John D. Rockefeller to justify himself self-righteously in front of a class of Sunday school children was not the product of an academic quack or a marginal crackpot philosopher. It came directly from the lectures and books of leading intellectual figures of the time, occupants of professional chairs at Harvard and Yale. Such is the power of an ideology that so neatly fits the needs of the dominant interests of society.

If one thinks about ideologies in America in 1970, one must be prepared to consider the possibility that a body of ideas that might seem almost self-evident is, in fact, highly distorted and highly selective; one must allow that the inclusion of a specific formulation in every freshman sociology text does not guarantee that the particular formulation represents abstract Truth rather than group interest. It is important not to delude ourselves into thinking that ideological monstrosities were constructed by monsters. They were not; they are not. They are developed through a process that shows every sign of being valid scholarship, complete with tables of numbers, copious footnotes, and scientific terminology. Ideologies are quite often academically and socially respectable and in many instances hold positions of exclusive validity, so that disagreement is considered unrespectable or radical and risks being labeled as irresponsible, unenlightened, or trashy.

Blaming the Victim holds such a position. It is central in the mainstream of contemporary American social thought, and its ideas pervade our most crucial assumptions so thoroughly that they are hardly noticed. Moreover, the fruits of this ideology appear to be fraught with altruism and humanitarianism, so it is hard to believe that it has principally functioned to block social change.

III

A major pharmaceutical manufacturer, as an act of humanitarian concern, has distributed copies of a large poster warning "LEAD PAINT CAN KILL!" The poster, featuring a photograph of the face of a charming little girl, goes on to explain that if children *eat* lead paint, it can poison them, they can develop serious symptoms, suffer permanent brain damage, even die. The health department of a major American city has put out a coloring book that provides the same information. While the poster urges parents to prevent their children from eating paint, the coloring book is more vivid. It labels as neglectful and thoughtless the mother who does not keep her infant under constant surveillance to keep it from eating paint chips.

Now, no one would argue against the idea that it is important to spread knowledge about the danger of eating paint in order that parents might act to forestall their children from doing so. But to campaign against lead paint *only* in these terms is destructive and misleading and, in a sense, an effective way to support and agree with slum landlords—who define the problem of lead poisoning in precisely these terms.

This is an example of applying an exceptionalistic solution to a universalistic problem. It is not accurate to say that lead poisoning results from the actions of individual neglectful mothers. Rather, lead poisoning is a social phenomenon supported by a number of social mechanisms, one of the most tragic by-products of the systematic toleration of slum housing. In New Haven, which has the highest reported rate of lead poisoning in the country, several small children have died and many others have incurred irreparable brain damage as a result of eating peeling paint. In several cases, when the landlord failed to make repairs, poisonings have occurred time and again through a succession of tenancies. And the major reason for the landlord's neglect of this problem was that the city agency responsible for enforcing the housing code did nothing to make him correct this dangerous condition.

The cause of the poisoning is the lead in the paint on the walls of the apartment in which the children live. The presence of the lead is illegal. To use lead paint in a residence is illegal; to permit lead paint to be exposed in a residence is illegal. It is not only illegal, it is potentially criminal since the housing code does provide for criminal penalties. The general problem of lead poisoning, then, is more accurately analyzed as the result of a systematic program of lawbreaking by one interest group in the community, with the toleration and encouragement of the public authority charged with enforcing that law. To ignore these continued and repeated law violations, to ignore the fact that the supposed law enforcer actually cooperates in lawbreaking, and then to load a burden of guilt on the mother of a dead or dangerously-ill child is an egregious distortion of reality. And to do so under the guise of public-spirited and humanitarian service to the community is intolerable.

But this is how Blaming the Victim works. The righteous humanitarian concern displayed by the drug company, with its poster, and the health department, with its coloring book, is a genuine concern, and this is a typical feature of Blaming the Victim. Also typical is the swerving away from the central target that requires systematic change and, instead, focusing in on the individual affected. The ultimate effect is always to distract attention from the basic causes and to leave the primary social injustice untouched. And, most telling, the proposed remedy for the problem is, of course, to work on the victim himself. Prescriptions for cure, as written by the Savage Discovery set, are invariably conceived to revamp and revise the victim, never to change the surrounding circumstances. They want to change his attitudes, alter his values, fill up his cultural deficits, energize his apathetic soul, cure his character defects, train him and polish him and woo him from his savage ways.

Isn't all of this more subtle and sophisticated than such old-fashioned ideologies as Social Darwinism? Doesn't the change from brutal ideas about survival of the fit (and the expiration of the unfit) to kindly concern about characterological defects (brought about by stigmas of social origin) seem like a substantial step forward? Hardly. It is only a substitution of terms. The old, reactionary exceptionalistic formulations are replaced by new progressive, humanitarian exceptionalistic formulations. In education, the outmoded and unacceptable concept of racial or class differences in basic inherited intellectual ability simply gives way to the new notion of cultural deprivation: there is very little functional difference between these two ideas. In taking a look at the phenomenon of poverty, the old concept of unfitness or idleness or laziness is replaced by the newfangled theory of the culture of poverty. In race relations, plain Negro inferiority—which was good enough for old-fashioned conservatives—is pushed aside by fancy conceits about the crumbling Negro family. With regard to illegitimacy, we are not so crass as to concern ourselves with immorality and vice, as in the old days; we settle benignly on the explanation of the ''lower-class pattern of sexual behavior,'' which no one condemns as evil, but which is, in fact, simply a variation of the old explanatory idea. Mental illness is no longer defined as the result of hereditary taint or congenital character flaw; now we have new causal hypotheses regarding the ego-damaging emotional experiences that are supposed to be the inevitable consequence of the deplorable child-rearing practices of the poor.

In each case, of course, we are persuaded to ignore the obvious: the continued blatant discrimination against the Negro, the gross deprivation of contraceptive and adoption services to the poor, the heavy stresses endemic in the life of the poor. And almost all our make-believe liberal programs aimed at correcting our urban problems are off target; they are designed either to change the poor man or to cool him out.

IV

We come finally to the question, Why? It is much easier to understand the process of Blaming the Victim as a way of thinking than it is to understand the motivation for it. Why do Victim Blamers, who are usually good people, blame the victim? The development and application of this ideology, and of all the mythologies associated with Savage Discovery, are readily exposed by careful analysis as hostile acts—one is almost tempted to say acts of war—directed against the disadvantaged, the distressed, the disinherited. It is class warfare in reverse. Yet those who are most fascinated and enchanted by this ideology tend to be progressive, humanitarian, and, in the best sense of the word, charitable persons. They would usually define themselves as moderates or liberals. Why do they pursue this dreadful war against the poor and the oppressed?

Put briefly, the answer can be formulated best in psychological terms—or, at least, I, as a psychologist, am more comfortable with such a formulation. The highly-charged psychological problem confronting this hypothetical progressive, charitable person I am talking about is that of reconciling his own self-interest with the promptings of his humanitarian impulses. This psychological process of reconciliation is not worked out in a logical, rational, conscious way; it is a process that takes place far below the level of sharp consciousness, and the solution—Blaming the Victim—is arrived at subconsciously as a compromise that apparently satisfies both his self-interest and his charitable concerns. Let me elaborate.

First, the question of self-interest, or, more accurately, class interest. The typical Victim Blamer is a middle-class person who is doing reasonably well in a material way; he has a good job, a good income, a good house, a good car. Basically, he likes the social system pretty much the way it is, at least in broad outline. He likes the two-party political system, though he may be highly skilled in finding a thousand minor flaws in its functioning. He heartily approves of the profit motive as the propelling engine of the economic system despite his awareness that there are abuses of that system, negative side effects, and substantial residual inequalities.

On the other hand, he is acutely aware of poverty, racial discrimination, exploitation, and deprivation, and, moreover, he wants to do something concrete to ameliorate the condition of the poor, the black, and the disadvantaged. This is not an extraneous concern; it is central to his value system to insist on the worth of the individual, the equality of men, and the importance of justice.

What is to be done, then? What intellectual position can he take, and what line of action can he follow that will satisfy both of these important motivations? He quickly and self-consciously rejects two obvious alternatives, which he defines as "extremes." He cannot side with an openly reactionary, repressive position that accepts continued oppression and exploitation as the price of a privileged position for his own class. This is incompatible with his own morality and his basic political principles. He finds the extreme conservative position repugnant.

He is, if anything, more allergic to radicals, however, than he is to reactionaries. He rejects the "extreme" solution of radical social change, and this makes sense since such radical social change threatens his own well-being. A more equitable distribution of income might mean that he would have less—a smaller or older house, with fewer yews or no rhododendrons in the yard, a less enjoyable job, or, at the least, a somewhat smaller salary. If black children and poor children were, in fact, reasonably educated and began to get high S.A.T. scores, they would be competing with *his* children for the scarce places in the entering classes of Harvard, Columbia, Bennington, and Antioch.

So our potential Victim Blamers are in a dilemma. In the words of an old Yiddish proverb, they are trying to dance at two weddings. They are old friends of both brides and fond of both kinds of dancing, and they want to accept both invitations. They cannot bring themselves to attack the system that has been so good to them, but they want so badly to be helpful to the victims of racism and economic injustice.

Their solution is a brilliant compromise. They turn their attention to the victim in his post-victimized state. They want to bind up wounds, inject penicillin, administer morphine, and evacuate the wounded for rehabilitation. They explain what's wrong with the victim in terms of social experiences *in the past*, experiences that have left wounds, defects, paralysis, and disability. And they take the cure of these wounds and the reduction of these disabilities as the first order of business. They want to make the victims less vulnerable, send them back into battle with better weapons, thicker armor, a higher level of morale.

In order to do so effectively, of course, they must analyze the victims carefully, dispassionately, objectively, scientifically, empathetically, mathematically, and hardheadedly, to see what made them so vulnerable in the first place.

What weapons, now, might they have lacked when they went into battle? Job skills? Education?

What armor was lacking that might have warded off their wounds? Better values? Habits of thrift and foresight?

And what might have ravaged their morale? Apathy? Ignorance? Deviant lower-class cultural patterns?

This is the solution of the dilemma, the solution of Blaming the Victim. And those who buy this solution with a sigh of relief are inevitably blinding themselves to the basic causes of the problems being addressed. They are, most crucially, rejecting the possibility of blaming, not the victims, but themselves. They are all unconsciously passing judgments on themselves and bringing in a unanimous verdict of Not Guilty.

If one comes to believe that the culture of poverty produces persons *fated* to be poor, who can find any fault with our corporation-dominated economy? And if the Negro family produces young men *incapable* of achieving equality, let's deal with that first before we go on to the task of changing the pervasive racism that informs and shapes and distorts our every social institution. And if unsatisfactory resolution of one's Oedipus complex accounts for all emotional distress and mental disorder, then by all means let us attend to that and postpone worrying about the pounding day-to-day stresses of life on the bottom rungs that drive so many to drink, dope, and madness.

That is the ideology of Blaming the Victim, the cunning Art of Savage Discovery. The tragic, frightening truth is that it is a mythology that is winning over the best people of our time, the very people who must resist this ideological temptation if we are to achieve nonviolent change in America.

"The Art of Savage Discovery: How to Blame the Victim" from his *Blaming the Victim*. New York: Pantheon Books, 1971, pp. 3–29.

C. Herbert J. Gans

Herbert Gans, professor of sociology at Columbia University, presents a study of the poor from the perspective of their role in society as a whole. Using a functional type of analysis, he describes the services they provide for the non-poor, services that often go unnoticed. Thus he raises to the level of consciousness many of the hidden dimensions of poverty's existence and bids us look at the poor not simply as "have-nots," but as contributors to the "haves."

It should be remembered, however, that functional analysis is not the same as causal analysis. Not all groups that benefit from poverty's functioning in our society constitute agents that create or perpetuate poverty. For example, the third function mentioned, that of providing employment for those who serve the poor in a variety of ways, arises after poverty has become a fact. Critics have pointed out that Gans has failed to show "the relationship between the function, the group it benefits, and that group's role in perpetuating poverty" (Janet and Jack Roach, "Commentary," American Journal of Sociology, 78 [May 1973], p. 1500).

If we review all of the functions Gans sets forth we find that most of them illustrate consequences of poverty once it is established and the uses that are made of its presence in society. Only the first two functions are causal in nature, and both of these are due to the paying of low wages.

The functional analysis, however, helps us see the difficulties involved in combating poverty. Although there are alternatives to most of the functions performed by the poor, many of them are unpalatable to the more affluent classes since they would create inconvenience and sacrifice. They have political ramifications as well. Gans' conclusion is that change will come about only if poverty becomes an intolerable condition for the non-poor, or when the poor themselves manage to form a power base sufficiently strong to bring it about. He is not very optimistic about either occurring in the near future.

Yet it is possible that Gans has fallen prey to the limited perspective of functional analysis itself. If we examine the functions closely we might conclude that some of them would disappear once the causal agents were removed. The interconnection of the functions and the dependency of some on others that bear primary responsibility for poverty's genesis and persistence are matters that call for closer scrutiny.

The Positive Functions of Poverty

The conventional view of American poverty is so dedicated to identifying the dysfunctions of poverty, both for the poor and the nation, that at first glance it seems inconceivable to suggest that poverty could be functional for anyone. Of course, the slum lord and the loan shark are widely known to profit from the existence of poverty; but they are popularly viewed as evil men, and their activities are, at least in part, dysfunctional for the poor. However, what is less often recognized, at least in the conventional wisdom, is that poverty also makes possible the existence or expansion of "respectable" professions and occupations, for example, penology, criminology, social work, and public health. More recently, the poor have provided jobs for professional and paraprofessional "poverty warriors," as well as journalists and social scientists, this author included, who have supplied the information demanded when public curiosity about the poor developed in the 1960s.

Clearly, then, poverty and the poor may well serve a number of functions for many non-poor in American society, and I shall describe 15 sets of such functions—economic, social, cultural, and political—that seem to me most significant.

First, the existence of poverty makes sure that "dirty work" is done. Every economy has such work: physically dirty or dangerous, temporary, dead-end and underpaid, undignified, and menial jobs. These jobs can be filled by paying higher wages than for "clean" work, or by requiring people who have no other choice to do the dirty work and at low wages. In America, poverty functions to provide a low-wage labor pool that is willing—or, rather, unable to be unwilling—to perform dirty work at low cost. Indeed, this function is so important that in some Southern states, welfare payments have been cut off during the summer months when the poor are needed to work in the fields. Moreover, the debate about welfare—and about proposed substitutes such as the negative income tax and the Family Assistance Plan—has emphasized the impact of income grants on work incentive, with opponents often arguing that such grants would reduce the incentive of—actually, the pressure on—the poor to carry out the needed dirty work if the wages therefore are no larger than the income grant. Furthermore, many economic activities which involve dirty work depend heavily on the poor; restaurants, hospitals, parts of the garment industry, and industrial agriculture, among others, could not persist in their present form without their dependence on the substandard wages which they pay to their employees.

Second, the poor subsidize, directly and indirectly, many activities that benefit the affluent. For one thing, they have long supported both the consumption and investment activities of the private economy by virtue of the low wages which they receive. This was openly recognized at the beginning of the Industrial Revolution, when a French writer quoted by T. H. Marshall pointed out that "to assure and maintain the prosperities of our industries, it is necessary that the workers should never acquire wealth.'' Examples of this kind of subsidization abound even today; for example, domestics subsidize the upper middle and upper class, making life easier for their employers and freeing affluent women for a variety of professional, cultural, civic, or social activities. In addition, as Barry Schwartz pointed out (personal communication), the low income of the poor enables the rich to divert a higher proportion of their income to savings and investment, and thus to fuel economic growth. This, in turn, can produce higher incomes for everybody, including the poor, although it does not necessarily improve the position of the poor in the socioeconomic hierarchy, since the benefits of economic growth are also distributed unequally.

At the same time, the poor subsidize the governmental economy. Because local property and sales taxes and the ungraduated income taxes levied by many states are regressive, the poor pay a higher percentage of their income in taxes than the rest of the population, thus subsidizing the many state and local governmental programs that serve more affluent taxpayers. In addition, the poor support medical innovation as patients in teaching and research hospitals, and as guinea pigs in medical experiments, subsidizing the more affluent patients who alone can afford these innovations once they are incorporated into medical practice.

Third, poverty creates jobs for a number of occupations and professions which serve the poor, or shield the rest of the population from them. As already noted, penology would be miniscule without the poor, as would the police, since the poor provide the majority of their "clients." Other activities which flourish because of the existence of poverty are the numbers game, the sale of heroin and cheap wines and liquors, pentecostal ministers, faith healers, prostitutes, pawn shops, and the peacetime army, which recruits its enlisted men mainly from among the poor.

Fourth, the poor buy goods which others do not want and thus prolong their economic usefulness, such as day-old bread, fruit and vegetables which would otherwise have to be thrown out, second-hand clothes, and deteriorating automobiles and buildings. They also provide incomes for doctors, lawyers, teachers, and others who are too old, poorly trained, or incompetent to attract more affluent clients.

In addition, the poor perform a number of social and cultural functions:

Fifth, the poor can be identified and punished as alleged or real deviants in order to uphold the legitimacy of dominant norms (Macarov 1970, pp. 31–33). The defenders of the desirability of hard work, thrift, honesty, and monogamy need people who can be accused of being lazy, spendthrift, dishonest, and promiscuous to justify these norms; and as Erikson (1964) and others following Durkheim have pointed out, the norms themselves are best legitimated by discovering violations.

Whether the poor actually violate these norms more than affluent people is still open to question. The working poor work harder and longer than high-status jobholders, and poor housewives must do more housework to keep their slum apartments clean than their middle-class peers in standard housing. The proportion of cheaters among welfare recipients is quite low and considerably lower than among income taxpayers. Violent crime is higher among the poor, but the affluent commit a variety of white-collar crimes, and several studies of self-reported delinquency have concluded that middle-class youngsters are sometimes as delinquent as the poor. However, the poor are more likely to be caught when participating in deviant acts and, once caught, to be punished more often than middle-class transgressors. Moreover, they lack the political and cultural power to correct the stereotypes that affluent people hold of them, and thus continue to be thought of as lazy, spendthrift, etc., whatever the empirical evidence, by those who need living proof that deviance does not pay. The actually or allegedly deviant poor have traditionally been described as undeserving and, in more recent terminology, culturally deprived or pathological.

Sixth, another group of poor, described as deserving because they are disabled or suffering from bad luck, provide the rest of the population with different emotional satisfactions; they evoke compassion, pity, and charity, thus allowing those who help them to feel that they are altruistic, moral, and practicing the Judeo-Christian ethic. The deserving poor also enable others to feel fortunate for being spared the deprivations that come with poverty.

Seventh, as a converse of the fifth function described previously, the poor offer affluent people vicarious participation in the uninhibited sexual, alcoholic, and narcotic behavior in which many poor people are alleged to indulge, and which, being freed from the constraints of affluence and respectability, they are often thought to enjoy more than the middle classes. One of the popular beliefs about welfare recipients is that many are on a permanent sex-filled vacation. Although it may be true that the poor are more given to uninhibited behavior, studies by Rainwater (1970) and other observers of the lower class indicate that such behavior is as often motivated by despair as by lack of inhibition, and that it results less in pleasure than in a compulsive escape from grim reality. However, whether the poor actually have more sex and enjoy it more than affluent people is irrelevant; as long as the latter believe it to be so, they can share it vicariously and perhaps enviously when instances are reported in fictional, journalistic, or sociological and anthropological formats.

Eighth, poverty helps to guarantee the status of those who are not poor. In a stratified society, where social mobility is an especially impor-tant goal and class boundaries are fuzzy, people need to know quite ur-gently where they stand. As a result, the poor function as a reliable and relatively permanent measuring rod for status comparison, particularly for the working class, which must find and maintain status distinctions be-tween itself and the poor, much as the aristocracy must find ways of distin-guishing itself from the *nouveau riche.*

Ninth, the poor also assist in the upward mobility of the non-poor, for, as Goode has pointed out (1967, p. 5), "the privileged . . . try systemati-cally to prevent the talent of the less privileged from being recognized or developed." By being denied educational opportunities or being stereo-typed as stupid or unteachable, the poor thus enable others to obtain the bet-ter jobs. Also, an unknown number of people have moved themselves or their children up in the socioeconomic hierarchy through the incomes earned from the provision of goods and services in the slums: by becoming policemen and teachers, owning "Mom and Pop" stores, or working in the various rackets that flourish in the slums.

In fact, members of almost every immigrant group have financed their upward mobility by providing retail goods and services, housing, entertain-ment, gambling, narcotics, etc., to later arrivals in America (or in the city), most recently to blacks, Mexicans, and Puerto Ricans. Other Americans, of both European and native origin, have financed their entry into the upper middle and upper classes by owning or managing the illegal institutions that serve the poor, as well as the legal but not respectable ones, such as slum housing.

Tenth, just as the poor contribute to the economic viability of a number of businesses and professions (see function 3 above), they also add to the social viability of noneconomic groups. For one thing, they help to keep the aristocracy busy, thus justifying its continued existence. "Society" uses the poor as clients of settlement houses and charity benefits; indeed, it must have the poor to practice its public-mindedness so as to demonstrate its su-periority over the *nouveaux riches* who devote themselves to conspicuous consumption. The poor play a similar function for philanthropic enterprises at other levels of the socioeconomic hierarchy, including the mass of mid-dle-class civic organizations and women's clubs engaged in volunteer work and fundraising in almost every American community. Doing good among the poor has traditionally helped the church to find a method of expressing religious sentiments in action; in recent years, militant church activity among and for the poor has enabled the church to hold on to its more liberal and radical members who might otherwise have dropped out of organized religion altogether.

Eleventh, the poor perform several cultural functions. They have played an unsung role in the creation of "civilization," having supplied the construction labor for many of the monuments which are often identified as the noblest expressions and examples of civilization, for example, the Egyptian pyramids, Greek temples, and medieval churches. Moreover, they have helped to create a goodly share of the surplus capital that funds the artists and intellectuals who make culture, and particularly "high" culture, possible in the first place.

Twelfth, the "low" culture created for or by the poor is often adopted by the more affluent. The rich collect artifacts from extinct folk cultures (although not only from poor ones), and almost all Americans listen to the jazz, blues, spirituals, and country music which originated among the Southern poor—as well as rock, which was derived from similar sources. The protest of the poor sometimes becomes literature; in 1970, for example, poetry written by ghetto children became popular in sophisticated literary circles. The poor also serve as culture heroes and literary subjects, particularly, of course, for the Left, but the hobo, cowboy, hipster, and the mythical prostitute with a heart of gold have performed this function for a variety of groups.

Finally, the poor carry out a number of important political functions:

Thirteenth, the poor serve as symbolic constituencies and opponents for several political groups. For example, parts of the revolutionary Left could not exist without the poor, particularly now that the working class can no longer be perceived as the vanguard of the revolution. Conversely, political groups of conservative bent need the "welfare chiselers" and others who "live off the taxpayer's hard-earned money" in order to justify their demands for reductions in welfare payments and tax relief. Moreover, the role of the poor in upholding dominant norms (see function 5 above) also has a significant political function. An economy based on the ideology of laissez faire requires a deprived population which is allegedly unwilling to work; not only does the alleged moral inferiority of the poor reduce the moral pressure on the present political economy to eliminate poverty, but redistributive alternatives can be made to look quite unattractive if those who will benefit from them most can be described as lazy, spendthrift, dishonest, and promiscuous. Thus, conservatives and classical liberals would find it difficult to justify many of their political beliefs without the poor; but then so would modern liberals and socialists who seek to eliminate poverty.

Fourteenth, the poor, being powerless, can be made to absorb the economic and political costs of change and growth in American society. During the 19th century, they did the backbreaking work that built the cities; today, they are pushed out of their neighborhoods to make room for "progress." Urban renewal projects to hold middle-class taxpayers and stores in the city and expressways to enable suburbanites to commute downtown have typically been located in poor neighborhoods, since no other group will allow itself to be displaced. For much the same reason, urban universities, hospitals, and civic centers also expand into land occupied by the poor. The major costs of the industrialization of agriculture in America have been borne by the poor, who are pushed off the land without recompense, just as in earlier centuries in Europe, they bore the brunt of the transformation of agrarian societies into industrial ones. The poor have also paid a large share of the human cost of the growth of American power overseas, for they have provided many of the foot soldiers for Vietnam and other wars.

Fifteenth, the poor have played an important role in shaping the American political process; because they vote and participate less than other groups, the political system has often been free to ignore them. This has not only made American politics more centrist than would otherwise be the case, but it has also added to the stability of the political process. If the 15% of the population below the federal ''poverty line'' participated fully in the political process, they would almost certainly demand better jobs and higher incomes, which would require income redistribution and would thus generate further political conflict between the haves and the have-nots. Moreover, when the poor do participate, they often provide the Democrats with a captive constituency, for they can rarely support Republicans, lack parties of their own, and thus have no other place to go politically. This, in turn, has enabled the Democrats to count on the votes of the poor, allowing the party to be more responsive to voters who might otherwise switch to the Republicans, in recent years, for example, the white working class.

I have described fifteen of the more important functions which the poor carry out in American society, enough to support the functionalist thesis that poverty survives in part because it is useful to a number of groups in society. This analysis is not intended to suggest that because it is functional, poverty *should* persist, or that it *must* persist. Whether it should persist is a normative question; whether it must, an analytic and empirical one, but the answer to both depends in part on whether the dysfunctions of poverty outweigh the functions. Obviously, poverty has many dysfunctions, mainly for the poor themselves but also for the more affluent. For example, their social order is upset by the pathology, crime, political protest, and disruption emanating from the poor, and the income of the affluent is affected by the taxes that must be levied to protect their social order. Whether the dysfunctions outweigh the functions is a question that clearly deserves study.

It is, however, possible to suggest alternatives for many of the functions of the poor. Thus, society's dirty work (function 1) could be done without poverty, some by automating it, the rest by paying the workers who do it decent wages, which would help considerably to cleanse that kind of work. Nor is it necessary for the poor to subsidize the activities they support through their low-wage jobs (function 2), for, like dirty work, many of these activities are essential enough to persist even if wages were raised. In both instances, however, costs would be driven up, resulting in higher prices to the customers and clients of dirty work and subsidized activity, with obvious dysfunctional consequences for more affluent people.

Alternative roles for the professionals who flourish because of the poor (function 3) are easy to suggest. Social workers could counsel the affluent, as most prefer to do anyway, and the police could devote themselves to traffic and organized crime. Fewer penologists would be employable, however, and pentecostal religion would probably not survive without the poor. Nor would parts of the second- and third-hand market (function 4), although even affluent people sometimes buy used goods. Other roles would have to be found for badly trained or incompetent professionals now relegated to serving the poor, and someone else would have to pay their salaries.

Alternatives for the deviance-connected social functions (functions 5–7) can be found more easily and cheaply than for the economic functions. Other groups are already available to serve as deviants to uphold traditional morality, for example, entertainers, hippies, and most recently, adolescents in general. These same groups are also available as alleged or real orgiasts to provide vicarious participation in sexual fantasies. The blind and disabled function as objects of pity and charity, and the poor may therefore not even be needed for functions 5–7.

The status and mobility functions of the poor (functions 8 and 9) are far more difficult to substitute, however. In a hierarchical society, some people must be defined as inferior to everyone else with respect to a variety of attributes, and the poor perform this function more adequately than others. They could, however, perform it without being as poverty-stricken as they are, and one can conceive of a stratification system in which the people below the federal "poverty line" would receive 75% of the median income rather than 40% or less, as is now the case—even though they would still be last in the pecking order. Needless to say, such a reduction of economic inequality would also require income redistribution. Given the opposition to income redistribution among more affluent people, however, it seems unlikely that the status functions of poverty can be replaced, and they—together with the economic functions of the poor, which are equally expensive to replace—may turn out to be the major obstacles to the elimination of poverty.

The role of the poor in the upward mobility of other groups could be maintained without their being so low in income. However, if their incomes were raised above subsistence levels, they would begin to generate capital so that their own entrepreneurs could supply them with goods and services, thus competing with and perhaps rejecting "outside" suppliers. Indeed, this is already happening in a number of ghettos, where blacks are replacing white storeowners.

Similarly, if the poor were more affluent, they would make less willing clients for upper- and middle-class philanthropic and religious groups (function 10), although as long as they are economically and otherwise unequal, this function need not disappear altogether. Moreover, some would still use the settlement houses and other philanthropic institutions to pursue individual upward mobility, as they do now.

The cultural functions (11 and 12) may not need to be replaced. In America, the labor unions have rarely allowed the poor to help build cultural monuments anyway, and there is sufficient surplus capital from other sources to subsidize the unprofitable components of high culture. Similarly, other deviant groups are available to innovate in popular culture and supply new culture heroes, for example, the hippies and members of other counter-cultures.

Some of the political functions of the poor would, however, be as difficult to replace as their economic and status functions. Although the poor could probably continue to serve as symbolic constituencies and opponents (function 13) if their incomes were raised while they remained unequal in other respects, increases in income are generally accompanied by increases in power as well. Consequently, once they were no longer so poor, people would be likely to resist paying the costs of growth and change (function 14); and it is difficult to find alternative groups who can be displaced for urban renewal and technological "progress." Of course, it is possible to design city-rebuilding and highway projects which properly reimburse the displaced people, but such projects would then become considerably more expensive, thus raising the price for those now benefiting from urban renewal and expressways. Alternatively, many might never be built, thus reducing the comfort and convenience of those beneficiaries. Similarly, if the poor were subjected to less economic pressure, they would probably be less willing to serve in the army, except at considerably higher pay, in which case war would become yet more costly and thus less popular politically. Alternatively, more servicemen would have to be recruited from the middle and upper class, but in that case war would also become less popular.

The political stabilizing and "centering" role of the poor (function 15) probably cannot be substituted for at all, since no other group is willing to be disenfranchised or likely enough to remain apathetic so as to reduce the fragility of the political system. Moreover, if the poor were given higher incomes, they would probably become more active politically, thus adding their demands for more to those of other groups already putting pressure on the political allocators of resources. The poor might continue to remain loyal to the Democratic party, but like other moderate-income voters, they could also be attracted to the Republicans or to third parties. While improving the economic status of the presently poor would not necessarily drive the political system far to the left, it would enlarge the constituencies now demanding higher wages and more public funds. It is of course possible to add new powerless groups who do not vote or otherwise participate to the political mix and can thus serve as "ballast" in the polity, for example, by encouraging the import of new poor immigrants from Europe and elsewhere, except that the labor unions are probably strong enough to veto such a policy.

In sum, then, several of the most important functions of the poor cannot be replaced with alternatives, while some could be replaced, but almost always only at higher costs to other people, particularly more affluent ones. Consequently, *a functional analysis must conclude that poverty persists not only because it satisfies a number of functions but also because many of the functional alternatives to poverty would be quite dysfunctional for the more affluent members of society.*

In one sense, my analysis is neutral; if one makes no judgment as to whether poverty ought to be eliminated—and if one can subsequently avoid being accused of acquiescing in poverty—then the analysis suggests only that poverty exists because it is useful to many groups in society. If one favors the elimination of poverty, however, then the analysis can have a variety of political implications, *depending in part on how completely it is carried out.*

If functional analysis only identifies the functions of social phenomena without mentioning their dysfunctions, then it may, intentionally or otherwise, agree with or support holders of conservative values. Thus, to say that the poor perform many functions for the rich might be interpreted or used to justify poverty, just as Davis and Moore's argument (1945) that social stratification is functional because it provides society with highly trained professionals could be taken to justify inequality.

Actually, the Davis and Moore analysis was conservative because it was incomplete; it did not identify the dysfunctions of inequality and failed to suggest functional alternatives, as Tumin (1953) and Schwartz (1955) have pointed out. Once a functional analysis is made more complete by the addition of functional alternatives, however, it can take on a liberal and reform cast, because the alternatives often provide ameliorative policies that do not require any drastic change in the existing social order.

Even so, to make functional analysis complete requires yet another step, an examination of the functional alternatives themselves. My analysis suggests that the alternatives for poverty are themselves dysfunctional for the affluent population, and it ultimately comes to a conclusion which is not very different from that of radical sociologists. To wit: *that social phenomena which are functional for affluent groups and dysfunctional for poor ones persist; that when the elimination of such phenomena through functional alternatives generates dysfunctions for the affluent, they will continue to persist; and that phenomena like poverty can be eliminated only when they either become sufficiently dysfunctional for the affluent or when the poor can obtain enough power to change the system of social stratification.*

"The Positive Functions of Poverty," *American Journal of Sociology*, 78 N. 2 (September 1972), Pp. 275–289.

D. Howard M. Wachtel

The conventional approach to poverty in this country has been to treat the poor as persons needing to be readapted to the prevailing economy and society. The emphasis has been upon job training, education, acculturation and developing individual traits and skills that make for success within the existing institutional framework. Wachtel offers a head-on challenge to this approach by taking the radical perspective. The term "radical" means going back to the root of something—in this case, the roots of poverty itself. In so doing the author directs our attention to the relationship of the poor to the institutions of the society in which the poor are destined to live. Is it really the poor who must change or is it the prevailing modes of industry and labor as well as the functioning processes of capitalism? Blaming the poor, Wachtel declares, is adding insult to injury and obscures the real source of their misery. It is the "normal functioning" of capitalism that causes poverty and not some aberration on the part of the poor. Most of Wachtel's essay is devoted to a demonstration of this thesis.

The cause-effect issue is, of course, the most debated—and one of the thorniest. The empirical evidence tends to be ambiguous at best since, as we have tried to show, the way in which that evidence is perceived depends heavily upon prior beliefs and perspectives. For the moment, however, let us follow Wachtel's argument. He sees the odds as stacked against the poor since society marshalls its forces against them. For the radical, the prevailing institutions of society have as their objective and raison d'être the perpetuating of their own power. Since government itself is complicit in this effort, little can be expected from its programs to serve as anything more than a bandaid or stopgap with only temporary effects. The poor are systematically excluded from any effective participation, lessening any prospect of long-term efforts that would deal with their plight successfully.

Wachtel's indictment has particular force and offers a needed vantage point on the problem of poverty and economic justice. Nevertheless a few questions emerge from an analysis of his attack. Note, for example, how he presents us with clear and disjunctive alternatives: either society or the poor themselves are to blame. The question may be raised as to whether these are the only alternatives and whether they are necessarily mutually exclusive. Another question is this: Has Wachtel taken a position (thesis) and then interpreted and selected all evidences for the purpose of supporting that thesis? If he has there may be something circular about his reasoning. That is, the thesis is true because the evidence supports it, and the evidence is valid because the thesis is the proper interpretation of it. Here it is worth pondering the nature of the evidence itself as well as the role and character of the thesis- and theory-formation. What kinds of arguments and evidences might count persuasively against Wachtel's analysis and its method?

Looking at Poverty from Radical, Conservative and Liberal Perspectives

Theories of Poverty

Examined from a perspective of radical political economics, poverty is the result of the normal functioning of the principal institutions of capitalism—specifically, labor markets, social class divisions and the state.

An individual's class status—his or her relationship to the means of production—provides the point of departure for an analysis of income inequalities and low incomes in an absolute sense. If an individual possesses both labor and capital, his chances of being poor or in a low income percentile are substantially less than if only labor is possessed. For individuals earning incomes under $10,000, nearly all income comes from labor. However, for individuals earning between $20,000 and $50,000 (in 1966), only slightly more than half comes from labor; while for individuals with incomes between $50,000 and $100,000 only a third comes from labor. And if you are rich—earning in excess of $100,000—only 15 percent comes from wage and salary earnings while two-thirds comes from capital returns (the balance is composed of "small business" income).

More important than the magnitude of capital income is its unequal distribution in our economy. Were we to redistribute this income, we could alleviate the purely financial aspects of low incomes. A direct transfer of income that would bring every family up to the Bureau of Labor Statistics' "Moderate but Adequate" living standard in 1966 (roughly $9,100) would have required $119 billion. This comes to about 20 percent of total personal income, slightly *less* than the proportion of personal income derived from ownership of capital.

Consequently, any meaningful discussion of the causes of income inequalities or low incomes must start with a discussion of Marx's class categories. The plain fact is that the probabilities of being both a capitalist and poor are slim compared with the opportunities for poverty if labor forms the principal means of acquiring income. And under capitalism, there is no mechanism for sharing the returns from capital—it all goes to the private owners of capital.

The individual's relationship to the means of production is only the starting point in the analysis. The labor market is the next institution of capitalism which must be analyzed to understand the causes of poverty. Given the fact that workers have no capital income, the chances of becoming poor

200

are increased. However, not all workers are poor in any sense of that ambiguous term. This leads us to our next concept in the analysis—*social stratification*. Social stratification refers to the divisions within a social class as distinct from the class itself. In this context, the divisions among workers in the labor market lead to social stratification among the class of workers which has had important implications for the cyclical and secular movements in class consciousness.

The functioning of labor markets, interacting with individual characteristics of workers, determines the wage status of any particular individual in stratified labor markets. The labor market causes poverty in several important ways. Contrary to conventional wisdom, nearly every poor person is or has been connected with the labor market in some way. Poor individuals sift into several categories. First, there are enormous numbers of *working poor*—individuals who work fulltime and full year, yet earn less than even the government's parsimonious poverty income. These people earn their poverty. Of all poor families attached to the labor force in 1968, about one-third (1.4 million) were fully employed workers. Of the more than 11 million families with incomes under $5,000 in 1968, nearly *30 percent* were headed by a fulltime wage earner. The incidence of the working poor is greater among black poor families and families with female heads. About 22 *percent* of all black poor families were headed by an individual working fulltime in 1968. And a *third* of all black families with incomes under $5,000 worked fulltime. The Department of Labor reports that 10 million workers in 1968 (nearly 20 percent of the private nonsupervisory employees) were earning less than $1.60 per hour—the wage rate that yields a poverty income if fully employed.

A second significant proportion of the poor are attached to the labor force but are not employed fulltime. Some of these individuals suffer intermittent periods of employment and unemployment, while others work for substantial periods of time and then suffer severe periods of long-term unemployment.

A third significant portion of the poor are handicapped in the labor market as a result of an occupational disability or poor health. However, these occupational disabilities are themselves related to a person's earlier status in the labor force. There are greater occupational hazards and opportunities for poor health in low wage jobs. Low incomes can contribute significantly to poor health, especially in the American markets for health care where enormous incomes or proper health insurance are an absolutely essential precondition for the receipt of medical care. Disabilities are widespread throughout the economy. In 1966, nearly *one-sixth* of the labor force was disabled for a period longer than *six months*. Only 48 percent of the disabled worked at all in 1966, while 12 percent of the employed disabled workers were employed only part-time. As a consequence of disability, many households with disabled heads are poor—about 50 percent.

Thus we see that nearly all of these poverty phenomena are endogeneous to the system—they are a consequence of the functioning of labor markets in the economy. This argument can be extended to birth defects as well. There is a growing body of evidence which suggests that many forms of birth defects are related to the nutrition of the mother which, in turn, is related to family income (itself dependent upon the class status of the family and the labor market status of the family wage earners). Even with the evidence as tentative as it is, we can say that the probability of birth defects is greater in families with low incomes and the resultant poor nutritional opportunities.

Another category of the poor are not presently attached to the labor market—the aged, the prison population, members of the military, the fully handicapped, and those on other forms of public assistance (principally women with dependent children). Though these individuals are not presently attached to the labor force, in many instances their low income is determined by past participation in the labor force.

For example, the ability of aged persons to cope with their non-employed status depends upon their wealth, private pension income, savings and public pension income (social security). Each of these, in turn, is related to the individual's status in the labor force during his working years. The one partial exception is social security which is typically cited as an income equalizing program where payments are only partially related to contributions. But even in this case, the redistributive effects of social security are not as great as they have been advertised, as we shall see later in this paper. This point aside, the payments for social security are so small that retired people, dependent solely on this source of income, end up in the government's poverty statistics.

The important elements of income for retirees are all associated with past labor force status and with the class status of the individual. High paid professional and blue-collar jobs typically provide private pension supplements to social security, while low paid jobs do not. Individuals with income from capital can continue to earn income from capital beyond the years they are attached to the labor force, while wage earners cannot. High income workers and owners of capital have vehicles for ensuring their security in old age, while medium and low wage earners have only social and financial insecurity to contemplate in their old age.

To a somewhat lesser extent other poor nonparticipants in the labor force attain their poverty as a result of their (or their spouse's) past association with the labor force. Even for the handicapped, the prisoner, or the welfare mother, the labor market is not a trivial determinant of their poverty status.

If labor force status provides such an important and inclusive explanation of poverty among individuals, the next question is: what determines an individual's status in the labor force? For simplicity, we will take occupation as an imperfect proxy for labor force status, bearing in mind that there is substantial variation in wage status within occupational categories as well as among occupational categories.

In broad terms, an individual's wage is dependent upon four types of variables:

1. Individual characteristics over which the individual exercises no control—age, race, sex, family class status, and region of socialization.
2. Individual characteristics over which the individual exercises degree of control—education, skill level, health, region of employment, and personal motivation.
3. Characteristics of the industry in which the individual is employed—profit rates, technology, product market concentration, relation of the industry to the government, and unionization.
4. Characteristics of the local labor market—structure of the labor demand, unemployment rate, and rate of growth.

One observation is immediately apparent: there are very few variables that lie within the individual's control that affect his labor market status. Even the individual characteristics placed in category two are not completely within the control of the individual. For example, as Coleman, Bowles and others have shown, education is heavily dependent upon the socioeconomic status of the family, an attribute which lies outside of individual control. Health is partially endogeneous to the system as discussed above. Geographic mobility depends upon income and wealth.

This classification scheme is a useful starting point, but a more formal analysis is needed to understand the way in which these several categories of variables interact in the labor market to yield low incomes.

The occupation an individual enters is *associated with* individual characteristics: educational quantity and quality, training, skills, and health. These attributes are normally defined as the *human capital* embodied in an individual. The differences in these variables among individuals, which influence their entry into occupations, are dependent upon race, sex, age and class status of the family. Although human capital is *defined* by the set of characteristics associated with the individual, the *determinants* of the differing levels of human capital among individuals are found in the set of individual characteristics that lie outside of the individual's control.

The story does not end here; the wage is not solely dependent upon the occupation of an individual. The fact that one person is a janitor, another a skilled blue-collar worker, tells us something about the wage that each will receive but not everything. There is a substantial variation in wage within each of those occupations that is dependent upon the industry and the local labor market in which an individual works. There are a variety of industrial and local labor market characteristics which yield different wages for essentially the same occupation and level of human capital. The wage will be higher for a given occupation in an industry with high profit rates, a strong union, highly productive technologies, a high degree of product market concentration, and a favorable status with the government. A similar type of analysis holds for the impact of local market conditions.

In sum, the individual has very little control over his or her labor force status. If you are black, female, have parents with low socio-economic status, and dependent upon labor income, there is a high probability that you will have relatively low levels of human capital which will slot you into low-paying jobs, in low wage industries, in low wage labor markets. With this initial placement, the individual is placed in a high risk category, destined to end up poor sometime during her working and nonworking years. She may earn her poverty by working fulltime. Or she may suffer either sporadic or long periods of unemployment. Or she may become disabled, thereby reducing her earning power even further. Or when she retires, social security payments will place her in poverty even if she escaped this fate throughout her working years. With little savings, wealth, or a private pension income, the retiree will be poor.

In contrast with this radical political-economic theory of the causes of poverty, both conservative and liberal political-economic theories look for the cause of poverty in terms of some individual characteristic over which the individual is presumed to exercise control. The conservative theory of poverty relies upon markets in labor and capital to provide sufficient mobility either within a generation or between generations to alleviate poverty. If one does not avail himself of the opportunities for social and economic mobility through the market, the individual is to blame. The poor cause their own poverty and its continuation. The individual is presumed to be master of his own destiny, and individualism will lead any deserving person out of poverty. (Of course, the people who posit these notions are the nonpoor.) For the undeserving poor, only institutionalization of one form or another will do. These people are trapped by their lower class life styles which prevent them from escaping poverty. If the poor would only work, there would be no poverty. The Elizabethan poor laws and their American counterpart considered unemployment a crime for which the penalty was work. Gilbert and Sullivan were appropriate when they said "let the penalty fit the crime."

The liberal (and dominant) theory of poverty grants some recognition to institutions as partial causes of poverty as well as social class as an intergenerational transmitter of poverty. But rather than seeking remedies by altering these social institutions or searching for ways to break class rigidities, liberals concentrate their energies on trying to find ways to use government either to ease the burden of poverty or assist the individual in adapting to prevailing institutions. The liberals reject exclusive reliance upon the market to foster social mobility and attempt to use government to equalize opportunities within the market or assist individuals in coping with their poverty status by direct income transfers. Nonetheless, their commitment to "alleviating" poverty without systemic changes is as deep as any conservative's. Manifestations of this orientation abound. The entire social work profession, borne out of liberal social reform, exists principally to help people cope with a rotten personal or family situation. Hungry people are given nutritional advice rather than access to food, which would involve structural changes in agricultural markets.

The objective of liberal social policy is equal opportunity—a random distribution of poverty—though we are far from that goal today. The radical challenge goes as follows: if you start from a position of inequality and treat everyone equally, you end up with continued inequality. Thus the need to create equality in fact rather than in opportunities.

Manpower programs, educational assistance, and the like are the principal policy results of the contemporary liberal human capital approach to social mobility. All of these programs are based on an essentially *untested* view of the labor market: namely, that personal characteristics over which the individual has control are the major causes of unequal and low incomes. These programs are quite similar in their ideological premise to virtually all the poor laws of capitalist society, starting with the Elizabethan poor laws. Poverty is associated with the absence of work for which work is the cure. The poor are incapable of managing their own affairs so they must be "social worked" to adapt to the rigor and needs of an industrialized and urbanized society.

This view of poverty is wrong in theory, in fact, and in social values. The causes of poverty lie outside the individuals' control in markets for labor and capital and class backgrounds. Equally important, something happens both to the people seeking to help the poor and to the poor themselves when we take as our starting point the premise that people are poor because of some manipulable attribute associated with the person.

Theories of the State and the Poor

Corresponding to the several political-economic theories of poverty are *theories of the state*, i.e., theories which discuss the origins and the role of government in eliminating poverty.

The *conservative* theory of the state views the origins of government as emerging from the consent of the governed. The proper economic role of the state is to leave things alone—*laissez faire*. The state exists solely to protect the basic institutions of capitalism—private property, markets in labor and capital, and markets in goods and services. It does this by providing both a domestic and a foreign military and by providing a system of courts to protect property and adjudicate disputes arising out of private property conflicts. The deserving poor will attain social mobility in this generation or the next via the normal functioning of markets. Any efforts by the state to interfere in this process will only distort these opportunities for mobility. Hence, the role of the state is simple: do nothing about the poor but protect their means to social mobility—free markets and capitalism.

Liberals view the state as a mediator between conflicting interest groups in a pluralistic society. Since market institutions work imperfectly at best, the role of the state vis-a-vis the poor is to compensate for these shortcomings of the market by providing the opportunities denied to individuals by markets. "Where *opportunities* are free, the poor will disappear," might be a good liberal slogan. While the conservative would retort: "where markets are free, the poor will disappear." Liberals also recognize the existence of a residual population for whom no amount of indirect compensation will prevent their poverty. For these people, public welfare—direct payments—is the only solution.

Radicals view the origin of the state in terms of a class of people who exercise dominant decision-making power in state institutions and who transmit their class power intergenerationally. One's relationship to the means of production is an essential, but not exclusive, determinant of power, and the education system is an intergenerational transmitter and legitimator of this power. This is not the place to probe deeply into this complicated subject, but ask yourself this question: who is powerful in your local community? Are these people workers or owners (and managers) of capital?

Given this view of power in the state, as distinct from the liberal pluralist view or the conservative consent-of-the-governed view, the role of the state is to ensure the continued survival and perpetuation of its class of decision-makers. If this analysis is valid, then the state becomes part of the problem rather than part of the solution. This does not mean that the same individuals or their inheritors have power in perpetuity, though this occurs—merely ponder the name Lodge, Harriman, or Rockefeller for awhile. This is why the term class is used, analytically distinct from a ruling elite or conspiracy theory of the state. In fact, liberals rather than radicals are the major proponents of conspiracy theories—witness the interest among liberals in a "military-industrial complex" conspiracy rather than a class analysis of the power of the military and its camp followers.

Several hypotheses flow from the radical theory of the state. First, government as a totality will reinforce the disequalizing tendencies of the market through its support of basic capitalist institutions even though liberals for the past 40 years have been attempting to do precisely the opposite. Second, programs to assist the poor will perhaps have some impact in the short run, but in the long run will either atrophy, become anemic in their impact, or become distorted in their purpose. Third, only those public programs that are compatible with the basic institutions of monopoly capitalism will see the light of day in the first instance and will survive to suffer the fate outlined above in the second hypothesis.

In contrast, liberals assume that the state intervenes on behalf of the underclass to redistribute wealth, opportunity, and privilege. In fact, the term used to characterize collective decision-making in economics is the *social welfare function*. As chapter three, "Government Spending and the Distribution of Income," shows, however, the possibility that state intervention buttresses the status quo, or even increases inequality in the distribution of income, cannot be dismissed.

"Looking at Poverty from a Radical Perspective," *Review of Radical Political Economics,* **Vol. 3, No. 3 (Summer 1971) pp. 1–19.**

VI. Approaches to Solution: Economic Justice at Work

There remains the question of how to deal with poverty in our society and with it a consideration of the proposed solutions running the gamut of viewpoints from the traditional laissez-faire position to that of the socialist. Two major issues are at stake here. One is the question of whether poverty can be cured or only remedied. If the members of society put their hearts and mind to it, could they banish poverty once and for all and prevent its reoccurrence? Or can we only expect to alleviate poverty when and where it occurs without any genuine prospect of its elimination? The other issue centers around the question of how much change within the existing organizational structure of our society is required if we are to deal with poverty effectively, and what costs are involved.

As to the first question of whether poverty can be cured, those who advocate this position usually hold also that the poor have certain rights or entitlements. Basing their positions on theories similar to those of Bowie and Simon who enunciate a right to well-being in an affluent society and of John Rawls whose second principle states that inequalities should be so arranged as to benefit the least advantaged, the proponents of this view would place priority upon the need, conditions and deserts of the poor over protecting the free market and defending pure capitalism. They contend that the economic inequalities of a prosperous society are inexcusable and call for vigorous efforts that would include the transformation of general economic conditions. Yet there is a variance in opinion as to what this entitlement on the part of the poor includes. Does it entail a guaranteed annual income for all who fall below a certain level? Does it require a guarantee of employment at a certain age, for example, for everyone who has completed his or her basic education, regardless of the demand and availability of jobs within the economy? Or does it mean providing opportunity for work through training programs that enable the poor to compete successfully within the private sector? Each of these questions implies answers that require different degrees and kinds of changes within existing arrangements. But whatever the costs involved, the proponents of this position generally hold that the violation of the poor's entitlements involve a far greater cost, one that should not be tolerated in our society.

Those who take the stance that poverty can only be alleviated are also the ones who oppose any extensive change in the economic order as it now exists. Some, such as Robert Lampman, would endeavor to eliminate its abuses while others, like Milton Friedman, would rely upon a negative income tax that would do away with the need for welfare programs and income supplements. Their emphasis is upon maintaining incentives among the poor so that they can become more effective participants in the marketplace and achieve self-sufficiency. They would be subject to the same criteria as the rest of the population: productivity, individual effort, social contribution, and ability. Their needs would be met accordingly. It is to the private sector that we must turn for the ultimate solution of poverty rather than the public. Any assistance from the latter should remain purely instrumental in boosting individuals and families so that they can maintain themselves without government programs.

A third issue that is related to the first two has to do with whether the capitalist free enterprise system is a training ground for character, as some of its classic defenders claim, inducing those traits and qualities that we identify with virtue such as self-discipline, ambition, prudence and resourcefulness, or whether it has the opposite effect upon some portion of the population and instead produces demoralization. Some have pointed out that the entrepreneur whom we generally regard as successful is often calloused and indifferent toward others, especially the less fortunate, and that self-interest engenders self-centeredness, a kind of look-at-me-I-made-it attitude. Others point out that those who grow up in an environment of want with little change to alter their circumstances become demoralized and passive as an adaptive response to their plight, and that the burden of responsibility should fall more on the society that produces such conditions and less on the individual. This issue is a complex one and needs a great deal more study and research, especially since the evidence itself is fraught with ambiguities. The interaction between person and conditions surrounding the individual may lead to varying conclusions depending upon cases, methods of study, and norms.

The history of our nation's attempts to deal with poverty has fluctuated between those various philosophies and according to the mood and reaction of the public at large. (An excellent account of this history can be found in James I. Patterson, *America's Struggle Against Poverty, 1900–1980.* Cambridge: Harvard University Press, 1981.) Just how to measure the success of these programs depends upon a number of factors. First it depends upon the criteria that are established to measure effectiveness, criteria that will naturally reflect the system of beliefs as well as the scope of our expectations and objectives. Related to this is the fact that many of the programs have promised more than they could deliver. The war on poverty during the 1960's is a case in point: it predicted the end of poverty within ten years, a forecast that was to produce widespread disappointment. Third, taking the long view we find that poverty has been reduced in relative terms over the span of the twentieth century since there has been a substantial reduction in the proportion of poor relative to the total population, but in terms of absolute numbers the poor still add up to the tens of millions and so constitute a sizable group. Moreover, the deep recession of the early 1980's has once again demonstrated how our cyclical economy can throw a large number of people out of work and onto the government dole. And we are encountering the phenomenon of ailing industries, especially steel and automotive, which may entail large-scale permanent layoffs.

Since the Great Depression of the 1930's the federal government has played a major role in dealing with poverty. Over the past five decades we have seen a multiplication of programs extending aid to members of our society in a variety of situations: the aged, homes without fathers, the unemployed, the unemployable, the disabled, and families that fall below a federally defined poverty level of income. Now with the rising rates of inflation, taxes, and federal budgetary deficits these programs have come under attack. The Reagan era marks a broad departure from the philosophy of the past administrations, introducing some deep cuts in federal spending for a broad spectrum of purposes and needs. The 1980's are destined to become a decade of controversy over both the effects of Reagonomics and the role that public funds and agencies should play in dealing with poverty.

Although the selections of this chapter were written before the inauguration of Reagan cutbacks, they nevertheless represent the major voices within the current debate. As you read them and attempt to draw some conclusions of your own it may be helpful to keep several questions in mind: Where does poverty fit into the total national agenda? That is, what priority does it have at present and what priority should it have? What changes would have to be made if poverty were to be dealt with effectively? What burdens or costs would be involved, and upon whom should these fall? What role should the private and public sectors each play, and how should they be held accountable?

A. Seymour Spilerman
and David Elesh

The question of how well theories fit the facts and serve as a basis for appropriate action is addressed here by two researchers from the University of Wisconsin. Their answer is a complex one. Instead of expecting a single model to provide a comprehensive and exhaustive schema by which to administer programs of assistance to the poor, we need to have some alternatives at our disposal. There are variables among the poor themselves that must be taken into account if we are to avoid negative results. For example, studies have shown that the intensity with which ethnicity permeates a neighborhood will make a difference in the way that the residents will respond to income maintenance measures. Moreover we may find it to be true generally that there are different reasons for poverty among different populations, which means that adjustment must be made from one situation to the next.

One of the important contributions Spilerman and Elesh make is to break down the notion of causality into three distinct forms or models—the lineal, cyclical, and path models—and show how each has its own set of implications for the kind of intervention called for. When it comes to testing each of the models, difficulties arise, however, and it may be virtually impossible to determine whether poverty is functional or cultural because the evidence may not clearly point to one kind of explanation. The issue raised is the danger posed to the theorist in interpreting what he or she sees as an observer. Either the person may not have looked carefully enough at the evidence or he or she is unprepared to consider alternative reasons for the response elicited by the particular measures of assistance applied.

The authors conclude that functional and cultural theories should not be considered as mutually exclusive but as applicable under different circumstances to different populations. The best-intentioned measure may turn out to be in vain unless there is a thorough understanding of the social and cultural context.

Alternative Conceptions of Poverty and Their Implications for Income Maintenance

The intent of this paper is to discuss some of the dimensions along which individual variation in response to an income maintenance program is likely to occur, and to indicate the relevance of different explanations of poverty to experimentation in income maintenance. Our perspective here is that (a) the different poverty theories predict divergent adaptations by recipients of income maintenance, (b) a given explanation of poverty is likely to be valid for some individuals but not for others, and only for particular correlates of low income, and (c) much of the inter-individual variation can be attributed to differences in response among *social* groups. Consequently, we propose that future research should be directed at identifying the characteristic types of adaptations which are likely to occur, and associating particular groups in poverty with each adaptation.

Alternative Theories of Poverty

Theories of poverty are broadly of two types, situational (commonly characterized by simple causality) and cultural (functional). Situational explanations view the behavioral characteristics of low income individuals as an adaptation to environment and circumstance. If a poor person tends not to defer gratification and invest in the future, it is because the future is precarious for him, too unstable for a long range perspective to be rational. If he mugs for a living, it is because the socially acceptable occupations which show similar financial returns are outside the pale of vocations available to him. Thus, the view that the destitute share a deviant culture, with values which are in opposition to those of the dominant society, is not invoked. The fact that in seemingly diverse settings poor persons exhibit similar behavioral characteristics is taken as evidence for their having to contend with analogous problems which permit few alternative adaptations, rather than their holding like deviant values.

By comparison, cultural explanations of poverty argue that the behavior and attitudes of poor persons are components of a coherent life style. These factors are seen as an expression of established rules or norms which prescribe what is desirable or important, rather than as an application of general societal values to the circumstance of the poor. Since cultural theories explain behavior and attitudes in terms of concepts like values, expectations and social pressure, cultural theories of poverty take the guise of "functional explanations." From this perspective, then, the poor in different settings behave in a similar fashion because they share common values.

These two types of explanations have very different underlying logical structures and often imply contradictory adaptations by recipients of income maintenance. Since our interest here is with developing the implications of the different theories by examining their logical structures, the substantive examples that are considered in the following sections will necessarily be elementary and are intended for illustrative purposes.

Situational explanations—In their most elementary form, situational explanations which relate low income to correlative behavioral characteristics may be paradigmed as causal sequences. For example, low and variable income leads to insufficient nutrition and inadequate housing, which result in poor health, impairing, in turn, the individual's ability to work. Or, low income implies inadequate home study conditions for children, poor nourishment, and a continual state of financial need by the family, which combine to reduce a child's ability to concentrate on school affairs. In each of these chains, as in causal theory generally, there is an implication that by manipulating a prior factor, the variable of primary interest can be altered; that an increase in family income would be translated into an improvement in work performance in the first illustration, and into an increase in scholastic attainment in the second example.

In order to obtain the most return from an intervention, it is vital that the variable chosen for manipulation be prior to most of the conditions which one is interested in altering. Thus, in the first example, if one improves the state of health of an individual by bringing exogenous factors to bear which impinge directly on health—providing vitamin pills rather than raising income—only the variables subsequent to state of health (the individual's work performance) will be improved by the manipulation. By intervening earlier in the causal sequence, however, (in this illustration by raising family income) a large number of factors can be altered *without particular attention having to be given to these disabilities.* From the perspective of altering the behavioral concomitants of poverty, then, an income maintenance program represents an assumption as to the causal ordering, namely that family income is causally prior to many of the other elements in the constellation of poverty characteristics.

There is another form of causal explanation, often employed in studies of the intergenerational transmission of poverty, in which it is less apparent that the link at which the intervention should occur is material. I refer to the "cycle of poverty" explanations. If a causal sequence can be closed by adding links to connect the final and initial variables (in the first illustration, low capacity to work can be linked to inadequate income in the succeeding time period; in the second, low academic attainment implies poor labor market situation which results in inadequate income), then, theoretically, intervention can be made at any link with a consequent improvement in the levels of all factors. In practice, however, even where a cycle provides a valid representation of reality, the selection of a variable for manipulation remains an important decision because the cost of intervention can differ considerably by link, and because societal values are more permissive of some manipulations (e.g., raising educational attainment, income maintenance) than of others (e.g., limiting family size).

More complex situational explanations can be represented as path models. Recent empirical work on the interrelations among poverty associated characteristics have used this methodology. It must be recognized that the use of a causal methodology such as a recursive system of equations represents an *assumption* regarding the validity of a situational explanation. A path model enables the variation in the dependent variable to be partitioned among the several paths (causal sequences). Only rarely, however, can the suitability of the underlying causal framework be tested.

There is a considerable literature, both theorizing and research, in support of a situational explanation for the behavioral and attitudinal correlates of poverty. In a now classic essay, Merton introduced a five-fold typology relating the goals which are pursued by individuals to the means employed. Merton contends that where the societal goals are accepted but the sanctioned means are unavailable, an innovative response—the use of illicit means—is likely to ensue. Applying this perspective to the poor, it would appear that precisely the individuals who subscribe to the middle-class conception of success—wealth and its appurtenances, to put matters crudely—would be most likely to resort to illegitimate means. Conversely, if well paid and steady work were available in the "respectable labor market," the muggers and pimps could presumably be enticed away from their current vocations.

Support for a situational perspective is also provided by Miller, Riessman, and Seagull. They argue that while impulse following and a preference for immediate gratification are characteristics of lower-class life styles, this behavior derives from the opportunity structure facing the poor, rather than from distinctive cultural values on their part. For a middle-class person the world is orderly and stable, making an investment in the future relatively secure and economically rational. By comparison, the present-time orientation of poor persons is a calculated response to an unstable reward structure, a world characterized by garnishment and unemployment. In this circumstance, one might well choose to get his kicks while he could rather than plan for extensive gratification in the future. Thus, in this view, it is not so much different orientations to time which account for the differential class tendency to invest in the future as it is the different futures of the poor and the affluent.

Liebow, in a study of Negro men who hang out at a particular street-corner, provides compelling descriptive evidence for the impact of the opportunity structure on their behavior, although in values and attitudes toward work the men are essentially middle class. Liebow argues that the lethargy and disinterest which these individuals bring to the job is due to their *acceptance* of the dominant societal values toward work. The jobs to which they have access are, typically, "hard, dirty, uninteresting and underpaid." More importantly, they are dead-end jobs, not stepping stones to better positions even for those who are willing to do them faithfully. "The busboy or dishwasher in a restaurant is not on a job track which, if negotiated skillfully, leads to chef or manager of the restaurant. The busboy or dishwasher who works hard becomes, simply, a hard working busboy or dishwasher.'' The disdain which these men have toward their work, then, is no different from the view which middle-class individuals accord to these same positions; they are accurately reflecting the values of the society.

These works are illustrative of research supporting a view of poverty which attributes the behavioral characteristics of poor persons to their material situation. The poor are not seen as carriers of an independent culture with values and aspirations that are at variance with those of middle-class society. Rather, their behavior deviates from established norms because the application of the societal values to their circumstance leads to different results. One immediate implication of situational theory for income maintenance is that the characteristics of low income individuals which are causally subsequent to income level will respond to a change in this variable. Indeed, it is expected that the resulting adaptation would approximate middle-class mores since, by assumption in this explanation, the values of the poor are not different from those of more affluent persons.

However, situational theory does not suggest what the waiting time would be for a particular response to income maintenance to develop. It is basically a theory of static relationships and rarely directs attention to the dynamic behavior of the adjustment process. Assuming the appropriateness of the situational assumption, other questions which must be addressed, in order to construct a particular situational explanation, concern the location of the income variable in the causal sequence, and the manner in which the linkage among variables differs by individual. These and related matters which impinge upon income maintenance are discussed after the logic of the cultural explanations has been outlined.

Cultural explanations—The main contrary thesis to situational explanations is represented by the cultural theories. In this perspective, individuals living in poverty share distinctive values and aspirations which set them apart from the dominant culture. Some of the values which are characteristic of this subculture are action seeking, impulse following, a strong present-time orientation, belief in luck or fate, and a predisposition toward authoritarianism. As derivative attributes, individuals subscribing to these values are generally hostile toward education (which is incompatible with action seeking and an orientation toward present-time gratification) and unable to identify with a job as a career.

Culture of poverty explanations, like much of functional theory, are weak in their ability to account for the emergence of the culture. The commonly presented view is that a poverty culture originates when a population has been economically depressed for a very long period of time. In this situation, values and aspirations develop which allow the population to achieve some modicum of success or status even in their deprived state. Individuals decide that the really important goals are ones which they can attain, that the standards according to which they should measure themselves are ones which they can reasonably compete for. Albert Cohen describes the adolescent gang culture in this vein: "Certain children are denied status in the respectable society because they cannot meet the criteria of the respectable status system. The delinquent subculture deals with these problems by providing criteria of status which these children can meet."

One assumption common to cultural explanations is that the values originating in this manner attain an existence which is relatively independent of the situational considerations which gave them birth. Moynihan suggests such a development in his controversial work on the Negro family. He is concerned with "whether the impact of economic disadvantage on the Negro community has gone on for so long that genuine structural change has occurred, so that a reversal in the course of economic events will no longer produce the expected response in social areas." He suggests that "three centuries of injustice have brought about deep-seated structural distortions in the life of the Negro American. At this point, the present tangle of pathology is capable of perpetuating itself without assistance from the white world" (U.S. Dept. of Labor). It is not our intention here to enter into a discussion concerning the substantive merit of his argument, only to illustrate a typical presentation of the origin of a culture of poverty.

The essential feature of a culture of poverty argument is that the value structure forms a self-maintaining system which perpetuates itself from generation to generation. By a self-maintaining value system we mean one in which the dominant norms and aspirations are accepted by members of the group, are interrelated in such a way as to sustain one another in an individual's internal organization of values, and are reinforced through social pressure upon deviants in the value setting institutions of the group (e.g., family, streetcorner gang).

According to a culture of poverty argument, then, a set of values has come into existence (perhaps as an adaptation to having lived in poverty for a long period) which discourages certain behavior such as investing time in education or developing a career orientation toward work. Were social agencies to intervene and increase the payoff or the probability of a return from these actions (by providing income maintenance to make the future more determinate and deferral of gratification more rational) the cultural values which support the status quo would be stressed by the traditional institutions of the group. Supplementing the effects from socialization to these values, individuals would be reminded of their obligations to kin, friends, and tradition, and thereby socially pressured to refrain from adopting life styles which are disvalued in the culture. As a consequence, one implication of a cultural explanation of poverty for income maintenance programs is that the behavioral correlates of low income may prove intractable to these manipulations and have to be treated directly. This, incidentally, is the type of policy recommendation which Moynihan makes in his assessment of the Negro family structure; and, in the context of a cultural explanation, it is an appropriate conclusion.

Conceptual distinctions between these explanations—In practice, circumstances in which a situational explanation provides an appropriate assessment for why individuals remain in poverty can be difficult to distinguish from ones in which a cultural explanation is valid. One reason is that "psychological maiming" may have occurred, and this would prevent individuals from responding to a change in conditions (such as might be provided by income maintenance), although one would predict such response from the values which they hold.

Psychological maiming refers to the complete demoralization of an individual as a result of repeated failure in the main institutions of society. For example, Liebow reports that the experience of being a dropout from school, continually having difficulty to find satisfying work, and failing to support adequately one's family, often generates low self-esteem and a fear of being tested. "Convinced of their own inadequacies, not only do they not seek out those few better paying jobs which test their resources, but they actively avoid them, gravitating in a mass to the menial, routine jobs which offer no challenge—and, therefore, pose no threat—to the already diminished images they have of themselves."

In this circumstance, the values to which the individual is socialized are those of the dominant culture, yet his ability to respond to an altered situation is drastically impaired. In Merton's paradigm, the condition is one of withdrawal or retreatism, and is exemplified by the "disreputable poor," the dregs, drifters, and hoboes. According to Gans, persons in this circumstance must be aided in reestablishing a link between values and behavior. "How much security, economic and other, must be provided for how long before people can take the risk of grasping at new opportunities and be able to give up present behavioral norms and associations?" Thus, the failure of an expected response to eventuate from a change in environment can result either when a causal explanation is correct but the linkage between the variables has been attenuated (psychological maiming), or when a functional (cultural) explanation is appropriate and the variable of interest is maintained at an approximately constant level through negative feedback.

Second, in circumstances for which a situational explanation is appropriate, the time to adjustment following the introduction of income maintenance may be considerable, incorrectly suggesting the operation of cultural values and aspirations which counter the requisite behavior for exploiting new conditions. However, the essence of a situational explanation is not that adjustments to an exogenous change are immediate; rather it is an absence of negative feedback structures which impede the adjustment. Thus, some behavioral correlates of low income, such as an inability to defer gratification, may be slow to disappear because poor persons may require several years of evidence that the income support payments are not a transitory phenomenon. Other possible adjustments, such as an increase in educational attainment by the family head, are unlikely ever to develop, even in the absence of cultural interference. The location of these individuals in the life cycle no longer permits a major response on this dimension. Unfortunately, existing analyses of adjustments to exogenously induced change rarely consider the dynamic aspects of the response. These studies are largely cross-sectional and focus on changes in the equilibrium relationships.

Third, even where a cultural explanation is appropriate, by drastically altering the environment, a *causal* response to the manipulated variable can often be effected. A self-regulating system such as a culture can maintain behavioral patterns homeostatically only for limited ranges of exogenously induced change. Therefore, concerning culturally supported behavior, the appropriate question is not whether it can be altered by exogenous manipulations but how extensive an input would be necessary. What is required is either a disintegration of the cultural values which normally prevent the response, which will occur if the traditional patterns are no longer viable in the altered context, or a readjustment of the culture of a new equilibrium in which the intended behavior is sanctioned (redefinition of the values). If alternative adaptations to a new situation are few, it is likely that the equilibrium would be in the direction of the dominant societal values, since these represent one adaptation with which all individuals have some familiarity. To illustrate, it may not be necessary to treat the instability of the Negro family directly, as Moynihan contends. Even accepting his evidence concerning the lack of responsiveness of the Negro family's stability to economic conditions, an *extensive* alteration of employment opportunities and the welfare structure may accomplish this purpose if it makes the matrifocal family less viable.

Elaborations and Implications for Research on Income Maintenance

In the preceding sections we have reviewed the logic of the main types of poverty theories and have indicated some immediate inferences to be been superficial in two ways. First, we have not differentiated among the various groups of persons in poverty to allow for the possibility that while a situational explanation may be appropriate to the circumstance of some, a cultural explanation may provide more accurate predictions of the response by others. Second, explanations should probably be behavior specific as well as population specific. As Gans has pointed out it is a mistake to view culture as a holistic system. In any culture some areas of behavior will tap few values or mores and, therefore, will respond situationally to exogenous interventions, while in other areas the culture will rigidly prescribe what is appropriate behavior.

Some early researchers into the relation between culture and poverty conceived of a universal poverty culture. Oscar Lewis, who has presented the most elaborate version of this type of explanation to account for the behavioral characteristics of low income individuals, argued that a poverty culture exists which "transcends regional, urban-rural, and national differences." While this contention of universality is probably extravagant, the reaction to the contrary evidence has been to discount the possibility that culture plays any role in the perpetuation of poverty. However, refuting the universality of this concept does not mean that culture is unimportant in every instance of poverty. What has been neglected is precisely the research which would permit specification of the range of conditions under which a cultural explanation is likely to be appropriate.

It is hardly controversial to claim that a diversity of groups live in poverty, and that much of the inter-individual variation in response to an anti-poverty program is likely to be explained by the group means. In designing income maintenance programs, for example, allowance is commonly made for different responses (in the size of the work disincentive, in educational investment) according to whether the family head is male or female, able-bodied or incapacitated, young or approaching retirement age. Our contention here is that *social* groupings will also differentiate among persons in their response to income maintenance and, furthermore, that cultural explanations will be appropriate for some of these groups, situational explanations for others. The importance of investigating the variance in the response is that alternate programs may be necessary to meet the needs of individuals who are unresponsive to an income support arrangement. To the extent that different groups can be associated with one or another of these theories (with respect to particular behavioral characteristics) their adjustments to income maintenance should be more predictable.

One factor which is likely to influence an individual's adaptation to income maintenance is ethnicity. Writing about the West Enders, an Italian community in Boston, Gans maintains that work, for them, is primarily means of obtaining income in order to maximize the pleasures of life within the family circle; type of work and considerations of job advancement are of secondary importance. ''Achievement and social mobility, for example, are group phenomena. In the current generation, in which the Italian is still effectively limited to blue-collar work, atypical educational and occupational mobility by the individual is frowned upon.''

The West Enders provide an example of an ethnic culture which would appear to retard economic mobility since group pressure functions to discourage exceptional attainment. However, an ethnic culture could also support this goal. The dominant Jewish-American and Japanese-American cultures are cases in point. In each, economic achievement and occupational status in the external society are encouraged by the group's values and also rewarded within the ethnic society.

More generally, there is considerable evidence that ethnic affiliation is an important component of social mobility, although there is some doubt as to whether the influence operates primarily through cultural values, oris a residue of the economic opportunities which were available to an immigrant group upon arrival to this country. There are reasons to believe that cultural factors play at least some part. Duncan and Duncan, using data which identify the country of origin for native white males of immigrant fathers, report that after controlling for father's SES (education and occupation), some 2.8 grades of schooling still separate the mean scores of the highest achieving and lowest achieving nationalorigin groups. ''Membership in a particular national-origin group can clearly constitute a substantial 'handicap' or 'bonus' in the stratification process'' apart from the class of social origin. Comparable findings are reported by Katzman in an analysis of the economic position of 14 ethnic groups: ''The educational at tain ment of the second generation is only weakly related to metropolitan educational opportunities and the educational level of their parents. Consequently, we interpret intergenerational gains as an expression of subcultural values.''

The intention of the above comments was to indicate that ethnicity may differentiate among persons in many areas of response to an income maintenance program. Extrapolating from the cited material we would suggest the following propositions:

(1) The *variability* of the response across individuals will be smaller among members of an ethnic group in which the traditional culture remains intact (in the sense of retaining distinctive values and institutions) than among individuals who lack an ethnic identity or for whom ethnicity no longer corresponds to a distinctive subculture in America.

(2) Although the presence of an ethnic culture should reduce the

within-group variance, the *direction and magnitude* of departure of the group mean from the average response by all persons in the program will reflect the particular cultural values. Consequently, among ethnic groups for whom cultural values influence the response to income maintenance, we can expect characteristic, and different, average group responses. Among individuals for whom the adaptation is situational rather than cultural, we can expect only a large variance in individual response.

These propositions must be qualified in two ways. First, as was indicated earlier, it is likely that with any ethnic group some behavioral correlates of poverty will be best approached through one type of theory, other characteristics through the second type of explanation. Second, the category of individuals upon whom the cultural mores tend to fall most heavily will probably differ by ethnic group. The constraints may be most severe on adult behavior, permitting children considerable flexibility in responding to altered conditions; or they may apply most rigidly to females, restricting their behavior, for example, as secondary wage earners. Research should, therefore, be directed at determining for which categories of persons, among ethnic groups with large numbers in poverty, behavior is likely to be prescribed by cultural mores, and what kinds of behavior are most likely to be so governed.

In the above discussion we have argued that ethnicity is likely to condition an individual's response to income maintenance in many important ways as it relates to whether his adaptation will be culturally specified or a situational adjustment. A second consideration involves the demographic and organizational characteristics of poor neighborhoods, since these factors will affect the strength of the cultural norms which can be exerted by an ethnic group.

In order for a culturally distinctive group to control behavior effectively it is necessary that an unambiguous rule exist for deciding when the norms of the external system are to be followed, and when the norms of the subculture are operative. Were this not the case, individuals would constantly find themselves cross-pressured, faced with contradictory specifications for behavior. Residential segregation provides one common way for avoiding this dilemma since the operation of the ethnic culture can be tied to geographic boundaries. Moreover, the fact that one resides with others of the same culture permits interpersonal pressure in support of the group's values to be exerted upon a deviant individual, especially when population turnover in the neighborhood is low, so that social bonds are stable. Extrapolating from these considerations, we can scale the likely ability of an ethnic group to control behavior effectively according to the following structural characteristics of a neighborhood:

(1) High cultural control over behavior	(2)	(3)	(4) Low cultural control over behavior
Single ethnic group in a neighborhood; stable population	Single ethnic group; geographically mobile population	Multi-ethnic neighborhood; stable population for the ethnic group under consideration	Multi-ethnic neighborhood; mobile population for the ethnic group under consideration

Holding neighborhood composition constant, a major determinant of a group's extent of control over its membership lies in its degree of institutional completeness (diversity of formal ethnic organizations). Residential segregation provides a setting which is conducive to the emergence of ethnic institutions—ethnic schools, churches, newspapers, and social clubs. However, the diversity of organizations which actually develops in a neighborhood will differ by ethnic group, reflecting such considerations as the magnitude of differences between the ethnic and native cultures. To the extent that these organizations do proliferate, an individual will have more of his social needs satisfied within the neighborhood, be embedded more thoroughly in ethnic networks, and be less likely to violate the expectations of the group. Such an argument suggests, for example, that the response to income maintenance by poor Italians (commonly an institutionally complete ethnic group) would be more closely governed by ethnic values and norms than would be the adjustment by poor Negroes (for whom ethnic institutions are less diverse).

In determining the response to an income maintenance program, these neighborhood characteristics would probably interact with ethnic membership in the following way: where an ethnic group does not place constraints on a behavioral response—deciding whether the wife should seek employment, for instance—the neighborhood social structure would be largely irrelevant to behavior. However, in cases where the ethnic values function either to prevent or encourage a particular adaptation, the organization of the neighborhood should be an important intervening consideration.

In the above discussion we have presented instances in which cultural groups are likely to influence the response to an exogenous intervention such as would be represented by income maintenance. The fact that an ethnic group may impede certain adjustments to income maintenance does not imply that the individuals actually desire to be poor. Rather, it is that the responses which are necessary in order to emerge from poverty are usually individualistic and detrimental to group cohesion, and may conflict with the values and mores which are central in the culture.

Conclusions

In the economic literature on income maintenance (Green, 1968; Kesselman, 1969), the analysis of work discentives and other effects from income manipulation proceeds as if, aside from universalistic considerations such as gender and physical condition of the family head, the poverty population can be treated as a homogeneous group. In this paper we have attempted to demonstrate the deficiency of that simplification. It is our contention that the diversity of adaptations to income maintenance which are likely to ensue cannot be adequately understood unless account is taken of the distinct social groups in poverty and of the different mechanisms which can maintain persons in that state.

Field experimentation with income maintenance is designed to answer a number of questions such as which behavioral correlates of poverty will respond to this intervention, what will be the time rate of response by different characteristics and, more generally, how should limited financial resources be allocated to maximize the rate at which individuals are removed from economic dependency. An appreciation of the different mechanisms through which persons are maintained in poverty is important to this enterprise for two reasons. This would allow for more efficient programming, enabling the range of response by different groups to be predicted beforehand. Also, if anti-poverty programs are actually to move persons to self-sufficiency and not merely maintain them above the poverty line, then an understanding of the diverse social contexts in which poor persons are embedded is a necessary preliminary for designing successful interventions.

"Alternative Conceptions of Poverty and Their Implications for Income Maintenance," from *Social Problems* 18 (Winter 1971), pp. 358–373.

B. Robert J. Lampman

Robert Lampman, professor of economics at the University of Wisconsin, thinks that poverty can be eliminated within the span of a single generation if we put our minds to it. The key is to recognize how the economic system at present selects some for poverty. Once we identify the forces that do the selecting we can counter them with effective measures. First are the events that place persons in poverty such as those that cause unemployment. Lampman proposes a variety of measures to deal with these. Second are the barriers that must be broken down which prevent the poor from having access to decent neighborhoods, education and needed services. Third are the deficiencies in ability and motivation which call for intensive educational and training programs to make the poor viable participants in the economy. There will be a continual need to study the comparative cost-benefit ratio of all programs so that they do not become wasteful or irrelevant.

Lampman's proposals are attractive in that they require little modification of the prevailing forces and institutions of our society and appeal to our conventional sense of practicality. But do they go far enough? Critics doubt that success in combating poverty can be achieved without some structural modifications, and they raise the question as to how the public assistance programs can be monitored and controlled so that they do not become obsolete or wasteful.

Approaches to the Reduction of Poverty

Why Poverty Persists

As background to strategic decisions, it is useful to categorize the causes of poverty in today's economy. But perhaps it is necessary first to brush aside the idea that there has to be some given amount of poverty. Most economists have long since given up the idea that a progressive society needs the threat of poverty to induce work and sobriety in the lower classes. Similarly, one can consign to folklore the ideas that some are rich only because others are poor and exploited, that if none were poor then necessary but unpleasant jobs would go undone, that the middle class has a psychological need to exclude a minority from above-poverty living standards, and that poverty is a necessary concomitant of the unemployment which necessarily accompanies economic growth.

Why, then, is it that there remains a minority of persons who are involuntarily poor in this affluent society? How does our system select the particular members for this minority? To the latter question we offer a three-part answer: (1) Events external to individuals select a number to be poor. (2) Social barriers of caste, class, and custom denominate persons with certain characteristics to run a high risk of being poor. (3) The market assigns a high risk of being poor to those with limited ability or motivations.

One cannot look at the data on who are the poor without sensing that many are poor because of events beyond their control. Over a third of the 35 million poor are children whose misfortune arises out of the chance assignment to poor parents. In some cases this poverty comes out of being members of unusually large families. Among the poor adults, about a third have either suffered a disability, premature death of the family breadwinner, or family dissolution. A considerable number have confronted a declining demand for services in their chosen occupation, industry, or place of residence. Some have outlived their savings or have lost them due to inflation or bank failure. For many persons who are otherwise ''normal'' poverty may be said to arise out of one or a combination of such happenings.

A second factor that operates in the selection of persons to be poor is the maintenance of social barriers in the form of caste, class, and custom. The clearest example of this, of course, is racial discrimination with regard to opportunities to qualify for and to obtain work. (It is perhaps worth emphasizing here that only a fifth of the present poor are nonwhite, and that only a minority of the nonwhites are presently poor.) Similar types of arbitrary barriers or market imperfections are observable in the case of sex, age, residence, religion, education, and seniority. They are formalized in employer hiring procedures, in the rules of unions and professional and trade associations, in governmental regulations concerning housing and welfare and other programs, and are informally expressed in customer preferences. Barriers, once established, tend to be reinforced from the poverty side by the alienated themselves. The poor tend to be cut off from not only opportunity but even from information about opportunity. A poverty subculture develops which sustains attitudes and values that are hostile to escape from poverty. These barriers combine to make events nonrandom; e.g., unemployment is slanted away from those inside the feudalistic walls of collective bargaining, disability more commonly occurs in jobs reserved for those outside the barriers, the subculture of poverty invites or is prone to self-realizing forecasts of disaster.

The third factor involved in selecting persons out of the affluent society to be poor is limited ability or motivation of persons to earn and to protect themselves against events and to fight their way over the barriers. To the extent that the market is perfect one can rationalize the selection for poverty (insofar as earnings alone are considered) on the basis of the abilities and skills needed by the market and the distribution of those abilities and skills in the population. But we note that ability is to some extent acquired or environmentally determined and that poverty tends to create personalities who will be de-selected by the market as inadequate on the basis of ability or motivation.

Countering "Events"

Approaches to the reduction of poverty can be seen as parallel to the causes or bases for selection recounted above. The first approach, then, is to prevent or counter the events or happenings which select some persons for poverty status. The poverty rate could be lessened by any reduction in early death, disability, family desertion, what Galbraith referred to as excessive procreation by the poor, or by containment of inflation and other hazards to financial security. Among the important events in this context the one most relevant to public policy consideration at this time is excessive unemployment. It would appear that if the recent level of over 5 percent unemployment could be reduced to 4 percent, the poverty rate would drop by about one percentage point. Further fall in the poverty rate would follow if—by retraining and relocation of some workers—long-term unemployment could be cut or if unemployment could be more widely shared with the nonpoor.

To the extent that events are beyond prevention, some, e.g., disability, can be countered by remedial measures. Where neither the preventive nor the remedial approach is suitable, only the alleviative measures of social insurance and public assistance remain. And the sufficiency of these measures will help determine the poverty rate and the size of the poverty income gap. It is interesting to note that our system of public income maintenance, which now pays out $35 billion in benefits per year, is aimed more at the problem of income insecurity of the middle class and at blocking returns to poverty than in facilitating exits from poverty for those who have never been out of poverty. The nonpoor have the major claim to social insurance benefits, the levels of which in most cases are not adequate in themselves to keep a family out of poverty. Assistance payments of $4 billion now go to 8 million persons, all of whom are in the ranks of poor, but about half of the 35 million poor receive neither assistance nor social insurance payments. One important step in the campaign against poverty would be to reexamine our insurance and assistance programs to discover ways in which they could be more effective in helping people to get out of poverty. Among the ideas to be considered along this line are easier eligibility for benefits, higher minimum benefits, incentives to earn while receiving benefits, ways to combine work-relief, retraining, rehabilitation, and relocation with receipt of benefits.

Among the several events that select people for poverty, the ones about which we have done the least by social policy are family break-up by other than death and the event of being born poor. Both of these could be alleviated by a family allowance system, which the U.S., almost alone among Western nations, lacks. We do, of course, have arrangements in the federal individual income tax for personal deductions and exemptions whereby families of different size and composition are ranked for the imposition of progressive rates. However, it is a major irony of this system that it does not extend the full force of its allowances for children to the really poor. In order to do so, the tax system could be converted to have negative as well as positive rates, paying out grants as well as forgiving taxes on the basis of already adopted exemptions and rates. At present there are almost $20 billion of unused exemptions and deductions, most of which relate to families with children. Restricting the plan to such families and applying a negative tax rate of, say 20 percent, to this amount would "yield" an allowance total of almost $4 billion. This would not in itself take many people out of poverty, but it would go a considerable distance toward closing the poverty income gap, which now aggregates about $12 billion.

It would, of course, be possible to go considerably further by this device without significantly impairing incentive to work and save. First, however, let me reject as unworkable any simple plan to assure a minimum income of $3,000. To make such an assurance would induce many now earning less than and even some earning slightly more than $3,000 to forego earnings opportunities and to accept the grant. Hence the poverty income gap of $12 billion would far understate the cost of such a minimum income plan. However, it would be practicable to enact a system of progressive rates articulated with the present income tax schedule. The present rates fall from 70 percent at the top to 14 percent at income just about $3,700 for a family of five, to zero percent for income below $3,700. The average negative tax rates could move, then, from zero percent to minus 14 percent for, say, the unused exemptions that total $500, to 20 percent for those that total $1,000 and 40 percent for those that total $3,700. This would amount to a minimum income of $1,480 for a family of five; it would retain positive incentives through a set of grants that would gradually diminish as earned income rose.

The total amount to be paid out (interestingly, this would be shown in the federal budget as a net reduction in tax collections) under such a program would obviously depend upon the particular rates selected, the definition of income used, the types of income-receiving units declared eligible, and the offsets made in public assistance payments. But it clearly could be more than the $4 billion mentioned in connection with the more limited plan of a standard 20 percent negative tax rate. At the outset it might involve half the poverty income gap and total about $6 billion. This amount is approximately equal to the total federal, state, and local taxes now paid by the poor. Hence it would amount to a remission of taxes paid. As the number in poverty fell, the amount paid out under this plan would in turn diminish.

Breaking Down Barriers

The approaches discussed thus far are consistent with the view that poverty is the result of events which happen to people. But there are other approaches, including those aimed at removing barriers which keep people in poverty. Legislation and private, volunteer efforts to assure equal educational and employment opportunities can make a contribution in this direction. Efforts to randomize unemployment by area redevelopment and relocation can in some cases work to break down "islands of poverty." Public policy can prevent or modify the forming of a poverty subculture by city zoning laws, by public housing and by regulations of private housing, by school redistricting, by recreational, cultural, and public health programs. It is curious that medieval cities built walls to keep poverty outside. Present arrangements often work to bottle it up inside cities or parts of cities and thereby encourage poverty to function as its own cause.

Improving Abilities and Motivations

The third broad approach to accelerated reduction of poverty relates to the basis for selection referred to above as limited ability or motivation. The process of economic growth works the poverty line progressively deeper into the ranks of people who are below average in ability or motivation, but meantime it should be possible to raise the ability and motivation levels of the lowest. It is interesting that few children, even those of below average ability, who are not born and raised in poverty, actually end up in poverty as adults. This suggests that poverty is to some extent an inherited disease. But it also suggests that if poor children had the same opportunities, including preschool training and remedial health care, as the nonpoor (even assuming no great breakthroughs of scientific understanding), the rate of escape from poverty would be higher. Even more fundamentally, we know that mental retardation as well as infant mortality and morbidity have an important causal connection with inadequate prenatal care, which in turn relates to low income of parents.

A belief in the economic responsiveness of poor youngsters to improved educational opportunities underlies policies advocated by many educational theorists from Bentham to Conant. And this widely shared belief no' doubt explains the emphasis which the Economic Opportunity Act places upon education and training. The appropriation under that Act, while it seems small relative to the poverty income gap, is large relative to present outlays for education of the poor. I would estimate that the half-billion dollars or so thereby added increases the national expenditure for this purpose by about one-seventh. To raise the level of educational expenditure for poor children—who are one-fifth of the nation's children but who consume about a tenth of educational outlay—to equal that of the average would cost in the neighborhood of $3 billion. Such an emphasis upon education and training is justified.

"*Approaches to the Reduction of Poverty*," *American Economic Review*, **55**:2 (**May 1965**), **pp. 521–529**.

C. Richard A. Cloward and Frances Fox Piven

Since the present laws actually entitle the poor to much more than they are getting (or at least such was the claim by the authors when this article was written), Cloward and Piven propose a massive drive to get more persons and families who are eligible for assistance onto the welfare rolls. Their immediate objective is to create a crisis, their ultimate one to obtain a national guaranteed annual income. The authors see the real obstacle to combating poverty as the conditional benefits that have been set up and which violate in many instances the civil rights of the poor. If a coalition of groups to organize the poor could be formed, the poor would have the beginnings of a constituency which in turn would provide a more solid basis for genuine reform. Present practices within the welfare system consist in setting up qualifications and restrictions which are largely self-serving and which prey upon the ignorance of welfare rights on the part of the poor. A drive to swell the welfare rolls would have the effect of creating a crisis of such magnitude that it would force legislative reform.

In considering such a proposal several questions arise. What are the costs as well as the benefits that it would entail? How should the burden of such a program be distributed? Would the private sector play a role in supporting a guaranteed income or would it fall exclusively upon the public sector? Would opportunity for jobs and job training be part of the program, or would these be left entirely to the operations of the free market?

A Strategy to End Poverty

How can the poor be organized to press for relief from poverty? How can a broad-based movement be developed and the current disarray of activist forces be halted? These questions confront, and confound, activists today. It is our purpose to advance a strategy which affords the basis for a convergence of civil rights organizations, militant anti-poverty groups and the poor. If this strategy were implemented, a political crisis would result that could lead to legislation for a guaranteed annual income and thus an end to poverty.

The strategy is based on the fact that a vast discrepancy exists between the benefits to which people are entitled under public welfare programs and the sums which they actually receive. This gulf is not recognized in a society that is wholly and self-righteously oriented toward getting people *off* the welfare rolls. It is widely known, for example, that nearly 8 million persons (half of them white) now subsist on welfare, but it is not generally known that for every person on the rolls at least one more probably meets existing criteria of eligibility but is not obtaining assistance.

The discrepancy is not an accident stemming from bureaucratic inefficiency; rather, it is an integral feature of the welfare system which, if challenged, would precipitate a profound financial and political crisis. The force for that challenge, and the strategy we propose, is a massive drive to recruit the poor *onto* the welfare rolls.

The distribution of public assistance has been a local and state responsibility, and that accounts in large part for the abysmal character of welfare practices. Despite the growing involvement of federal agencies in supervisory and reimbursement arrangements, state and local community forces are still decisive. The poor are most visible and proximate in the local community; antagonism toward them (and toward the agencies which are implicated with them) has always, therefore, been more intense locally than at the federal level. In recent years, local communities have increasingly felt class and ethnic friction generated by competition for neighborhoods, schools, jobs and political power. Public welfare systems are under the constant stress of conflict and opposition, made only sharper by the rising costs to localities of public aid. And, to accommodate this pressure, welfare practice everywhere has become more restrictive than welfare statute; much of the time it verges on lawlessness. Thus, public welfare systems try to keep their budgets down and their rolls low by failing to inform people of the rights available to them; by intimidating and shaming them to the degree that they are reluctant either to apply or to press claims, and by arbitrarily denying benefits to those who are eligible.

A series of welfare drives in large cities would, we believe, impel action on a new federal program to distribute income, eliminating the present public welfare system and alleviating the abject poverty which it perpetrates. Widespread campaigns to register the eligible poor for welfare aid, and to help existing recipients obtain their full benefits, would produce bureaucratic disruption in welfare agencies and fiscal disruption in local and state governments. These disruptions would generate severe political strains, and deepen existing divisions among elements in the big-city Democratic coalition: the remaining white middle class, the white working-class ethnic groups and the growing minority poor. To avoid a further weakening of that historic coalition, a national Democratic administration would be constrained to advance a federal solution to poverty that would override local welfare failures, local class and racial conflicts and local revenue dilemmas. By the internal disruption of local bureaucratic practices, by the furor over public welfare poverty, and by the collapse of current financing arrangements, powerful forces can be generated for major economic reforms at the national level.

The ultimate objective of this strategy—to wipe out poverty by establishing a guaranteed annual income—will be questioned by some. Because the ideal of individual social and economic mobility has deep roots, even activists seem reluctant to call for national programs to eliminate poverty by the outright redistribution of income. Instead programs are demanded to enable people to become economically competitive. But such programs are of no use to millions of today's poor. For example, one-third of the 35 million poor Americans are in families headed by females; these heads of family cannot be aided appreciably by job retraining, higher minimum wages, accelerated rates of economic growth, or employment in public works projects. Nor can the 5 million aged who are poor, nor those whose poverty results from the ill health of the wage earner. Programs to enhance individual mobility will chiefly benefit the very young, if not the as yet unborn. Individual mobility is no answer to the question of how to abolish the massive problem of poverty now.

It has never been the full answer. If many people in the past have found their way up from poverty by the path of individual mobility, many others have taken a different route. Organized labor stands out as a major example. Although many American workers never yielded their dreams of individual achievement, they accepted and practiced the principle that each can benefit only as the status of workers as a whole is elevated. They bargained for collective mobility, not for individual mobility; to promote their fortunes in the aggregate, not to promote the prospects of one worker over another. And if each finally found himself in the same relative economic relationship to his fellows as when he began, it was nevertheless clear that all were infinitely better off. That fact has sustained the labor movement in the face of a counter pull from the ideal of individual achievement.

But many of the contemporary poor will not rise from poverty by organizing to bargain collectively. They either are not in the labor force or are in such marginal and dispersed occupations (e.g., domestic servants) that it is extremely difficult to organize them. Compared with other groups, then, many of today's poor cannot secure a redistribution of income by organizing within the institution of private enterprise. A federal program of income redistribution has become necessary to elevate the poor en masse from poverty.

Several ways have been proposed for redistributing income through the federal government. It is not our purpose here to assess the relative merits of these plans, which are still undergoing debate and clarification. Whatever mechanism is eventually adopted, however, it must include certain features if it is not merely to perpetuate in a new guise the present evils of the public welfare system.

First, adequate levels of income must be assured. (Public welfare levels are astonishingly low; indeed, states typically define a "minimum" standard of living and then grant only a percentage of it, so that families are held well below what the government itself officially defines as the poverty level.) Furthermore, income should be distributed without requiring that recipients first divest themselves of their assets, as public welfare now does, thereby pauperizing families as a condition of sustenance.

Second, the right to income must be guaranteed, or the oppression of the welfare poor will not be eliminated. Because benefits are conditional under the present public welfare system, submission to arbitrary governmental power is regularly made the price of sustenance. People have been coerced into attending literacy classes or participating in medical or vocational rehabilitation regimes, on pain of having their benefits terminated. Men are forced into labor on virtually any terms lest they forfeit their welfare aid. One can prize literacy, health and work, while still vigorously opposing the right of government to compel compliance with these values.

Conditional benefits thus result in violations of civil liberties throughout the nation, and in a pervasive oppression of the poor. And these violations are not less real because the impulse leading to them is altruistic and the agency is professional. If new systems of income distribution continue to permit the professional bureaucracies to choose when to give and when to withhold financial relief, the poor will once again be surrendered to an arrangement in which their rights are diminished in the name of overcoming their vices. Those who lead an attack on the welfare system must therefore be alert to the pitfalls of inadequate but placating reforms which give the appearance of victory to what is in truth defeat. . .

In order to generate a crisis, the poor must obtain benefits which they have forfeited. Until now, they have been inhibited from asserting claims by self-protective devices within the welfare system: its capacity to limit information, to intimidate applicants, to demoralize recipients, and arbitrarily to deny lawful claims.

Ignorance of welfare rights can be attacked through a massive educational campaign. Brochures describing benefits in simple, clear language, and urging people to seek their full entitlements, should be distributed door to door in tenements and public housing projects, and deposited in stores, schools, churches and civic centers. Advertisements should be placed in newspapers; spot announcements should be made on radio. Leaders of social, religious, fraternal and political groups in the slums should also be enlisted to recruit the eligible to the rolls. The fact that the campaign is intended to inform people of their rights under a government program, that it is a civic education drive, will lend it legitimacy.

But information alone will not suffice. Organizers will have to become advocates in order to deal effectively with improper rejections and terminations. The advocate's task is to appraise the circumstances of each case, to argue its merits before welfare, to threaten legal action if satisfaction is not given. In some cases, it will be necessary to contest decisions by requesting a "fair hearing" before the appropriate state supervisory agency; it may occasionally be necessary to sue for redress in the courts. Hearings and court actions will require lawyers, many of whom, in cities like New York, can be recruited on a voluntary basis, especially under the banner of a movement to end poverty by a strategy of asserting legal rights. However, most cases will not require an expert knowledge of law, but only of welfare regulations; the rules can be learned by laymen, including welfare recipients themselves (who can help to man "information and advocacy" centers). To aid workers in these centers, handbooks should be prepared describing welfare rights and the tactics to employ in claiming them.

Advocacy must be supplemented by organized demonstrations to create a climate of militancy that will overcome the invidious and immobilizing attitudes which many potential recipients hold toward being "on welfare." In such a climate, many more poor people are likely to become their own advocates and will not need to rely on aid from organizers. . . .

Movements that depend on involving masses of poor people have generally failed in America. Why would the proposed strategy to engage the poor succeed?

First, this plan promises immediate economic benefits. This is a point of some importance because, whereas America's poor have not been moved in any number by radical political ideologies, they have sometimes been moved by their economic interests. Since radical movements in America have rarely been able to provide visible economic incentives, they have usually failed to secure mass participation of any kind. The conservative "business unionism" of organized labor is explained by this fact, for membership enlarged only as unionism paid off in material benefits. Union leaders have understood that their strength derives almost entirely from their capacity to provide economic rewards to members. Although leaders have increasingly acted in political spheres, their influence has been directed chiefly to matters of governmental policy affecting the well-being of organized workers. The same point is made by the experience of rent strikes in

Northern cities. Their organizers were often motivated by radical ideologies, but tenants have been attracted by the promise that housing improvements would quickly be made if they withheld their rent.

Second, for this strategy to succeed, one need not ask more of most of the poor than that they claim lawful benefits. Thus the plan has the extraordinary capability of yielding mass influence *without* mass participation, at least as the term "participation" is ordinarily understood. Mass influence in this case stems from the consumption of benefits and does not require that large groups of people be involved in regular organizational roles.

Moreover, this kind of mass influence is cumulative because benefits are continuous. Once eligibility for basic food and rent grants is established, the drain on local resources persists indefinitely. Other movements have failed precisely because they could not produce continuous and cumulative influence. In the Northern rent strikes, for example, tenant participation depended largely on immediate grievances; as soon as landlords made the most minimal repairs, participation fell away and with it the impact of the movement. Efforts to revive tenant participation by organizing demonstrations around broader housing issues (e.g., the expansion of public housing) did not succeed because the incentives were not immediate.

Third, the prospects for mass influence are enhanced because this plan provides a practical basis for coalition between poor whites and poor Negroes. Advocates of low-income movements have not been able to suggest how poor whites and poor Negroes can be united in an expressly lower-class movement. Despite pleas of some Negro leaders for joint action on programs requiring integration, poor whites have steadfastly resisted making common cause with poor Negroes. By contrast, the benefits of the present plan are as great for whites as for Negroes. In the big cities, at least, it does not seem likely that poor whites, whatever their prejudices against Negroes or public welfare, will refuse to participate when Negroes aggressively claim benefits that are unlawfully denied to them as well. One salutary consequence of public information campaigns to acquaint Negroes with their rights is that many whites will be made aware of theirs. Even if whites prefer to work through their own organizations and leaders, the consequences will be equivalent to joining with Negroes. For if the object is to focus attention on the need for new economic measures by producing a crisis over the dole, anyone who insists upon extracting maximum benefits from public welfare is in effect part of a coalition and is contributing to the cause.

The ultimate aim of this strategy is a new program for direct income distribution. What reason is there to expect that the federal government will enact such legislation in response to a crisis in the welfare system?

We ordinarily think of major legislation as taking form only through established electoral processes. We tend to overlook the force of crisis in precipitating legislative reform, partly because we lack a theoretical framework by which to understand the impact of major disruptions.

By crisis, we mean a *publicly visible* disruption in some institutional sphere. Crisis can occur spontaneously (e.g., riots) or as the intended result of tactics of demonstration and protest which either generate institutional disruption or bring unrecognized disruption to public attention. Public trouble is a political liability; it calls for action by political leaders to stabilize the situation. Because crisis usually creates or exposes conflict, it threatens to produce cleavages in a political consensus which politicians will ordinarily act to avert.

Although crisis impels political action, it does not itself determine the selection of specific solutions. Political leaders will try to respond with proposals which work to their advantage in the electoral process. Unless group cleavages form around issues and demands, the politican has great latitude and tends to proffer only the minimum action required to quell disturbances without risking existing electoral support. Spontaneous disruptions, such as riots, rarely produce leaders who articulate demands; thus no terms are imposed, and political leaders are permitted to respond in ways that merely restore a semblance of stability without offending other groups in a coalition.

When, however, a crisis is defined by its participants—or by other activated groups—as a matter of clear issues and preferred solutions, terms are imposed on the politicians' bid for their support. Whether political leaders then design solutions to reflect these terms depends on a two-fold calculation: first, the impact of the crisis and the issues it raises on existing alignments and, second, the gains or losses in support to be expected as a result of a proposed resolution.

If this strategy for crisis would intensify group cleavages, a federal income solution would not further exacerbate them. The demands put forward during recent civil rights drives in the Northern cities aroused the opposition of huge majorities. Indeed, such fierce resistance was evoked (e.g., school boycotts followed by counter-boycotts), that accessions by political leaders would have provoked greater political turmoil than the protests themselves, for profound class and ethnic interests are at stake in the employment, educational and residential institutions of our society. By contrast, legislative measures to provide direct income to the poor would permit national Democratic leaders to cultivate ghetto constituencies without unduly antagonizing other urban groups, as is the case when the battle lines are drawn over schools, housing or jobs. Furthermore, a federal income program would not only redeem local governments from the immediate crisis but would permanently relieve them of the financially and politically onerous burdens of public welfare—a function which generates support from none and hostility from many, not least of all welfare recipients.

We suggest, in short, that if pervasive institutional reforms are not yet possible, requiring as they do expanded Negro political power and the development of new political alliances, crisis tactics can nevertheless be employed to secure particular reforms in the short run by exploiting weaknesses in current political alignments. Because the urban coalition stands weakened by group conflict today, disruption and threats of disaffection will count powerfully, provided that national leaders can respond with solutions which retain the support of ghetto constituencies while avoiding new group antagonisms and bolstering the urban party apparatus. These are the conditions, then, for an effective crisis strategy in the cities to secure an end to poverty.

No strategy, however confident its advocates may be, is foolproof. But if unforeseen contingencies thwart this plan to bring about new federal legislation in the field of poverty, it should also be noted that there would be gains even in defeat. For one thing, the plight of many poor people would be somewhat eased in the course of an assault upon public welfare. Existing recipients would come to know their rights and how to defend them, thus acquiring dignity where none now exists; and millions of dollars in withheld welfare benefits would become available to potential recipients now—not several generations from now. Such an attack should also be welcome to those currently concerned with programs designed to equip the young to rise out of poverty (e.g., Head Start), for surely children learn more readily when the oppressive burden of financial insecurity is lifted from the shoulders of their parents. And those seeking new ways to engage the Negro politically should remember that public resources have always been the fuel for low-income urban political organization. If organizers can deliver millions of dollars in cash benefits to the ghetto masses, it seems reasonable to expect that the masses will deliver their loyalties to their benefactors. At least, they have always done so in the past.

"A Strategy To End Poverty," *The Nation*, 202:18 (May 2, 1966), pp. 510–517.

D. Milton Friedman

Milton Friedman, a classical libertarian and champion of the free enterprise system, thinks we can avoid the whole welfare burden by adopting a negative income tax. Poverty, he contends, is solely a matter of economic need. It can be attacked by allowing those who fall below a certain level of income to receive funds to supplement their wages. Compensation will depend upon the degree to which such persons fall below the minimum standard.

The proposal has particular appeal because it promises to do away with all the complexities and expenses of government programs. But it entails a number of questions that need to be addressed, such as who will set the minimum income level and on what basis, whether the poor will have any voice in the matter, whether there will be any incentives offered to assist and encourage persons out of poverty, whether any medical care will be provided (especially for children of the poor), and whether any measures will be offered to ensure opportunity, not only of employment, but of education and training as well. The crucial concept is that of the minimum income itself. The poor and the non-poor may have quite different conceptions of it. How arrive at a figure that is truly "just"?

The Alleviation of Poverty

The extraordinary economic growth experienced by Western countries during the past two centuries and the wide distribution of the benefits of free enterprise have enormously reduced the extent of poverty in any absolute sense in the capitalistic countries of the West. But poverty is in part a relative matter, and even in these countries, there are clearly many people living under conditions that the rest of us label as poverty.

One recourse, and in many ways the most desirable, is private charity. It is noteworthy that the heyday of laissez-faire, the middle and late nineteenth century in Britain and the United States, saw an extraordinary proliferation of private eleemosynary organizations and institutions. One of the major costs of the extension of governmental welfare activities has been the corresponding decline in private charitable activities.

It can be argued that private charity is insufficient because the benefits from it accrue to people other than those who make the gifts—again, a neighborhood effect. I am distressed by the sight of poverty; I am benefited by its alleviation; but I am benefited equally whether I or someone else pays for its alleviation; the benefits of other people's charity therefore partly accrue to me. To put it differently, we might all of us be willing to contribute to the relief of poverty, *provided* everyone else did. We might not be willing to contribute the same amount without such assurance. In small communities, public pressure can suffice to realize the proviso even with private charity. In the large impersonal communities that are increasingly coming to dominate our society, it is much more difficult for it to do so.

Suppose one accepts, as I do, this line of reasoning as justifying governmental action to alleviate poverty; to set, as it were, a floor under the standard of life of every person in the community. There remain the questions, how much and how. I see no way of deciding "how much" except in terms of the amount of taxes—by which I mean the great bulk of us—are willing to impose on ourselves for the purpose. The question, "how," affords more room for speculation.

Two things seem clear. First, if the objective is to alleviate poverty, we should have a program directed at helping the poor. There is every reason to help the poor man who happens to be a farmer, not because he is a farmer but because he is poor. The program, that is, should be designed to help people as people not as members of particular occupational groups or age groups or wage-rate groups or labor organizations or industries. This is a defect of farm programs, general old-age benefits, minimum-wage laws, pro-union legislation, tariffs, licensing provisions of crafts or professions, and so on in seemingly endless profusion. Second, so far as possible the program should, while operating through the market, not distort the market or impede its functioning. This is a defect of price supports, minimum-wage laws, tariffs and the like.

The arrangement that recommends itself on purely mechanical grounds is a negative income tax. We now have an exemption of $600 per person under the federal income tax (plus a minimum 10 per cent flat deduction). If an individual receives $100 taxable income, i.e., an income of $100 in excess of the exemption and deductions, he pays a tax. Under the proposal, if his taxable income minus $100, i.e., $100 less than the exemption plus deductions, he would pay a negative tax, i.e., receive a subsidy. If the rate of subsidy were, say, 50 per cent, he would receive $50. If he had no income at all, and, for simplicity, no deductions, and the rate were constant, he would receive $300. He might receive more than this if he had deductions, for example, for medical expenses, so that his income less deductions, was negative even before subtracting the exemption. The rates of subsidy could, of course, be graduated just as the rates of tax above the exemption are. In this way, it would be possible to set a floor below which no man's net income (defined now to include the subsidy) could fall—in the simple example $300 per person. The precise floor set would depend on what the community could afford.

The advantages of this arrangement are clear. It is directed specifically at the problem of poverty. It gives help in the form most useful to the individual, namely, cash. It is general and could be substituted for the host of special measures now in effect. It makes explicit the cost borne by society. It operates outside the market. Like any other measures to alleviate poverty, it reduces the incentives of those helped to help themselves, but it does not eliminate that incentive entirely, as a system of supplementing incomes up to some fixed minimum would. An extra dollar earned always means more money available for expenditure.

No doubt there would be problems of administration, but these seem to me a minor disadvantage, if they be a disadvantage at all. The system would fit directly into our current income tax system and could be administered along with it. The present tax system covers the bulk of income recipients and the necessity of covering all would have the by-product of improving the operation of the present income tax. More important, if enacted as a substitute for the present rag bag of measures directed at the same end, the total administrative burden would surely be reduced.

A few brief calculations suggest also that this proposal could be far less costly in money, let alone in the degree of governmental intervention involved, than our present collection of welfare measures. Alternatively, these calculations can be regarded as showing how wasteful our present measures are, judged as measures for helping the poor.

In 1961, government amounted to something like $33 billion (federal, state, and local) on direct welfare payments and programs of all kinds: old age assistance, social security benefit payments, aid to dependent children, general assistance, farm price support programs, public housing, etc. I have excluded veterans' benefits in making this calculation. I have also made no allowance for the direct and indirect costs of such measures as minimum-wage laws, tariffs, licensing provisions, and so on, or for the costs of public health activities, state and local expenditures on hospitals, mental institutions, and the like.

There are approximately 57 million consumer units (unattached individuals and families) in the United States. The 1961 expenditures of $33 billion would have financed outright cash grants of nearly $6,000 per consumer unit to the 10 per cent with the lowest incomes. Such grants would have raised their incomes above the average for all units in the United States. Alternatively, these expenditures would have financed grants of nearly $3,000 per consumer unit to the 20 per cent with the lowest incomes. Even if one went so far as that one-third whom New Dealers were fond of calling ill-fed, ill-housed, and ill-clothed, 1961 expenditures would have financed grants of nearly $2,000 per consumer unit, roughly the sum which, after allowing for the change in the level of prices, was the income which separated the lower one-third in the middle 1930's from the upper two-thirds. Today, fewer than one-eighth of consumer units have an income, adjusted for the change in the level of prices, as low as that of the lowest third in the middle 1930's.

Clearly, these are all far more extravagant programs than can be justified to "alleviate poverty" even by a rather generous interpretation of that term. A program which *supplemented* the incomes of the 20 per cent of the consumer units with the lowest incomes so as to raise them to the lowest income of the rest would cost less than half of what we are now spending.

The major disadvantage of the proposed negative income tax is its political implications. It establishes a system under which taxes are imposed on some to pay subsidies to others. And presumably, these others have a vote. There is always the danger that instead of being an arrangement under which the great majority tax themselves willingly to help an unfortunate minority, it will be converted into one under which a majority imposes taxes for its own benefit on an unwilling minority. Because this proposal makes the process so explicit, the danger is perhaps greater than with other measures. I see no solution to this problem except to rely on the self-restraint and good will of the electorate.

Writing about a corresponding problem—British old-age pensions— in 1914, Dicey said, "Surely a sensible and a benevolent man may well ask himself whether England as a whole will gain by enacting that the receipt of poor relief, in the shape of a pension, shall be consistent with the pensioner's retaining the right to join in the election of a Member of Parliament."

The verdict of experience in Britain on Dicey's question must as yet be regarded as mixed. England did move to universal suffrage without the disfranchisement of either pensioners or other recipients of state aid. And there has been an enormous expansion of taxation of some for the benefit of others, which must surely be regarded as having retarded Britain's growth, and so may not even have benefited most of those who regard themselves as on the receiving end. But these measures have not destroyed, at least as yet, Britain's liberties or its predominantly capitalistic system. And, more important, there have been some signs of a turning of the tide and of the exercise of self-restraint on the part of the electorate.

Liberalism and Egalitarianism

The heart of the liberal philosophy is a belief in the dignity of the individual, in his freedom to make the most of his capacities and opportunities according to his own lights, subject only to the proviso that he not interfere with the freedom of other individuals to do the same. This implies a belief in the equality of men in one sense; in their inequality in another.

Each man has an equal right to freedom. This is an important and fundamental right precisely because men are different, because one man will want to do different things with his freedom than another, and in the process can contribute more than another to the general culture of the society in which many men live.

The liberal will therefore distinguish sharply between equality of rights and equality of opportunity, on the one hand, and material equality or equality of outcome on the other. He may welcome the fact that a free society in fact tends toward greater material equality than any other yet tried. But he will regard this as a desirable by-product of a free society, not its major justification. He will welcome measures that promote both freedom and equality—such as measures to eliminate monopoly power and to improve the operation of the market. He will regard private charity directed at helping the less fortunate as an example of the proper use of freedom. And he may approve state action toward ameliorating poverty as a more effective way in which the great bulk of the community can achieve a common objective. He will do so with regret, however, at having to substitute compulsory for voluntary action.

The egalitarian will go this far, too. But he will want to go further. He will defend taking from some to give to others, not as a more effective means whereby the "some" can achieve an objective they want to achieve, but on grounds of "justice." At this point, equality comes sharply into conflict with freedom; one must choose. One cannot be both an egalitarian, in this sense, and a liberal.

"The Alleviation of Poverty," from *Capitalism and Freedom*. Chicago: University of Chicago Press, 1962, pp. 190–195.

E. Michael Harrington

Michael Harrington, probably the best-known advocate of socialism in this country, declares that even the welfare state with all of its relief programs will not do justice to the problem of poverty. The existing forms of capitalism systematically exclude a certain segment of the population from sharing the wealth. Furthermore, they make it impossible for our society to develop any long-term and comprehensive economic plan that would deal with poverty effectively. Although Harrington acknowledges that welfare programs offer some benefits, they are at best stopgap measures. Even so, they seldom meet real human need.

Harrington proposes a socialism brought about by democratic means. He believes it possible for a coalition of groups within America to join with the poor to bring about structural changes that would redistribute the wealth and maintain greater equality of compensation. In spite of all the modifications that have been made over the years to the laissez-faire system, he asks whether any amount of alteration will remove its inherent destructive tendencies: its favoring of the affluent classes, its emphasis on short-term profits, its inability to provide for public goods and services, its discriminatory tax structure, and its endemic production of unemployment.

Some advocates of capitalism insist that the system has never been given a proper chance to work at optimum efficiency in this country, and that many of the modifications, especially the welfare system, have brought more ill than good. Thus the libertarians have joined the voices of socialism in criticizing existing conditions. But Harrington's main point of attack is that capitalism in any form means, ultimately, liberty for some at the expense of others. The only cure is more control and planning at the highest level of government, not only to curb capitalism's excesses but to transform some of its industries into publicly-owned and operated ones for the benefit of all.

Just what the full consequences of the socialist proposal are remains a matter of some conjecture since we have never experienced this form of economy. There emerge a number of concerns, such as how power shall be distributed, what safeguards will be established to prevent abuse of power in the hands of those who plan and control, and what lines shall be drawn between those aspects of our life that will be planned and those that will be left for individuals and private groups to determine. Finally, what role will be given to the poor in such a society? Will they be included in the social planning? What measures would be taken to prevent the general blueprint from merely following the interests of the prevailing middle class in our society?

Why We Need Socialism in America

America needs socialism. Our technology has produced unprecedented wealth, rotted great cities, threatened the very air and water, and embittered races, generations, and social classes.

Our vision of society, even when most liberal, is too conservative to resolve these contradictions, for they are aspects of a system that has a deep, even principled commitment to the wrong priorities. And while significant reforms—often socialist in inspiration—have modified some of the extreme forms of capitalist injustice, the post-Keynesian welfare state still allows huge corporations to make decisions of fundamental social importance without consulting either those who are affected or those who work for them.

But isn't it an act of leftist nostalgia to indict American society in this way? Today, one is told, the United States is the richest country in the history of mankind, and its remaining problems can be taken care of by pragmatic technicians acting within the framework of the welfare state.

It is precisely this conventional assumption about our present and future that I propose to challenge. I will show that our affluence is so misshapen that it does not even meet the needs of the majority of the people. The most humane of technocrats cannot cope with the basic causes of these antisocial policies, if only because they are located in an entrenched and possessive system of power. Only a democratic mass movement could challenge this vested interest in our current crises. And it is just possible that the "success" of American capitalism will accomplish what its sweatshops failed to do: make socialism politically relevant.

I say these things with a full knowledge of the ways in which the socialist idea has been confused, betrayed, and eviscerated during the past 150 years. Indeed, one of the aims of this essay is to try to face up to these difficulties with candor and to make the idea of socialism more precise. If that attempt is successful, what will emerge at the end of this study will not be the promise of a magical cure-all to bring complete and eternal happiness to all men but a more modest yet still audacious program for making America a good society.

Is Reform of the Welfare State Enough?

There are three basic reasons why the reform of the welfare state will not solve our most urgent problems:

- the class structure of capitalist society vitiates, or subverts, almost every such effort toward social justice;

- private, corporate power cannot tolerate the comprehensive and democratic planning we desperately need;
- and even if these first two obstacles to providing every citizen with a decent house, income, and job were overcome, the system still has an inherent tendency to make affluence self-destructive.

In thus documenting the limits of the welfare state it may seem that I am contemptuous of past reforms or of those liberals who do not share my conviction that there must be fundamental, structural change. Nothing could be further from the truth. The welfare state was an enormous advance over the cruelty and indifference to human suffering that characterized early capitalism. It was achieved through struggle and great sacrifice—sometimes of life itself—on the part of "ordinary" people who, even though they had usually been denied an adequate education, tutored the wealthy in some of the fundamentals of social decency. And to the extent that there is a mass "left wing" in the United States, it is composed largely of precisely those groups—trade unionists, minorities, middle-class idealists—which fought these great battles and are determined to preserve the gains they brought.

Far from being simply a matter of keeping the record straight, this point has profound political implications for the future. It is important that socialists demonstrate the inherent inability of the welfare state, based as it is upon a capitalist economy and social structure, to deal with problems that demand anticapitalist allocations of resources. But that does not mean, as some young leftists in recent times have thought, that the welfare state is to be dismissed as a "fraud" that prevents the people from coming to truly radical conclusions. For if millions of Americans are to become socialists they will do so because, in the struggle to make that welfare state respond to their immediate needs they will have discovered that they must go beyond it. If socialists were arrogantly to dismiss these battles as irrelevant, they would play no role when masses of their fellow citizens turned left.

Socialists, then, must be in the forefront of every fight to defend and extend the welfare state, even as they criticize its inability to solve fundamental problems and even as they propose alternatives to it. In this context, the following analysis of the severe limits capitalism imposes upon the welfare state is designed not to prove that liberals are foolish and deluded, but that their liberal values can only be completely realized on the basis of a socialist program.

The welfare state, for all its value, tends to provide benefits in inverse relationship to human need. And not—the point is crucial—because there is a conspiracy of the affluent, but as a "natural consequence of the division of society into unequal social classes."

Through vigorous and radical reforms it is possible to offset—though not to remove—this inherent tendency within capitalist society to distribute public benefits according to the inequalities of private wealth. Any movement that attempts to carry out such reforms will be going against the grain of the system itself. This has not kept socialists from participating in every one of these struggles, nor will it in the future. But if the gains are to be permanent, if they are not to be reversed when a period of social innovation is followed by a swing back to capitalist normality, then there must be basic, structural changes. Instead of episodic victories within an antisocial environment, there must be a concerted effort to create a new human environment.

How Inequality is Built into the System

The class divisions of welfare capitalism which are the root cause of this problem are not, it must be stressed, simply unfair in some abstract sense. Were that the case, a sophisticated conservative argument might be persuasive: since to some extent the growth of the economy benefits everyone, even those who are worst off, there is no point in endangering these gains on behalf of a vision of egalitarianism. What really concerns the poor, this argument continues, is not the rise or fall of their *relative* share of affluence but the steady increase in their absolute standard of living. In fact, however, inequality means not merely that there are sharply unequal proportions of goods distributed among the various social sectors of the population. It also signifies a socioeconomic process, at once dynamic and destructive, which determines that public and private resources shall be spent in an increasingly antisocial way, thereby threatening the well-being of the entire society.

Housing is a crucial case in point. Even under liberal administrations, the government has been much more solicitous about the comfort of the rich than the shelter of the poor. Not only is this policy morally outrageous; it has had disastrous social consequences. Yet it must be emphasized that in thus investing billions in the creation of public problems, Washington did not act maliciously but only followed—unconsciously, automatically, "naturally"—the priorities structured into our society's class divisions. Thus:

• in 1962 the value of a single tax deduction to the 20 percent of Americans with the highest incomes was worth twice as much as all the monies spent on public housing for the one-fifth who were poorest, and this figure does

not even take into account the government support for below-market rates
of interest to build suburbia;
- in 1969, the *Wall Street Journal* reported, the $2.5 billion for urban free-
ways was a far greater subsidy to car owners who daily fled the central city
than was the $175 million subsidy to mass transit, and Richard Nixon's
1970 Budget continued this perverse allocation of resources by providing
public transportation with only 6 percent of the funds assigned to highways;
- as the National Commission on Civil Disorders (the "Riot Commission"
of 1968) computed the figures, during roughly the same 30-year period the
government helped to construct over 10 million housing units for home
builders, i.e. for the middle class and the rich, but provided only 650,000
units of low-cost housing for the poor.

Skewed Priorities and Social Consequences

It would be a mistake to think Washington discriminated only against
the poor. For, as a White House Conference told President Johnson in
1966, *the entire lower half of the American population is excluded from the
market for new housing,* a market that could not exist without massive federal support. This point needs special emphasis if only because many people, with the best of intentions, concluded from the rediscovery of poverty
in America in the sixties that the bulk of the nation was affluent while only
a minority was poor. The statistics, far from describing a simple division
between the rich and the poverty-stricken, show that we have in this country a *majority*—composed of the poor, the near-poor, more than half the
workers and lower-middle class—which does not even have a "moderate
standard of living" as defined by the government.

When Washington used its powers to improve conditions for a wealthy
elite, the poor suffered most because they had the most urgent claim on the
funds thus squandered on the upper class; but a majority of the people, including tens of millions who were not poor, were also deprived of benefits
that should have rightfully been theirs. Worse, in carrying out these discriminatory policies, the federal programs did positive harm to those most
in need. As an American Presidential commission recently reported, ". . .
over the last decades, government action through urban renewal, highway
programs, demolitions on public housing sites, code enforcement, and
other programs has destroyed more housing for the poor than government
at all levels has built for them." But then this is a familiar injustice: "Fifty
years ago," wrote Alvin Schorr in 1968, "a British Royal Commission for
Inquiry into the Housing of the Working Classes observed, with dismay,
that poor people rarely benefited when land was cleared and model housing
erected."

In the America of the seventies these fantastically skewed priorities will have momentous social consequences. For Washington has, in effect, been aggravating the very social problems to which it points with alarm. By financing the flight of the middle class from the metropolis and helping industry locate in the suburbs, the central city has been allowed to rot—with federal encouragement. As a result such related evils as violence, bitter old age, intensified racism, the decay of the traditional centers of culture, all grew worse. A study commissioned by the government and chaired by Milton Eisenhower gave the darkest view of these trends. The National Commission on the Causes and Prevention of Violence said that, "lacking effective public action," the centers of the great American cities would be safe only in the daytime when crowds gave the individual a sense of security, and that they would be dangerous and empty at night. The big downtown apartment buildings would become "fortified cells for upper-middle and high-income populations living at prime locations in the city." The ghettos would become "places of terror with widespread crime, perhaps entirely out of police control during nighttime hours." And the surburbs would be ringed by freeways patrolled by lightly armored cars.

So the government's discriminatory social policies have done much more than to exacerbate inequality; they have helped to promote a fantastic anti-design for living. How then can we explain why sincere and dedicated men—as those who presided over these disastrous programs often were— would lavish public funds to aggravate social problems? The answer is to be found in the class character of American society and in the commercial logic which both derives from it and pervades governmental decisions.

The 1969 Report of the Council of Economic Advisers provides candid documentation of this pattern. "Investing in new housing for low-income families—particularly in big cities—is usually a losing proposition," the Council said. "Indeed the *most profitable investment* is often one that demolishes homes of low-income families to make room for business and higher-income families." (Emphasis added.) It is obvious that the criterion of profitability to which the Council refers is private since, as the gloomy projections of the Violence Commission demonstrate, the social cost of the present system is bankrupting the society. Yet precisely this private calculus is the one the government follows. As the Urban Problems Commission put it, ". . . renewal was and is too often looked upon as a federally financed gimmick to provide relatively cheap land for a miscellany of profitable or prestigious enterprises."

In a society based on class inequality and suffused with commercial values, it just doesn't "make sense" to waste resources on social uses or beauty—or anything that cannot be quantified in dollars and cents. Our legislators, drawn almost exclusively from the middle and upper classes, cannot bring themselves to forget those principles that are sacred to a private economy. To them it seems logical to invest the federal dollar in undertakings that run the lowest risk and will show the highest and most immediate return.

Housing is only one example of how the welfare state observes the priorities of maldistributed wealth even when it attempts to serve the common good. Other cases in point can be found in literally every department of government. The American welfare system in the sixties reached only a third of the poor and provided them, on a national average, with only half of what they needed. Meanwhile, in 1969, the richest one-sixth among the farmers (individuals and corporations) received two-thirds of the agricultural subsidies, or about $2.5 billion. Given the relation of social classes in this field, America's commitment to promote "agriculture" is also a commitment to help the rich at the expense of the poor. And if one considers the various deductions in the tax codes as an indirect form of government expense—by not collecting money from an individual, Washington increases his income as surely as if it had sent him a check—one will note that they total up to $50 billion, with the bulk of that sum going to oil men, home builders, stockmarket speculators, and other from the top of the economic pyramid.

Education and Social Inequality

It is in education that the effect of systematic inequality is most damaging. America is becoming a "knowledge economy" in which higher and higher educational credentials are required, sometimes unnecessarily, in order to get a good job. This is one of the most important areas of socialized effort since, either through public schools or aid to private education, the state supplies the modern economy with "its decisive factor of production, which is trained manpower." Although public spending on education in the sixties increased at a rate faster than that of the Gross National Product, those Americans in the most desperate straits were not reached.

So it is that in the sixties a rather optimistic study of social mobility in the United States found that there is an "oversupply" of youth at the bottom of the economic structure: the *Manpower Report of the President, 1969,* reported that the unprecedented recent boom had clearly revealed "economic expansion alone was insufficient to employ many people who had been bypassed in the general advance because of inexperience, lack of skills, and cultural deprivation." Now it is bad enough that such a group should exist at all. What is truly intolerable is the extent to which the social class structure denies it effective access to tax-supported education and works and thereby makes it both self-perpetuating and hereditary.

For if, as Christopher Jencks and David Riesman document in *The Academic Revolution,* society is divided into blue- and white-collar groups, the high school seniors from the white-collar background are four times as likely to score in the top rather than in the bottom 10 percent, while the blue-collar students are twice as likely to be at the bottom rather than at the top. One way of coping with such depressing statistics is to argue that they reflect the ''middle-class bias'' of the tests used to evaluate students. There have been demands to do away with IQ tests and standard grading, to assign each racial and ethnic group a quota of admissions in state-supported colleges (the top 10 percent of Negroes, Puerto Ricans, Mexican-Americans, and others would have places reserved for them, so there would be competition only within these communities but not among them or with the non-ethnics).

To those who charge that the tests are ''unfair to the poor,'' Riesman and Jencks cogently reply, ''Life is unfair to the poor. Tests are merely the results. Urban middle-class life in general and professional work in particular seem to nourish potential academic skills and interests in parents, while lower-class life does the opposite.'' The conclusion they come to is much more radical than that offered by people who simply denounce ''educational racism''—or even propose separate but inferior college faculties for the children of the poor and the minorities. Riesman and Jencks write:

> So long as the distribution of power and privilege remains radically unequal, so long as some children are raised by adults at the bottom while others are raised by adults at the top, the children will more often than not turn out unequal. . . . We suspect that these differences account for more of the class variation in college changes than all other differences combined.

Jencks and Riesman then raise a basic psychological point. Suppose by an act of political will the schools could be transformed so as to favor the minorities while the fundamental social inequalities were left intact. That, they hold, ''could be a formula for misery. A mobile, fluid society in which men move up and down is simultaneously a competitive, insecure, and invidious society.'' ''What America needs,'' they conclude, ''is not more mobility but more equality. So long as American life is premised on dramatic inequalities of wealth and power, *no* system for allocating social roles will be very satisfactory.'' Exactly!

In education, housing, and agriculture, in welfare and every other area of social life, it is therefore necessary to attack the systematic concentration of economic power in order to achieve serious reform. The fulfillment of liberal values, in short, requires structural changes in our class relationships, changes transcending the capitalist limits of today's welfare state.

"Why We Need Socialism in America," *Dissent,* **17:3 (May–June 1970), pp. 240–246.**

F. Mary Fish and Vergil Williams

Fish and Williams, both professors at the University of Alabama, take a prag-matic approach which attempts to mediate between philosophies of public assist-ance and those of free enterprise. They do so by centering their attention on what they conclude is the real problem: that of increasing productivity of the poor and en-abling the poor to help themselves. In the short run relief and income subsidies may be needed. But these measures are to serve the long-run solution which is to produce self-sustaining members of the work force. Thus the reform of the welfare program recently initiated and the concentration on removing barriers of health, prejudice, and educational opportunities are, in the view of the authors, right on target. Such measures mean that poverty can be attacked and perhaps cured through the existing structures of our economy and without undue interference from the public sector.

At the same time Fish and Williams recognize that their approach is still a promise of things to come rather than accomplished fact. For the task of enabling the poor to help themselves by removing all the barriers has just begun.

From the standpoint of the theorist the essential concern is whether the plan takes account of all the forces at work in the economy as well as the total set of con-ditions that comprise poverty. For example, how would it deal with unemployment, a problem deeply enmeshed with other factors besides the incentives and skills of the poor? In particular, what solution would it offer to a population like that found in Appalachia where the options for work are extremely limited due to the regional factors themselves?

Economic Philosophy and the Distribution of Income

Welfare and Incentive Issue

Since the 1930's the number of people receiving some form of welfare assistance from the government has gradually increased. This has caused a considerable amount of consternation among adherents of classical eco-nomics. They are concerned about the motivational system in a market so-ciety. A market society is free of the need for central planning and coercion by human authority. The motivational force is self-interest; that is, each in-dividual in the society works for his personal benefit as he performs his specialized work. Nonetheless, this self-interest serves society, because the tasks the individual performs in his own self-interest are necessary for the operation of society. Thus the self-interest of the individual benefits society as well as the individual.

The classical supposition about the nature of man raises a problem, however. Man, it is supposed, is torn between the desire for ease and comfort and the need to wrest sustenance from a parsimonious nature. Insecurity and inequality are therefore necessary in order for society to prosper. The individual must be driven to work by need or by desire for vertical mobility in the society which can be bought with material wealth. Believing man's nature to be thus, the classicists led their students to believe that insecurity and inequality must be preserved for the good of mankind, for without it workers would lay down their tools and rest in the shade while the economy languished. Welfare payments from the government did not pose a threat to this outlook so long as they were confined to caring for the needs of orphans and widows and providing the bare necessities of life for the disabled. Opposition to welfare arose when government payments began to be made to able-bodied workers who, for one reason or another, were in need. The classicists sincerely and desperately feared that the economic society would crumble due to the destruction of the incentive to produce. To cling to the rigid marginal productivity theory of income distribution was a protection for society. It would preserve the inequality and insecurity necessary to overcome man's supposed indolence.

Despite opposition to welfare activity by classicists, public assistance payments have been increasing at the rate of ten percent annually in recent years. In absolute dollar terms, current welfare payment activity is some fourteen billion dollars per year counting state, local and federal expenditures. This is a substantial sum, yet one might say that this is a small price to pay for eliminating pockets of poverty and misery in an affluent society. The sad truth is that these vast expenditures are *not* eliminating poverty, and some critics argue that the welfare system as it stands in the early months of 1971 acts to perpetuate poverty. Their main criticisms may be grouped into five categories:

1. Roughly one-half of the poor people get no help at all even though they are as destitute as welfare recipients. Proposed reform would bring more of these people onto welfare rolls as the Aid to Dependent Children Plan is replaced with the Nixon Family Assistance Plan.

2. States determine the level of benefits. Some states keep welfare payments so low that welfare recipients may find it to their advantage to migrate into crowded urban ghettos where benefits are somewhat higher. Reform proposals will attempt to establish a "floor" under several types of direct welfare payments by providing states with federal aid for this purpose.

3. Administration of the assistance has been prohibitively expensive and wasteful primarily because the bulk of the social worker's time has been spent in investigating eligibility for welfare payments. This extensive investigation has consumed one dollar of every three available for relief in recent years. Welfare reform proposes to reduce administrative expense by foregoing these extensive investigations and making only spot checks similar to the Internal Revenue checking on income tax statements.

4. Until recently, most localities reduced benefits by one dollar for every dollar earned by a recipient. This acted as a 100 percent tax on the earnings of the poor and discouraged work—especially where working would create extra expenses such as baby sitting fees. Currently, more care is given to phasing out welfare payments as the recipients become self-supporting.

5. The Aid to Families with Dependent Children program was designed to provide welfare to women with children. An employable male in the house made the family ineligible for assistance. This, of course, stemmed from the classical viewpoint of avoiding paying any assistance to prospective workers for fear of destroying their will to work. Unexpectedly, it succeeded only in breaking up families by causing desertions, separations, and divorces as destitute men left home in order to at least make their families eligible for welfare. The Family Assistance Program attempts to avoid this problem by making the employable males and the working poor eligible for benefits.

Whether or not the old system has perpetuated poverty is a moot question. One can say with more certainty that it has not cured poverty. Rather, poverty has been allowed to perpetuate itself for generations in the same family. It is worthy to provide urgently needed necessities for the destitute, but it would be more worthy, and more practical, to go one step farther and solve the problem by transforming the poor into dignified self-supporting citizens.

New Light on Old Problem

As indicated in the discussion above, the United States has overcome its fear of welfare to a large extent and has built a system of income redistribution designed to alleviate some problems of poverty. Unfortunately, the system is half-hearted and ill-conceived. The program has not solved the problem despite substantial expenditures. It is encouraging that the faults of the system are now widely recognized and the United States stands on the verge of a major overhaul of the welfare system which will constitute a new approach. The new approach not only will provide more adequate help for the needy but will also take the additional step of attempting to lift the needy out of poverty permanently by increasing their productivity.

Let us review one of the events in the United States which has partially overcome resistance to increased efforts to aid the indigent. It is important to understand why society is more willing to tackle the problem now than it has been in the recent past. The most encouraging force at work is the new understanding of the old incentive issue.

Perhaps it would be more correct to say that we are beginning to realize that the old incentive issue was a misconception all along. Man's nature is not such that he lays down his tools and sits in the shade at the slightest encouragement. New empirical evidence has been uncovered in a study being conducted by the Office of Economic Opportunity. This is the first and only available experiment of this type. The study is not complete but a tentative report has been published, entitled *Preliminary Results of the New Jersey Graduated Work Incentive Experiment*. The Director of the OEO has aptly commented that this may be the most significant social science experiment that has ever taken place.

The project is a well-financed OEO experiment, funded by a five-million dollar grant. Some 575 working-poor families are involved in the experiment in Trenton, Jersey City, Passaic, and Paterson, New Jersey, and an additional 150 families from Scranton, Pennsylvania. In 1968 a subcontractor began contracting to provide families with a guaranteed basic income ranging from $1700 a year to $4200 for a three-year period. The families are required to fill out questionnaires in return for income payments. The questionnaires provide a record of whether or not the income guarantee affects the recipient's work experience. A control group of 634 families have also signed contracts. These families receive no guaranteed income but do receive ten dollars a month as payment for filling out similar forms.

Since the project was designed to test the old classical proposition regarding the effect of welfare payments, the families involved are headed by employable males who are free to choose whether or not to work. Furthermore, people in the program are not required to accept any type of job training. Such freedom of choice was vital if the experiment were to test the old ideas.

The first reports of the project indicate that there is no evidence that those families receiving a guaranteed income have reduced their work efforts. In fact, there is evidence that families receiving the guaranteed income have increased their efforts as compared to the control group. Average incomes on a weekly basis rose for 53 percent of the guaranteed income group while at the same time income rose for only 42 percent of the control group. The initial conclusion is that the urge to work has been badly underestimated for this group of people.

Evidence of a strong urge to work is reinforced by a benefit reduction feature built into the program. That is, benefits are reduced as income rises so that, in effect, the reductions are the same as a sharply progressive tax on earned income. For some project families benefits are cut as much as 70 percent on each dollar earned. Other evidence, provided by in-depth interview of recipients, indicates that 65 percent would like a better job, 55 percent are willing to take a cut in salary to train for a better job, and 60 percent are willing to take second jobs to supplement their incomes. Of course, the experiment is far from over, and it is too early to discard the hypothesis that welfare payments reduce the supply of labor. Still, the evidence being gathered indicates that the effect of welfare payments on the willingness to work is much less important than the classicists would have one believe.

Motivation versus Ability

The Office of Economic Opportunity experiment seems to suggest that motivation or lack of motivation to work—as an inherent characteristic in man—may not be the key to making the decisions necessary in constructing a workable social welfare system. Let us turn to an alternative hypothesis. Instead of attempting to dig further into man's psyche and attempting to determine his reaction to a sum of welfare money, let us instead estimate his opportunities in a society which is still largely basing its rewards for work effort on the marginal productivity of the individual. As a practical matter, the marginal productivity theory of income distribution rewards the individual in direct proportion to his contribution to the value being created in the society. If he is illiterate or discriminated against on the hiring line, or if he is too ill to work, he cannot hope to contribute much to production of desired goods and services. If he cannot contribute much, he cannot get much in return.

Society has essentially three choices. It can leave him in poverty to die or to subsist on the margin or it can redistribute income sufficiently to support him at some satisfactory level or it can find ways to raise his level of productivity in order to enable him to get a reasonable share of the national wealth through his own efforts. It is this latter alternative that presents the greatest hope for solving the problem of poverty permanently without changing the basic nature of our economic system. The key to the problem is in raising the productivity of the poor through education, training, elimination of economic prejudices stemming from race and sex differences, and helping the poor to attain health standards adequate for participation in productive work effort. Only then can they achieve a self-supporting dignified existence. If the poor cannot achieve this by their own efforts, one can hardly expect them to be motivated to work at menial tasks for rewards scarcely greater than those offered by the social welfare system. Conversely, their motivation can be expected to be better if they are given a roadmap showing them the way to upward social and economic mobility.

This notion of expending effort to raise the productivity of the poor amounts to a philosophy of treating human beings as an important national resource to be improved and cultivated just as other national resources have been improved and cultivated. The philosophy is neither very new nor very old. It began to develop in the decade of the 1950's in the writings of economists. Many noted welfare economists (so designated because they freely make value-judgments) picked up the theme and incorporated it into the body of their writings. Thus, the theme is found in a vast volume of writings by these economists. It is precisely for that reason that we need to revive it, reiterate it, and make it as explicit as possible at a time when the welfare system is being overhauled. The idea has not been generally accepted and understood for a number of reasons. The writings of these economists are read primarily by the academic community or that relatively small portion of the academic community interested in the literature of economics. Furthermore, the theme is often not made explicit because the author is dealing with a wide range of ideas in a book. Still worse, the idea is not understood because of political philosophies. The reader who classifies himself as a conservative may become angry and feel that the welfare economist is constantly advocating more government giveaway programs. Frequently, the welfare economist is doing precisely that as a short-run part of his program to rejuvenate the welfare recipient so his productivity can be increased. The reader may become disenchanted long before he realizes that the long-run solution being presented is not unpalatable to the conservative.

Thus, we argue that in the writings of the welfare economists there is a common theme which states that the long-run solution to poverty is in raising productivity by making short-run efforts to spend more on helping the poor to increase their ability to help themselves. The long-run solution does not imply basic changes in our economic system or increasing centralization of government or any of those things that conservatives find so distasteful. On the contrary, it is perfectly in keeping with the conservative economist's craving for solutions brought about through free market forces with a minimum of government interference.

The welfare reform movement under way currently seems to have captured the essence of this approach to the problem of poverty and is making a tentative step toward converting it from an abstract philosophy to a pragmatic approach to the problem. It is refreshing to have a new practical approach, but the actual task of increasing the ability and opportunities for the poor is still ahead of us.

"**Economic Philosophy and the Distribution of Income,**" *Midwest Quarterly,* **13,** October **1971, pp. 47–64.**